EAT WHAT IS SET BEFORE YOU

A MISSIOLOGY OF THE CONGREGATION IN CONTEXT

SCOTT HAGLEY

EDITED BY ANDREW WOOD

URBAN LOFT PUBLISHERS | SKYFOREST, CA

Eat What is Set Before You
A Missiology of the Congregation in Context

Urban Loft Publishers
P.O. Box 6
Skyforest, CA 92385
www.urbanloftpublishers.com

Senior Editors: Stephen Burris & Kendi Howells Douglas
Track Editor: Andrew Wood
Copy Editor: Marla Black
Graphics: Elisabeth Arnold
Cover Art: "Garfield Farm" by Tim Englehardt
www.engelhardtdesigns.net"

ISBN-13: 978-1-949625-00-4

For Maribeth,
whose faith envisions a world where peace is offered
and received

In memory of Jannie Swart,
who could always imagine God

ENDORSEMENTS

"I have known Scott as a teammate, friend and colleague. Most of all, I know him to be a follower of Jesus who teaches as much with his life as he does in the classroom about what it means to join God on mission. This is an outstanding book, which I will use in my church, my networks and the classroom. It is full of stories and a depth of wisdom about how we may encourage people in our congregations to live out the gospel in our current contexts."

Dr. Cameron Roxburgh
VP of Missional Initiatives for NAB, National Director of Forge Canada, and Senior Pastor of Southside Community Church

"If your church sets out to become a life-giving presence in the neighborhood, you're in for a wild ride! It all seems simple enough, until you start doing it. That's why you need this book. It is going to give you astonishing insight into what you have been going through as a church. It is going to give you a rich practical theology for understanding how to improvise for what's coming next. And it is taken from a deeply personal and particular account of Scott Hagley's experience of participating in a neighborhood church, which makes it resonate deeply and concretely with your real experience. This is one of the most helpful guidebooks I have encountered in the past twenty years of parish ministry."

Paul Sparks
Co-Author of the award-winning book *The New Parish: How Neighborhood Churches Are Transforming Mission, Discipleship, and Community* and Co-founding Director of the Parish Collective.

"Having given a lecture on the future of theological education that focused on "being hosted as well as hosting" a Dean of a major Protestant denominational Seminary asked me an honest question, "I know how to host, and I have a few experiences of being hosted, of course, but how does theological education place the emphasis on "being hosted" in such a diverse culture as ours?" Scott Hagley's book answers that question at many levels: firstly, he tells the story of a local church, Midtown Baptist; secondly, the nests that story in the story of Christian mission; thirdly, he nests that story in the life of the Triune God; fourthly, he provides both a theological and sociological reflection that takes very seriously the realities of a late modern (some say post-modern) culture. He does theology in, with, under, against, and for a local church within a deep reading of contemporary culture. Good reading for teachers of theology and local lay and clergy leaders of the practice of missional church. Bravo!"

Patrick R. Keifert
Professor Emeritus of Systematic Theology
Luther Theological Seminary
President and Director of Research
Church Innovations Institute

"Finally—a book that develops a usable congregational missiology! The author presents a biblically and theologically framed, yet profoundly practical missiology for any and every congregation to take seriously its participation in God's mission within its own local context. By probing deeply and then reflecting insightfully on the lived experience of a particular congregation, the author invites the reader to understand the process as well as the principles of pursuing this work. I heartily recommend this reading to lay leaders, pastors, and denominational officials."

Dr. Craig Van Gelder
Emeritus Professor of Congregational Mission, Luther Seminary

ACKNOWLEDGEMENTS

I have been ruminating over this book ever since I started my Ph.D. work at Luther Seminary and began working with congregations. It commenced in earnest after I completed my dissertation and started noticing congregations like Midtown wherever I traveled as a researcher and consultant for Church Innovations Institute and Forge Canada. Because the argument developed slowly, chapters have been written alongside my work in three very different contexts – St. Paul, Vancouver, and now Pittsburgh – and while working with congregations and theological schools across the United States and Canada. The book is inconceivable apart from the hospitality so many have offered me, inviting me to teach and consult with congregations, taking my ideas seriously enough to challenge them, and offering encouragement along the way. I'm profoundly grateful for conversation partners cultivated over such a wide terrain.

The initial idea for this research came together through my work at Church Innovations Institute. I'm thankful for Pat Taylor Ellison, who helped me dive into the deep waters of congregational research and for Pat Keifert and Gary Simpson, who taught me to think theologically about such work. My colleagues at Southside Community Church and Forge Canada helped me to see the significance of place for shaping congregational mission. I'm thankful for Cam Roxburgh, my partner in ministry at both Southside and Forge, whose passion for neighborhood-based missional communities has shaped a whole cadre of church leaders in Canada. Pittsburgh Theological Seminary, with its renewed commitment to cultivating missional and pioneering leaders, has provided a rich context to bring these different ideas together. I am grateful to my colleagues and conversation partners in this new space.

Many people read early drafts and significantly improved this work. I offer thanks to Craig Van Gelder, whose careful critique and encouragement kept me on track to finish the project. Thanks, also to Dwight Zscheile, Kirby Stoll, Laura Bentley, Ron Saari, Jane Larson, Chris Brown, Karen Wilk, Craig Bosnick, and John Ogren. Your comments, feedback, questions, and encouragement significantly improved the final outcome. Andrew Wood has been a patient, gracious, insightful, and incredibly competent editor, offering feedback and encouragement at all stages of production. Of course, any inadequacies in the book remain my own.

During the writing of this book, my dear friend Jannie Swart unexpectedly died while playing Frisbee with students on the lawn at Pittsburgh Seminary. Jannie had this way of subverting one's theological imagination by consistently turning the conversation to God's gracious hospitality to us through the stranger. I miss him, and offer this work in his memory. His voice, no doubt, is reflected in these pages.

We all write from within a particular situation. Mine has been as a father and a husband. I have been working on this book for almost half my daughters' lives. Hannah and Isabelle have enriched and complicated my life in beautiful ways; I am grateful for how they have helped me see and live in the world differently. Finally, I dedicate this book to my partner of almost two decades, Maribeth Hagley. Her theological work is always done in relationship to the concrete cares and concerns of neighbors and strangers. It is hard not to be drawn into the world she cultivates; and so the shape of this work draws inspiration and insight from her life and witness. I am so grateful for her partnership and love.

TABLE OF CONTENTS

INTRODUCTION

Eat What is Set Before You 12

    Time for Table Manners.. 12

    God's Love, Alive in the West End: Midtown Baptist Church 16

    The Journey Ahead 22

    How to Use This Book 26

CHAPTER 1

The Crisis of Mission.. 31

    Faith Forged in Crisis 34

    Conclusion: Mission as Crisis 49

CHAPTER 2

Living and Learning: Ethnography of a Crisis 53

    An Ethnographic Account of Missional Crises.. 55

    Eat What is Set Before You: Three Capacities for Mission 76

    Conclusion.. 78

PART II: THE CRISIS OF CALL 81

CHAPTER 3

Suffering the Call: Encountering God On The Way 83

    Trumpets at the Tomb 83

    The Faith of Abraham, Mission History, and the Global Church 86

    For God so Loves the World… 91

    The Triune *missio Dei* 92

    Participation in the Triune Life 96

    The God who bears.. 104

Conclusion...107

CHAPTER 4

Faith Disclosed: Discerning God's Call...*109*

Everything You Know is Wrong 109

Who Am I to Stand in the Way of God? Discernment in Mission 111

Discernment Gives Us the Scriptures... 115

A Picture of Theological Discernment 118

Paying Attention 121

Risky Speech 124

Act and Reflect... 127

Adaptive Theological Leadership for Our Missional Era........................... 130

PART III: CRISES OF CULTIVATION AND CONTEXT 137

CHAPTER 5

Heroes and Hope...*138*

Introduction... 138

Heroism, Hope, and the World-Changing Missionary 142

Understanding the [Modern] Missionary Imagination............................. 148

Midtown and the Modern Missionary Imagination 158

Why We Cannot Change the World: Or, Mission as Perduring Presence 161

CHAPTER 6

Cultivating Missional Partnerships *165*

Introduction... 165

If Not a Hero, Then What? 170

Toward Trustworthy Public Companionship 178

The Church in the Neighborhood... 182

The Church with the Neighborhood... 184

Public Improvisational Leadership 190

Yes . . . and 191

"Yes . . . let's try . . .".. 193

"Yes . . . we are . . .".. 195

Conclusion...197

CHAPTER 7

The Crisis of Context 199

Introduction...199

Sketching the Crisis: How Does One Join a Family? 203

Contextualization and Assimilation...209

Cultivating Connection to Place 218

Conclusion..227

CHAPTER 8

Discovering God's Love in the Neighborhood 229

Contextualization and Identity...231

Hospitality and Missional Formation..238

Discerning Shared (Worldly) Practices 240

Practices Perform the Gospel 243

Rhythms of Welcome: 'Making Room' in the Congregation and
Community..253

Discerning Welcome: Cultivating a Connection to Place 256

God's Love, Alive in the West End: Conclusion 257

EPILOGUE..**259**

APPENDIX **267**

LIVING AS A GUEST...**267**

Receive...267

Pray..270

Eat..272

INTRODUCTION
EAT WHAT IS SET BEFORE YOU

Go on your way. See, I am sending you out like lambs into the midst of wolves. Carry no purse, no bag, no sandals... (Luke 10:3-4)

Time for Table Manners

I met Ruben several months before I began research at Midtown Baptist Church. A father of six, elder at the church, and a fundraiser at a Christian liberal arts college, Ruben had a firm handshake and infectious smile. When I first met him, I had just attended my first worship gathering at Midtown and we talked about weather and work, kids and the state of higher education. It was the fall of 2007, and the conversation begun on that Sunday stretched out for several weeks, from Sunday to Sunday, year to year. We became acquaintances and, in time, friends. Ruben knew I was not only attending Midtown, but also researching it as part of my doctoral program. We often talked about what I was learning as I tested out things that I heard or observed with him. He became a significant informant for my work. By marriage and longevity, he was part of the church family, but also able to interpret the family for outsiders like me.

He started attending Midtown in college, when he began dating and eventually married Beth – a woman who had grown up in the church. It was during one of these conversations, near the end of my research, that he stumped me with a question elegant in its simplicity: "So what is it that you want to say to us?" I had written pages and pages of field notes, transcribed interviews, and facilitated focus groups; I had placed this fieldwork into conversation with core disciplinary literature in mission studies and theology with enough coverage and depth to earn an academic degree. I had talked for hours with pastors and lay leaders, people like Ruben who loved this church and wanted to learn with me and from me. But I did not know how to answer him. "It's complicated." I wanted to say. We continued our conversation, and before moving to a new city for a new job, I tried to address his question more directly, but we both knew that my thoughts were only partially formed and my suggestions closer to conjecture than wisdom. In some ways, this book is a long overdue response to Ruben's question.

If I could drop in on my conversation with Ruben now, I would tell him that it is time for some table manners. A table has been set and food has been prepared, and now it is time for Midtown to sit down and eat the food that has been given with those who have been gathered. Table manners: "eat what is set before you." It sounds simple, but often it is not. The table magnifies our vulnerabilities and subsequently discloses our insecurities. As any parent of toddlers can attest, power struggles in the home tend to start at the table with cut vegetables on a plastic plate. Both toddler and parent want control, and since the toddler doesn't prepare the food, there is only one way such control can be exercised. As children get older, the words, "you can't make me" become a dinnertime mantra. Thankfully, we grow out of toddler willfulness, but not entirely. Whenever we eat in the home of a stranger or cross boundaries of culture or language, our ignorance makes us feel vulnerable. "What am I putting into my mouth?" "Will I pay for this later?" "What is the appropriate way to eat this?" "How long do I have to sit here?" Of course, food allergies dramatically intensify our vulnerability in such settings.

In worship, we gather at a table to practice receiving bread and wine in gratitude. During the Eucharist, we receive the gift of Christ and rightly give thanks for his life poured out for us and embodied with us. In so doing, we seek to live in the way of Christ, with gratitude, hope, and trust. But we should not confuse the gift of the communion table with safety. For when we break bread and pour wine we also say "on the night that Jesus was *betrayed*"—and must remember that the betrayer was also munching on bread with thirty pieces of silver rattling in his pocket. Table manners, at least according to the gospel of Jesus Christ, do not remove us from such ambiguities and vulnerabilities. Rather, when Jesus says "take and eat," or when he tells his disciples to "eat what is set before you," he thrusts us right into the middle of all that is confounding, difficult, and ambiguous about faithful witness to the gospel. This is why we need table manners for mission.

When Jesus instructs the seventy before they go out ahead of him in Luke 10, he provides a basic orientation in the table manners of the "sent ones" when living as guests. When they encounter a person of peace, Jesus tells them to stay with that person, not moving around from house to house. Remain in that house, Jesus says, eating and drinking whatever they provide. They should stay put and eat up. The one sent by Jesus to heal and proclaim the good news of the Reign of God will be able to do so only by being dependent upon the gifts and hospitality of others. This person will graciously receive what is offered in food and shelter, while also offering the healing power and word of God. Jesus gives table manners for mission because the disciples participate in an ecosystem of gift and care; they discover people of peace even as they offer the peace of God.

Of course, this is easier said than done. Those of us raised on the heroic stories of the modern missionary movement, or who entertain notions of churches transforming neighborhoods, do not always catch the import of Jesus' table manners for mission. Nor do we always like them when they are given. When talking about preaching the gospel or helping those less fortunate, we prefer to be in control, to set the table, provide the food, and "strongly encourage" people when they decide they don't want to eat the chopped broccoli we've lovingly put on their plastic plate. When we've had enough encounters with people inadequately thankful for our ministry, we decide it is time to move on to a group more likely to need us and express gratitude for us.

Of course, I am no longer talking only about food, but about the kinds of relationships Christians and congregations have with those to whom God sends them. Jesus' instruction in Luke 10 draws our attention to the fact that the missionary *joins* an existing relational ecology, *depends* upon it, and *discovers* opportunities to heal and witness to the gospel. Thus, Jesus' table manners for mission offer a means by which we can attend to this ecology and receive the gifts it has to offer, even as we contribute to the welfare and wellbeing of the community. A church with a long history of generous giving, Midtown exemplifies the many ways in which a congregation can and should contribute to the welfare and peace of its city.

However, demographic changes in the neighborhood and congregation have created tension precisely at the places of intersection with the neighborhood. On the one hand, the old ways of exercising care were no longer financially tenable for the congregation. On the other hand, the congregation had cultivated wonderful relationships in the neighborhood that actually sustained the congregation's public presence. I suspect it is now time for Midtown to *depend* upon the gifts that God offers them through various neighborhood partners, to *discover and join* the people of peace in the neighborhood, and to *discern* the good news of the gospel within this relational ecosystem. They should take a seat at the table that has already been set, and take part in the meal that has been served out of gratitude for God. Learning to eat what is set before it, the congregation will be formed in ways that neither Ruben nor I can predict, but that will be necessary for Midtown to participate in God's mission within the particularities of this context. This book is about *why* I think such table manners for mission is good congregational missiology, and *how* this might be developed for Midtown and congregations in countless other contexts across North America.

God's Love, Alive in the West End: Midtown Baptist Church

Midtown Baptist Church[1] looks like thousands of other urban congregations located in a major metropolitan area. Its neighborhood, the West End, bears all the expected marks of urban transition, blight, and redevelopment. Freeways mark its western and southern boundaries and it adjoins a fairgrounds and liberal arts private university on its northern edge. Not surprisingly, the northern part of the neighborhood houses young professionals alongside generations of blue-collar families, a mix of parks, coffee shops, and small ethnic restaurants. The south end, however, bears the marks of transition and blight. One can walk block-by-block in the southern part of the neighborhood and encounter entirely different neighborhoods on the same street, with blocks of manicured lawns and renovated properties followed by long stretches of rental properties, crumbling sidewalks, and chain-link fences.

A busy East-West thoroughfare cuts through the southern half of the neighborhood. Once, a streetcar ran down the middle of this avenue before suburban development and freeways undermined the financial and cultural viability of public transit. Now, ironically, a street-level light rail project has just been completed, a sign of this neighborhood's participation in the urban renaissance marking the first decades of the twenty-first century. While the new transit system promises higher rents and new luxury condominiums in its path, the southern half of the West End shows few signs of gentrification. Mostly, it bears the marks of neglect. Empty warehouses sit adjacent to crumbling sidewalks. Rows of empty car lots witness to dealerships that left for the suburbs intermixed with long-abandoned industrial buildings. One small stretch was redeveloped twenty

---

[1] All names and places are changed to protect the identity of the congregation and those who participated in the study.

years ago into a four-block stretch of strip malls. Large parking lots serve a mixture of foot and car traffic toward two major food chains, a Walmart, and a host of other stores. Coffee shops and storefront businesses are notably absent.

On a Sunday morning, those who worship at Midtown use a parking garage across the street from the strip-mall development. The three-story parking garage rests adjacent to a boxy, shimmering-green building with few windows. It was built to offer office and street-level commercial space. At one time, it had an Applebee's and jewelry store at street level, with many other businesses renting space on the upper floors. Now, it sits mostly vacant except for an emergency pet care service and the off-street parking it provides for Midtown Baptist and Bethany Lutheran Churches. On a typical Sunday morning, a sign directs Midtown worshippers to the parking ramp in the vacant green building. Booming chords of classical music, echoing off the concrete structure, greet worshippers stepping out of their cars.

When the weather is nice, the corner just beyond the ramp is already pulsing with bus and foot traffic by the time worship starts. The crowds at this particular corner encapsulate the demographic diversity of the neighborhood: roughly 60% white, 30% African American, and 10% a mixture of ethnicities, including many new immigrants. The neighborhood is trending younger and poorer than the city average, though education levels are slightly higher. The groups streaming into Midtown Baptist, however, appear older, whiter, wealthier, better educated, and much more culturally monotone (that is, Swedish Baptist) than the crowds of people going about their Sunday morning business on the other side of the parking ramp. Like many aging and urban churches throughout North America, Midtown faces the distinct challenge of embracing and nurturing a Reformation Christendom heritage in a post-Christian, transient, vibrant, and culturally dynamic neighborhood.

It is a two-block walk from the parking garage and past Bethany Lutheran to Midtown. Despite their close proximity, Bethany and Midtown collaborate in only a couple activities. In the fall, they host a neighborhood block party together; the churches block the adjacent street, barbeque burgers and hot dogs, play music, and set up a bounce house for the kids. The event draws from the immediate residential neighborhood and mixes the two congregations. Bethany also helps Midtown with "Family Assistance;" a month-long ministry to homeless families, in which Midtown turns itself into an overflow shelter for the county in partnership with the area Council of Churches. Bethany provides volunteers for Midtown for this resource intensive service.

Members of Midtown can still remember when they needed no help to pull off big events. At one time, it was a flagship congregation in its denomination. Building its first sanctuary in 1913, it was an early arrival to the growing West End neighborhood. During this time, the denominational seminary also moved into the city, a mile from the church, and developed into a four-year college after World War II. In the middle of the twentieth century, the college and seminary supplied a steady stream of students, professors, families, and young professionals. Demographically, Midtown resembled its neighborhood: white (Scandinavian), middle-class, professional families. However, by the mid-1970s, it became clear that the neighborhood was changing in ways that challenged Midtown's identity as an ethnic Baptist church. Suburban space drew away the college and seminary, along with many Midtown members. Midtown's median age crept higher, even as the surrounding neighborhood, with its large number of rental properties, remained young. The church's membership remained Scandinavian in both ethnicity and in their pietistic Baptist culture, even as the neighborhood grew increasingly diverse.

However, in the mid-1970s, Midtown made a decision to stay in the neighborhood. In the years since that decision, they have learned to articulate their call to the city, thanks in part to their Senior Pastor of twenty-three years, Robert Samuelson. "While Pastor Robert began his tenure after Midtown discerned its place in the city, he enabled the church to lean into this call by connecting Midtown to other urban ministries and congregations. Robert exhibits an unassuming confidence, which creates the conditions for the competence of others to flourish. Former pastors of Midtown have found refuge in the congregation, along with retired professors and a wide variety of professionals. Robert's easygoing leadership style has also created space for a spectrum of theological and ideological differences, making Pastor Robert an unlikely champion for different causes in the theologically conservative denomination and across the city.

Under Pastor Robert's leadership, Midtown has not only remained in the West End neighborhood, but has made the neighborhood central to Midtown's sense of mission and call. The congregation endured the changes taking place and remained present *within* and *to* the West End. Today, the church prominently professes their commitment to the neighborhood with a sign that reads "God's love, alive in the West End." Conversation with Midtown leaders discloses a sense of gratitude that the congregation has found new life in this place. God's love is alive in the story of the church. Midtown leaders also imagine the persevering presence, benevolence, and hospitality of the congregation as a sign of God's love for the neighborhood. They discerned God's call to the city and now their life together bears witness to God's love for the city and God's presence in the city. It is not just talk. Midtown is present to, in, and with the neighborhood. On any given day, the church buzzes with the frenetic energy of a tutoring program, food bank, day care, or any of the anti-poverty or new immigrant services launched by its non-profit social services agency. Midtown hosts its neighbors frequently, attending to their physical, emotional, and spiritual needs. To host all these programs,

Midtown actively seeks community partnerships with other churches, non-profits, or volunteer organizations as a way of being present with their neighbors. Two of the church's biggest community engagement projects are impossible apart from cooperation with outside organizations. During the month of September, the church building becomes an overflow homeless shelter in partnership with the area council of churches and the county government; and Midtown's tutoring program runs in partnership with the neighborhood elementary school.

The Midtown story, however, is not a generic 'success' story, where the congregation now stands as a model for others to mimic. It is a story that remains fluid and uncertain. Although Midtown now has a growing number of young urban families, professionals and students, its story is still open. The conclusion may not be one of organizational survival in a fluid urban context. For although hundreds of families and kids in the neighborhood are engaged on a regular basis by Midtown, few will ever attend a service or join a small group or attend Sunday school. In part, this is due to the fact that Midtown's energetic engagement with the neighborhood has largely been an activity of *extension* accomplished by keeping the core identity of the church untouched and untroubled. Other than funding these practices, the open hospitality, acts of benevolence and ongoing public conversation do not impinge too much on the worship and community of many in the congregation. While social service activities have engaged the vulnerable at the margins, the church itself continues to function as a white, middle class congregation. This dynamic between center and periphery divides the congregation by age, economics, and ethnicity. The result is that a declining number of aging wealthy members funds Midtown's robust engagement with its neighborhood.

However, the center-periphery dynamic does not make Midtown a cold or condescending neighborhood partner. They imagine their presence participating in God's love for the neighborhood, and in turn, the West End neighborhood loves Midtown as a church. But its ministries of extension and engagement struggle for finances and volunteers as the congregation itself searches for a plausible and coherent sense of identity. Over the years, Midtown has remained present *in* the neighborhood, learned how to serve its neighbors, and exists *for* the neighborhood. However, with the demographic pressures facing many congregations, urban and otherwise, this does not seem to be enough. Shrinking budgets and aging members beg another question: Can Midtown learn presence *with* the neighborhood? This remains a critical question, not only for Midtown, but also for the broader field of missiology. When congregations remain within the neighborhood they seek to serve, they will find themselves shaped by the neighborhood in a variety of ways. Learning to live "in" and "for" an urban neighborhood necessitates presence *with*. Mission precipitates a crisis for congregations, where they learn to bear witness to the gospel not only by serving the neighborhood, but also by suffering in solidarity with it. This suffering challenges the very core of Midtown's identity as a Scandinavian Baptist church, as a middle-class benefactor for the neighborhood. It marks the challenge of congregational missiology.

This is a book about Midtown and the missiological implications of congregational presence in and with the neighborhood: the why and how of learning table manners for mission as guests. I suggest that in Midtown's commitment to stay in one place, and in Midtown's determination to trust God for ministry in this place, the congregation is being invited by God to place its very identity at risk. For the mission of God places the congregation within a relational ecology not of its own making and forces the congregation to work with conditions and partners that it has not chosen. Saying "yes" to God's mission in this place at this time means they must sit down and eat what is set before them with those who are gathered: learning to depend upon partners and the gifts of the neighborhood, joining the rhythms and wellbeing of their neighborhood, so that they might discern faithful Christian witness for this time and in this place. This is both the way of God's mission and the means of participation in God's mission through suffering-love. Thus, Midtown's *perduring presence* in and with the neighborhood *bears witness* to the gospel of Jesus Christ, even as the work of God in the neighborhood surprises, shapes, and clarifies the call of the congregation.[2] Along with Midtown, congregations across North America find themselves in a similar setting, where perduring presence provides both possibility and challenge for the congregation. Despite our claims to the contrary, our congregations are *shaped by* the neighborhoods we are called into even as we hope to change or transform the neighborhood.

The Journey Ahead

Sociologically speaking, congregations are inevitable participants in the relational ecology of neighborhoods, communities, and cities. In *Congregation & Community,* Nancy Ammerman uses an evolutionary/ecological metaphor to understand the symbiotic relationship between a congregation and its community.[3] In her extensive study of twenty-one congregations, Ammerman attends to ways in which congregations adapt to changing neighborhood contexts. While some congregations seem to thrive, others struggle as the world changes around them. Yet, congregations and communities affect one another, sometimes in surprising ways. While the "social processes" of different communities shape "the rise and fall" of congregations, Ammerman notices that congregations generate "spiritual energies" that shape the "social

---

[2] "Perdure" comes from the Latin *perdurare:* "to continue." Perdure means "to continue, endure, last on." I choose "perdure" to communicate both *endurance* and *steadfast continuance* for the church. I intentionally use a term outside of our normal vernacular to provoke reflection on the *relational* dimensions of mission, as a presence-with rather than a project-for. Thanks to Gary Simpson for this insight. See J.A. Simpson and E.S.C. Weiner, *The Oxford English Dictionary,* 2nd ed., Vol. XI (Oxford: Oxford University Press, 1989), 531.

[3] Nancy Tatom Ammerman, *Congregation & Community* (New Brunswick: Rutgers University Press, 1997).

structures of communities."[4] In other words, congregations do not get to determine the cultural practices, symbols, hopes, or narratives within which they are working. They don't get to determine how people will make sense of things or what people will value. They do, however, move and gather people in particular ways and toward particular ends. Her study does not say that congregations have zero effect on neighborhoods; it just emphasizes the complex symbiosis between congregation and community. It is in the faithful, enduring presence—*perduring presence*—where the mission of God is discerned and discovered. The perduring presence of Midtown Baptist Church, I argue, is an ongoing achievement, something they must continue to learn how to do, and this requires them to develop postures of availability to God's call, new partners, and the broader cultural dynamics of the West End neighborhood. This is not only good strategy for adaptation, but rather good missiology: in mission, we learn to participate in the suffering-love of God.

I have organized this book into three sections. The first section develops a theological account for the way in which God's mission precipitates crisis moments for the church. In the first chapter, I argue that because the living God encounters us within the limitations of creaturely life and in the midst of the real world, faith is often forged in response to crisis moments. God sends God's people into the world; God calls God's people in the midst of the world. In both of these situations, we can say that mission evokes crisis for our faith. The second chapter explores this thesis in the life of Midtown, accounting for three different kinds of crises they are encountering as they seek to remain faithfully present and steadfast in their neighborhood. In each of these cases, mission *limits* Midtown's agency in some way, causing the congregation to rethink and reimagine their life together, learning to be a guest in the neighborhood.

---

[4] Ammerman, *Congregation & Community,* 2-3.

23

The experience, practice, and reflections of Midtown Baptist Church guide this project. This is not because Midtown is a model urban mission church, but because Midtown's experience is typical as a progressive evangelical congregation in a rapidly changing neighborhood in an urban center. No doubt, many church leaders will recognize their own concerns and vulnerabilities in various aspects of Midtown's life. Others may find Midtown not quite conservative enough, or liberal enough. That is okay. This is not a book that holds up one congregation as an example to be followed, or a cautionary tale to avoid. Rather, it is a book expects close attention to the particularities of experience can yield abundant insights for others. The ethnographer James Clifford writes about ethnography as allegory, where deep understanding of another's cultural practices can yield insight into one's own.[5] Similarly, Paul Ricoeur explores the ways a close reading of a text functions "disclosively," that is, texts open us up to new possibilities and worlds.[6] I draw from Midtown's experiences in trust that the experience of one congregation in mission is sufficiently rich to inspire, challenge, provoke, and surprise the rest of us in contexts that may or may not map precisely onto Midtown's.

In the second part of the book, I develop a theo-practical vision of how Midtown might find its place at the table God has set for it in the neighborhood. By this, I mean to suggest ways in which the encounter with the "other" can challenge, surprise, and equip Midtown to discern a faithful, contextual response to the gospel of Jesus Christ. Chapter 3 draws from the story of Midtown to develop a missional theology for

---

[5] See James Clifford, "On Ethnographic Allegory," in *Writing Culture: The Poetics and Politics of Ethnography*, eds. James Clifford and George E. Marcus (Berkley: University of California Press, 1986), 98-121.

[6] See Paul Ricœur, *From Text to Action: Essays in Hermeneutics II*, trans. Kathleen Blamey and John B. Thompson (Evanston: Northwestern University Press, 1991). See also my essay reflecting on the role of the text in shaping ecclesial leadership Scott Hagley, "Cultivating Response-Able Leadership Postures: Ricoeur's Hermeneutic Phenomenology and the Biblical Text," *Journal of Religious Leadership* 15, no. 2 (Fall 2016), 81-108.

congregations and their communities.[7] Midtown's crises of mission suggest that we *suffer* the mission of God, for in mission we *participate* in the love and fellowship of the triune *missio Dei*. By "suffer," I draw attention to the fact that God's mission is constituted in matrices of relationship. The congregation does not complete projects on behalf of God, but rather *is moved* by God *with* others and *in* the neighborhood. These three actors— God, others, and neighborhood/place—each contribute to the shape of congregational mission.

Chapter 4 introduces the need for adaptive congregational leadership and the practice of discernment. When the church practices discernment, it carefully attends to worldly experience with *theological* interest. Learning to practice discernment enables the church to learn from its encounters with others and the neighborhood as it seeks faithful, contextual Christian practice. The crises of call, cultivation, and context are different ways in which the church suffers the Other as a means of discerning faithful Christian witness.

The third section works out the theological and practical implications of mission as participation in suffering-love. Having established the significance of engaging God's mission as guests in the neighborhood and the centrality of the practice of discernment, we turn to how congregations might learn to share space, initiative, and resources with the various partners God has given them. Invited to a table they have not prepared, congregations must learn to share in and with those gathered around various neighborhood initiatives and movements. Chapters 5 and 6 explore what I call the *crisis of cultivation*. In order to

---

[7] By "missional," I refer to the broader missional church conversation, which emerged from the work of the Gospel and Our Culture Network in the late 1990s. While there are many contemporary uses for the term "missional," I agree with those who insist that it names a theological orientation for both mission and church. Chapter three makes this argument directly in reference to Trinitarian theology. For an overview and evaluation of different contemporary uses for the term "missional," see Craig Van Gelder and Dwight J. Zscheile, *The Missional Church in Perspective: Mapping Trends and Shaping the Conversation* (Grand Rapids: Baker Academic, 2011), 186.

remain present *with* its neighbors, Midtown will need to cultivate new relationships in the neighborhood and civil society. This means navigating a shift in the imagined end of congregational mission, from changing the world to dwelling faithfully within it. Chapters 7 and 8 address what I call the *crisis of context.* Faithful Christian mission takes place *somewhere,* which means learning to attend to a place, and to witness to the gospel in that place. The congregation must contextualize its witness and practice of the faith. The concluding chapter turns to the hospitality tradition as one that both equips the church for mission and witnesses to the gospel in a contextually sensitive way.

These final four chapters identify places where the presence of the church in the neighborhood raises fundamental questions of identity for the congregation. By identifying these places of challenge, which I name as "crises," I aim to offer a pathway forward for missional leaders. Throughout, I suggest that mission raises fundamental questions of identity for congregations, which must be navigated by adaptive, sensemaking, discerning leaders. Such leadership is exercised by setting the table for engaging in experiments, and helping the church to identify where tables have already been set. Leadership in such a setting seeks to help the congregation *learn* responsiveness to the leading of the Spirit while they also seek to *clarify* or *understand* the calling and gifts of God for this time and place. Such leadership is both adaptive and theological, and is much needed in congregations across the continent and indeed around the world.

How to Use This Book

While Ruben provided the initial impetus for this book, I have more than Midtown in mind in each chapter. As a missiology for congregations in context, I intend this book for congregational leaders in rural and urban, suburban and exurban contexts. I think close attention to one congregation can identify and surface important issues for other congregations. In my consulting and teaching work, I have seen congregations learn from one another for exactly this reason. As an aid to leadership teams, pastors, students, and teachers, I have included an appendix at the end of the book with suggested experiments and practices for learning from and with one's context in the ways suggested by Midtown's story. The appendix is organized to reflect on themes of the book: receive, pray, and eat. Though these themes invite us to consider the rhythm of a meal, they are to be considered as *also* evoking broader metaphorical resonance to the dynamics of congregations and context, as elements whereby we learn to live as guests in the contexts God has placed us.

Receive

When we *receive* the broken bread at the communion table, we recognize the gift of Christ and receive his invitation to his table. We are guests at the table set by Jesus Christ, who recognize and receive the gifts Christ offers us. Guests receive and recognize what is set before them, and if congregations are to participate in the mission of God, they will receive and recognize the gifts of God in Christ as they live in their respective neighborhoods. But we do not naturally know how to do this. We must learn to receive and recognize; we must learn to adjust our expectations in relationship to neighborhood cultures and dynamics, to learn to pay careful attention, to receive others and receive their norms and ideas. In other words, we must learn to live as guests.

From January to March, I play pick-up hockey on Friday nights at an outdoor ice rink near my house in Pittsburgh. At midnight, after the Friday night skating sessions end, anywhere from fifteen to twenty-five men gather for an hour and half of skating in the freezing west Pennsylvania winter. We do not play at a high level, but we do have a good time pretending we are fitter and better versions of ourselves. One evening last year, five young players in their twenties showed up to the game with matching uniforms and a little too much swagger. Ignoring the norms that structure pick-up games of all kinds of sports across the continent, the players played in a way that failed to recognize the culture, skill level, and general ethos of the group. They created their own line, subbed together as a unit, dominated ice time, and started belittling and trash-talking some of the older (and slower) players on the ice. Clearly, they were having fun and they raised the level of play. However, they failed to realize that an established culture, with its own practices, norms, and hierarchy created the space where they were currently playing. They failed to recognize and receive what was already *there* in the hockey game, preferring instead to insert themselves into the middle of the group with little regard or concern for what existed before. Of course, hockey has its own ways of policing the violations of such norms, and the game eventually descended into the chaos of pushing, swearing, punching, and the like.

What happened at the pick-up hockey game could be described as a failure of hospitality. The five who joined the pick-up game were unable to recognize and receive the established realities of Friday night hockey. They did not recognize their identity as guests of an existing community. In addition, the "established" pick up players missed key opportunities to host the newcomers. We could have invited them to participate in ways that would have allowed them to understand how pick-up hockey in the middle of the night differs from league play.

The same dynamics guide any host-guest interaction, with similar risks and opportunities. We often focus on the role of 'host' when thinking about church and mission. My contention is that congregations must learn to live as guests of the neighborhood in which God has placed them. Guests must have a clear sense of their own expectations and experiences, while also attending to the social, cultural, and material offerings of the host. This kind of dual attentiveness – to self and to other – I will hold together under the verb "receive." By "receive", I picture hands and eyes open to *that which is present* in any social or cultural setting: attentiveness to what we bring and to the others we hope to join. The "Receive" section will invite congregations into practices of attentiveness to the dynamics and realities of both congregation and context.

Pray

For the Christian, hospitality provides an image of the gospel. We are simultaneously the guest and the host of the Triune God. So also, we relate to one another in a fluid interchange between guest and host. "Welcome one another," Paul says, "just as God, in Christ, has welcomed you" (Rom. 15:7). For this reason, the practices that help us learn to receive and recognize our own gifts and the dynamics of the places where God sends us cannot only be socially attentive, they must also be theologically attentive. In the "Pray" section, I will introduce practices for discerning God's leading and God's call while in the midst of our everyday lives. While "Receive" invites congregations to pay attention to fluid dynamics of congregation and community, "Pray" cultivates within congregations the capacity to reflect theologically within and upon these dynamics.

Eat

Even in our fast-paced, post-everything, i-device world, we express solidarity by eating with others. We are not only what we eat, but also those with whom we eat shape us. The Luke 10 narrative, where Jesus invites the seventy to eat what is set before them, assumes the reality of shared meals, of expressions of solidarity around the table. More broadly, congregational attentiveness to the realities of their neighborhoods and discerning prayer regarding God's presence and leading, will lead to companionship (literally, 'breaking bread with') with those to whom they have learned to dwell among. The "Eat" portion of the appendix will invite congregations to consider basic practices that build capacity for expressions of companionship and solidarity with neighborhood partners.

CHAPTER 1

THE CRISIS OF MISSION

Eat what is set before you;
heal the sick who are there
and say to them
'the Kingdom of God has come near to you.'
(Luke 10:8b-9)

"Ten years ago, that was me" Gary shouted as he nodded at a group of young high school boys wrestling over a loose basketball as a group of girls stood nearby, mildly interested in the outcome. It was an ordinary Wednesday at Midtown Baptist, and about forty-five students from the neighborhood had descended upon the church building for some combination of basketball, foosball, dodgeball, food, fun, and Bible Study. At the other end of the shortened basketball court, a group of older boys took turns shooting from behind the three-point line while a dispassionate game of soccer worked its way along the center of the court. Some young adults were intermixed in each of the games while a few huddled around the foosball table to check in and make plans for the upcoming evening. This loosely choreographed chaos was one of Midtown's clear success stories.

About ten years earlier, Keith, the youth pastor, realized that with few young families in the congregation, he could no longer depend upon the church to supply a steady stream of students. He also recognized that the neighborhood provided few safe and constructive spaces for young people. Thus, he began to make himself more present in the neighborhood and the church invested in a van to help transport students. Over the course of several years, Midtown's youth ministry began to reflect the racial and socioeconomic diversity of the neighborhood.

Gary was one of the early beneficiaries of this shift. He describes himself as a troubled kid who medicated family instability with drugs and cynicism. Checking out a youth drop-in night for the first time, he was surprised to find himself accepted by Keith and other leaders. At first, he attended sporadically and had trouble making sense of Keith's caring presence in his life. The consistent care and availability of an adult role model unsettled Gary, creating in him a crisis of belief. While he still scoffed at religion, he started to find himself moved by stories of God's love and new life in Jesus. Eventually, Gary turned toward Jesus in faith and slowly integrated into the life of the church. Several years later, Gary began serving as a volunteer leader in the youth group. I'm not sure which of the kids he nodded at, but my guess was he could identify with a good percentage of them.

According to the leadership team, the Midtown youth ministry has about a dozen "core" members who attend every week and involve themselves in the broader life of the church. The other 75% of the group is fluid from week-to-week, attending sporadically on Wednesday nights. The leaders hope for many more stories like Gary's—this is the vision that motivates this basketball-infused mess. It is why Keith has driven through the neighborhood nearly every Wednesday night for the past ten years to nurture relationships with hundreds of young people. In over a decade of ministry, Keith has cultivated a group where kids from the community and a few kids from the church gather, play basketball, and build friendships.

In many ways, Midtown's youth ministry mirrors the story of the congregation. Over the past decade, the church has responded to changes in the neighborhood by building bridges and creating a "come as you are" space.[1] Because of this, Gary embodies one of Midtown's most cherished images of itself, as a place where "God's love" is "alive in the West End."[2] Midtown celebrates those who have moved from stranger to family, from drug-addicted to regenerated. Yet, Midtown tells few stories about how the concept of "come as you are" shapes the identity and self-understanding of the church. Yes, people like Gary are changed in relationship with Midtown, but how is Midtown changed by its presence with and among strangers in the neighborhood? What are the implications, for instance, of a youth ministry with very few "church" kids and more than three quarters from the neighborhood?[3] Such questions lurk at the edges of Midtown's perduring presence in the West End neighborhood. When Gary showed up at the Midtown youth group several years ago, the love he encountered precipitated a crisis. He suddenly had to reckon with a different way of conceptualizing God, self, and world; now Midtown celebrates his confession of faith and journey of discipleship. He is one of their "success" stories. But what if the crisis goes the other way as well? What if Gary's presence at Midtown also precipitates a crisis *for the church?*

The next two chapters consider three ways in which Midtown's commitment to the West End neighborhood precipitates a crisis for the church. As with the case of Gary's conversion narrative, I suggest that crisis describes one condition of possibility for an encounter with the living

---

[1] The phrase "come as you are" was used repeatedly in focus groups and interviews by members and leaders of the church to describe their ethos and values. It is one of their cherished images of themselves.

[2] On the front of the church, a sign reads "God's love, alive in the West End!"

[3] Of course, there are other ways to talk about the participants in a youth ministry. I am using the designation made by the congregation itself, where people distinguish between "church kids" and "community kids." Midtown bases this distinction upon family relationships, not faith commitments. Some "community kids" have made professions of faith, but still do not participate in the broader life of the church. They distinguish between "church" and "community" kids based upon kinship. If a student is related to long-standing church families, they are considered "church kids." Midtown styles itself a family, which presents some challenges to its missional calling. I will address these questions in chapters seven and eight.

God. Because God is alive and active in God's church and world, and because God's ways are not our ways, we can expect God-encounters to cause disturbance and to upset our cherished notions of self and world. When we look at common biblical narratives of faith, we see that God-encounters precipitate crisis while various crises of life cultivate the kind of creativity and attentiveness needed to know or encounter God in a new way.

My argument in this chapter is relatively simple: God forges our faith in in the midst of crisis because the living God calls us as creatures within our creaturely, worldly lives to live for the sake of joining God in mission. After establishing this relationship between crisis and mission, we return to the experience of Midtown's perduring presence in the next chapter, as Midtown learns to recognize God's care for them by receiving what the neighborhood offers.

Faith Forged in Crisis

All of these died in faith without having received the promises, but from a distance they saw and greeted them. They confessed that they were strangers and foreigners on the earth, for people who speak in this way make it clear that they are seeking a homeland. If they had been thinking of the land that they had left behind, they would have had opportunity to return. But as it is, they desire a better country, that is, a heavenly one. Therefore God is not ashamed to be called their God. (Heb 11:13-16 NRSV)

The Danish philosopher Søren Kierkegaard begins his book *Fear and Trembling* with an extended meditation on Abraham as the father of faith. He portrays five different scenarios of Abraham sacrificing Isaac. Kierkegaard understands this episode as a crisis moment, and as one that discloses the nature of faith: what it means to struggle and to trust God. Kierkegaard sees Abraham as the picture of faith for us in the modern world as well, for faith is forged in crisis, asking us to take a leap into the unknown to trust God.[4] Abraham hears God's call within the desires, hopes, and limitations of creaturely and embodied existence. This call is not abstract, but concerns Abraham's family, his progeny, his fears, and hopes. Abraham's journey with Isaac and the lifting of the knife also have worldly implications in the sense that Isaac exists as a promise not only to Abraham, but also to a world in need of blessing.

David Bosch explains in *Transforming Mission* that the Japanese character for "crisis" contains both the character for "danger" and "opportunity."[5] Bosch draws upon this anecdote to reframe anxieties regarding the global missions movement. In spite of rapid and uncertain change, Bosch insists that the story of mission needs to be told and reimagined. Yes, the church faces certain risks and dangers, but the crisis in missions offers leaders and researchers an opportunity to see clearly, to act imaginatively, and to love boldly. I offer a similar use of "crisis" here. To say that faith forms in crisis is to reflect upon the possibilities for faith that risk and uncertainty create. In what follows, we explore themes of crisis in Scripture in relationship to faith: the crisis precipitated by God's call to us as creatures and for participation in God's mission. Tracing several situations of danger and opportunity in the biblical narrative, I outline three different ways in which crisis confronts the people of God in a way that builds faith: a crisis of *call*, a crisis of *cultivation*, and a crisis of *context*.

---

[4] See Søren Kierkegaard, *Fear and Trembling; Repetition*, trans. Howard V. Hong and Edna H. Hong, Vol. 6 (Princeton: Princeton University Press, 1983), 420. For Kierkegaard, faith forms in crisis, and constitutes a fundamental part of the human experience. He writes of Abraham: "you had to draw the knife before you kept Isaac...in 130 years you got no further than faith" (23).

[5] David Jacobus Bosch, *Transforming Mission: Paradigm Shifts in Theology of Mission*, 20th anniversary ed., Vol. 16 (Maryknoll: Orbis, 2011), 3.

Faith Disclosed: The Crisis of Call

The author of Hebrews follows Paul in chapter 11 by making Abraham the paradigmatic figure of faith for those in Christ.in making Abraham our paradigmatic figure of faith. In Genesis 12:1-3, Abraham hears God's call, which comes in the form of a promise and vocation. God promises Abraham land and descendants for the purpose of blessing the entire world. The promise is in service of the vocation. The vocation issues from the promise. Abraham and his children are blessed to be a blessing. The substance of God's call, however, is preceded by an imperative: "Go ... to the land that I will show you." In Abraham's life, the voice of God unsettled his plans and disrupted his family. No longer would Abraham live in his father's house and receive his father's inheritance. No longer would Abraham live among "his" people.

The promise and call of God interrupts Abraham's path and creates a crisis in Abraham's life. This is what God's voice and promise does. Crisis accompanies the promise and call of God, for promise necessarily looks forward to fulfillment. It calls attention to what is not yet by conditioning the future.[6] Imagine, for example, the promise a parent makes to a child: "I promise to attend your choir concert tonight." The promise only makes sense if the concert has not yet happened. It places a condition and now an expectation or anticipation on the future. As such, it creates a disruption for both the promiser and promised: the child now lives in anticipation of fulfillment and the parent must order her or his life accordingly. Perhaps previously, the child had a vague sense of parental support for the choir concert. Now, after the promise is spoken, the child has a concrete hope, expectation, and anticipation of actual presence. The

---

[6] Gregory Walter argues that promise is a type of gift: "promise consists of two moments of giving, both the pledge and then the actual giving of the promise, with the doubled gift extended over time in between the two" (6). Walter draws attention to the fact that promise creates particular social conditions, which he describes as gift. The promise given creates a social bond between the promiser and the promised, as well as the actual gift given when the promise is fulfilled. See Gregory Walter, *Being Promised: Theology, Gift, and Practice* (Grand Rapids: Eerdmans, 2013).

promise permanently alters the child's *imagined future* and subsequently shapes the child's *desire*. The child will now anticipate the concert as an event shared with the parent; the child will imagine singing to the parent in the audience and desire some kind of parental recognition, show of support, or response. Now, if circumstances intervene and the parent does not arrive at the concert or arrives late and sits in a place where the child cannot see, the child will anxiously scan the crowd throughout the performance and register disappointment at the absence. Before the promise, such an imagined future and desire may have been present, but it would not be as concrete. A promise alters, disrupts, and changes a social relationship in concrete ways by looking forward to fulfillment, giving new shape to the life and expectations of the parties involved in the promise. The bigger the promise – "I promise to love you in sickness and in health" – the more potentially disruptive it becomes.

The examples of faith in Hebrews 11 are marked by such disruption, for the faithful hear God's promise and learn to desire concretely what they (perhaps) only vaguely sensed. Through promise, they learn to desire "a better country, a heavenly one." In Abraham's case, God promises land and a family. At the time, Abraham is part of a transient family and without children. The desire for land and family would certainly be expected in his cultural environment. However, God's promise gives that desire new form, for now God promises to fulfill these particular hopes in a particular way. Children and land are no longer things that might just happen if circumstances allow (similar to the child's vague sense that the parent supports the choir concert), they are now a future possibility in relationship to this God; there is an agent, a Subject responsible for land and family. This creates a crisis point for Abraham; it provokes Abraham to respond in one way or another. There is no return to 'normal' or status quo.

God's word of promise works in relationship to calling, or one's vocation. Vocation also offers a horizon or a vision of the future that gives concrete shape to one's imagination. If promise shapes expectation and anticipation, then vocation shapes one's sense of purpose or meaning. Promise invites one to anticipate a certain situation or outcome, shaping one's desires and life accordingly. Vocation offers a *telos* or the orientation of meaning for one's life, interjecting a "so that" into the midst of one's activity. This "so that" also creates a type of crisis, in that it invites a response of participation which inevitably shapes the imagination and the practices of the one called and invited.

Current approaches to early childhood education utilize some features of a vocational call. Researchers have discovered the value of play for teaching children things like discipline and self-control.[7] Through play, children construct narratives with other children as a means of disciplining one another's behavior. A child becomes capable of standing at attention for long periods if she imagines herself guarding a castle. The narrative constructed through play provides a horizon of meaning for the child's activities, which empowers the child to learn new things, to exercise self-control, to work with others, etc. Adults are not much different, in that we yearn to make sense of our lives, to have a *telos* or horizon toward which we live: a "so that." When God promises Abraham a family and land, God also invites Abraham into a particular "so that." Abraham's life is to now be lived *so that* all the nations on earth can be blessed through him (Gen. 12:1-3). This vocation, however, requires participation. Once heard, Abraham must enter the story God is telling, must make God's "so that" his own. The promise invites anticipation; vocation invites participation. The two come together in the imperative "Go."

Abraham and the others highlighted in Hebrews 11 are celebrated for their faith because the call and promise of God elicited a real response

---

[7] Research into play is fascinating and multi-faceted. See, for example, Robin Maranz Henig, "Taking Play Seriously," *New York Times Magazine* (February 17, 2008).

from them. They each went to the land that God would show them. Their desires were shaped according to the promise given by God; their self-understanding determined by the vocation bestowed upon them. They lived as "strangers and foreigners" in anticipation of a "homeland" to be given by God (Heb. 11:13). They embraced the fragments of fulfilled promises, understanding their lives as caught up in a grand and epic narrative, thus seeing and "greeting" the promises of God while they were still far off. The voice and presence of God disrupted and interrupted them. And they responded in faith, by leaving what was once settled and comfortable. They received the promise and they participated in the call. Their desires began to be shaped according to the promise and they began to imagine their lives as participating in the story of God. This is faith; this is why faith must always be accompanied by disruption and interruption. Such themes are expressed in stories of the faithful again and again. But the disruption comes, not only from God's call, but also by the earthly, creaturely conditions of the called. The call does not elevate one above creaturely existence, but rather, orders one within it. The creaturely conditions of God's call, then, provide another lens through which we might consider the crisis of faith. The faith of Israel formed in exile provides our example here.

Faith Dislocated: The Crisis of Cultivation

The call of Abraham and other heroes of the faith underscore the disruptive nature of God's invitation to relationship. The promise and call of God precipitates a crisis in our lives by offering an alternative future and horizon to which we are invited to respond. When the voice of God breaks the silence, we are confronted with the new and unexpected; a horizon opens up that previously was not imagined or of which we were only vaguely aware. We are placed in a position to respond; to *go to the land that God shows us*. Of course, Abraham physically went to the land of Canaan, a land that was new and unfamiliar. Other persons recounted in

Hebrews 11 did not physically relocate but had some concrete means of response—of embarking on a journey of faith and risk.

The speech of God creates a faith-forming crisis that moves God's people. But it is not the only such crisis. In the biblical narrative, the Exile offers another picture of faith forged in the midst of crisis. The forced relocation of Israel, the burning and plundering of her cities, the destruction of her temple, the capture of her young men and women to be conscripted into Foreign Service, is preceded by prophetic warnings to an idolatrous and self-satisfied people. Isaiah and Jeremiah make clear the connection between callous disinterest in the voice and call of God and the resulting experience of exile. Exile is judgment. The people are forced into movement they never expected and greatly feared. Their faith was irretrievably fractured in suffering and violence. Yet, such a crisis creates new ground for faith; an insight not lost on Bible scholars. If the voice of God creates a crisis of *response*, creaturely life and worldly events force upon Israel a crisis of *identity*.

Israel inherited God's promise and call through the Abrahamic and Mosaic covenants. Their religious and national identity had been cultivated over centuries of religious and political practices, sustained institutionally by the Priesthood, the Temple, and the Monarchy. These institutions provided more than social order and religious/governmental services; they functioned symbolically, along with the Torah and the Land, to provide a sense of coherence for Israel's story and self-understanding.[8] Israelite *culture* and Israel's *cultural institutions* provided a reliable orientation and means for Israel's faith. What does it mean to be Yahweh's people? It means that Israel has received Land and Torah, is governed by Yahweh's chosen servant, and hosts the very dwelling place of God on Mount Zion.

---

[8] N.T. Wright, in *The New Testament and the People of God,* argues for Temple, Land, Torah, and Israel as core symbols for sustaining Jewish identity and practice. See N. T. Wright, *The New Testament and the People of God*, Vol. 1 (Minneapolis: Fortress Press, 1992), 215ff.

The Exile lays waste to each of these symbols and institutions except, to some extent, the Torah.

By all accounts, the Exile left Judah devastated. The temple lay in ruins. Jerusalem was burned to the ground, and David's heir was impotent in the face of Babylonian aggression. Those carried off into exile now faced an identity crisis with massive theological and doxological implications. Israel understood herself as the people of God who received the land promised to Abraham, the Law given to Moses, the Kingdom given to the Davidic dynasty, and the temple built by Solomon. Babylon's victory meant a sudden and violent end to nearly all these carriers of identity. Although they still had the Law, they lacked the political power to implement it as a complete social program. As such, Israel's exilic theological crisis goes beyond the usual questions of theodicy (Where are you, God? Why?), and provokes deeper questions of identity and faith: *Who and whose are we now that this has happened? What is the state of the promise given to our people?*

These questions led to theological searching: *Can God be trusted?* The exilic Psalm asks, "How can we sing the Lord's song in a foreign land?" (Psalm 137:4). The Psalmist's question addresses God, Israelite identity, and matters of religious practice. What does it look like to worship God as a religious and cultural minority, while swimming in the shark-infested waters of exile? How can we observe the commandments of the Lord as social and cultural minorities? How do we sing the Lord's song while in a foreign land? In the course of Psalm 137, God's silence so frustrates the Psalmist that he even envisions dashing Babylonian infants on the stones! Indeed, the Exile elicits a broad range of responses, from anger and questions to the promises of Deutero-Isaiah and the stories of Ezra, Nehemiah, Esther, and Daniel. The breadth of material points toward a people finding their way and rediscovering the faithful presence of the God who goes with them into exile.

Some exilic texts seek to reestablish a lost identity, as with the Ezra-Nehemiah accounts of return from captivity. However, other texts, such as Jeremiah's letter to the captives and the stories of Daniel, wrestle with issues of faithfulness and identity within an altogether new cultural and social setting. Daniel, in particular, embodies a concern for Israelite identity, worship, and theology while living in the center of the imperial machine. Although Daniel is conscripted into pagan service, he refuses to eat the rich food of the upper class. Although Daniel excels as a young professional among Babylon's politicians, he refuses to offer sacrifices and pray to an earthly King. An ambiguous tension plays out in Daniel's life.

While complete and total removal from the pagan empire remains impossible, Daniel discerns faithful practices and practical resistance to the assumptions and ways of the empire. Through this discernment, Daniel discovers a new shape for Israel's exilic identity. They are still God's holy people set apart and blessed to be a blessing. But they now receive the blessing of God from within a vulnerable social location and proceed to offer blessing to a foreign land and a pagan nation. The identity and theological crises lead to a theological breakthrough: God is trustworthy, and God's blessing is meant to be shared!

Putting down roots, seeking the *shalom* of Babylon while still discerning and cultivating a unique Jewish identity among the pagans, these difficult tasks constitute some of the most theologically creative and insightful texts of the Hebrew canon. In the midst of these tasks, the book of Isaiah[9] instructs the exiles to put out of their mind the things of old, for God is about to do something altogether new. The exilic (and post-exilic) texts provide visions like Isaiah 60, where the nations now travel to a

---

[9] The book of Isaiah reflects prophecies addressing three different historical periods for Israel. Generally, chapters 1-39 warn Israel about the impending exile, 40-55 reflect the exilic condition, and 56-66 their post-exilic condition. I recognize that my language here conflates the second and third sections, referring to the announcement of something new, which features primarily in 56-66. I do this because I agree with New Testament scholars, like N.T. Wright, who argue that Israel was still waiting to be rescued from Exile in the First Century. That is, their return to the land remained ambiguous and problematic.

restored temple and offer to God their cultural riches. The exilic texts put the creaturely conditions of God's call into sharp relief. Will God keep the promise? Can God be trusted? Is God here in Babylon? As such, it forces questions of culture and cultivation; can God be worshipped outside of Jerusalem? Can we worship God among these people? Here is the tension in biblical faith: it is always an embodied faith that demands the cultivation of community, language, practices, and institutions for its expression and proclamation. The Israelite faith knew no alternative but an all-encompassing one, which touches all of one's life. Yet, as Israel discovers in exile, cultural practices, institutions, and symbols are not always readily amenable to biblical faith. The Exile forces Israel to cultivate new and creative responses to Babylonian culture, even as they live their lives among Babylonian people.

Not all Judeans were carried off into exile. Some were able to stay behind and work the now devastated land. Ezra and Nehemiah provide a glimpse of those who were left behind. Although they shared in the theological crisis of the exiles, they were not able to share in or experience the same theological breakthrough. Those who were carried into exile entered a learning curve not of their own design; their suffering and discernment and crisis of identity gave shape to what Walter Brueggemann considers Israel's most productive and creative period theologically.[10] Similarly, Jehu Hanciles observes, "The Jerusalem remnant, too, mourned over the fate that had befallen their nation and longed for its restoration. But it settled into a precarious existence, barely sustained by fading memories of yesteryears. Settledness, such as it was, bred religious decay."[11]

---

[10] See Walter Brueggemann, *Theology of the Old Testament: Testimony, Dispute, Advocacy* (Minneapolis: Fortress Press, 1997).

[11] Jehu Hanciles, *Beyond Christendom: Globalization, African Migration, and the Transformation of the West* (Maryknoll, N.Y.: Orbis Books, 2008), 147.

Here lies the tension. The suffering and forced migration of the Exile created an identity crisis for an idolatrous and self-satisfied Israel. Those carried off do, in fact, learn to understand themselves differently through practices of both resistance and blessing in the midst of a pagan empire. More importantly, as they go, they discover Yahweh powerful and present among the nations. This discovery influences the further development of Israel's Scriptures in a profound way, giving shape to the current redaction of the creation stories that makes a clear contrast with the violence of Babylonian creation myths. The Exile leads Israel to collect and formalize its canon. The Exile brings into Israel's prophetic consciousness a concern for and angst about the nations, as Second-Isaiah's (Isa. 40-55) focus on the Servant demonstrates. The prophet imagines the servant as not only a gift for Israel, but also a light to the nations. Furthermore, the Exile gives space for Israel to recognize the dead-end that is self-satisfied worship. The context of blessing, promise, and vocation is placed back into the world of the nations. Perhaps some of these theological breakthroughs could have come from an Israel settled permanently in the land, but they did not. Instead, the ones who remained in the land did not reimagine and reframe Israel's identity as God's people in this time of transition and crisis. Nor are they the ones who are able to encounter Yahweh in the same expansive and transformative terms of the exilic community. Sometimes we can lose our way without ever leaving home. Indeed, "settledness," and the stasis of identity that it brings in a changing and fluid world, can lead to spiritual, theological, and religious decay.

At times, this mobility happens as a response of faith to God's call: "Go." At other times, it is a mobility thrust upon God's people from sin or war or even exile. The biblical faith is and has been formed within the crisis and ambiguity of real-world events. Crises such as the Exile give shape to the faith in a way that is almost inconceivable before. The real-world conditions of our lives, our creaturely limitations and possibilities, are not accidental to our theological understanding, but rather constitutive. Like a farmer preparing ground for seed, faith must be cultivated as the promise and presence of God addresses everyday life. What we learn is that God's people are formed as God's people while on the way and while working through historical processes. In Israel's reflection, the Exile was understood as God's judgment. The result of the Exile, however, was an expansive understanding of God and a beautifully adaptive and resilient *diaspora* faith: a faith formed from and made for the road. This is part of the biblical faith. The real-world crises, particularly crises of identity, give shape to our faith and theology. We come to know God, not in an escape from the world, but as we stretch to live faithfully within it. Faith is *cultivated* while on the way.

Faith Discovered: The Crisis of Context

Abraham is called, promised, and sent. Judah is carried off into exile. Both events precipitate a crisis of identity and theology. Both events call into question the status quo and invite God's people into a different understanding of God. The theological reflection that emerges from both events leaves an indelible mark on the biblical faith. Faith forms in crises of disclosure and dislocation, it is reformed as we learn to respond to God's call and cultivate new forms of faith and witness in the midst of real-world events. As such, biblical faith is creaturely and embodied. The danger in what has been developed so far is that the crisis of faith might be interpreted existentially, as an internalized crisis of identity. However, the biblical narratives do not allow us this interpretation for God's call. Given in the midst of our everyday lives, the call is always for the sake of God's world. We not only receive God's call within the possibilities and limitations of our creaturely existence, but we also *discover* what that call means under these same conditions. What I mean by this is that exile was not the backdrop or muse for theological formation, but that real Israelite encounters with the imperial "Other" allowed Israel to discover God's presence, identity, and power in new ways. Daniel and others find theological companionship in unlikely places. This theme of discovery becomes clearer as we consider the discoveries of the early church in the book of Acts, where companionship with the Gentiles leads to crisis and discovery.

Luke writes the paradigmatic text for Gentile inclusion in Acts 10-15. The events are well known. Peter, lounging on the rooftop of Simon the tanner, receives a vision of unclean animals and hears the instruction to "kill and eat" (Acts 10:13). When Peter protests, claiming his purity as one who has never allowed anything unclean or impure to touch his lips, a voice responds, "what God has made clean, you must not call profane" (Acts 10:15). This happens three times right before Peter receives a knock on the door. The reader knows that Cornelius, a devout centurion in Caesarea, had received a vision from God instructing him to send to Joppa for Simon called Peter. Peter does not yet know what the vision means, but the reader suspects that it just might have something to do with this devout centurion who has sent men to find Peter. Standing at the door, Peter hears additional confirmation from the Holy Spirit, so Peter goes with the servants of Cornelius.

In this story, God calls Peter into God's mission. Luke's narrative leaves the agency completely in the hands of God. It is God who appears to Cornelius. It is God who speaks to Peter. It is the Spirit who tells Peter to go while he is still scratching his head over the vision. Peter responds in faith and goes to the place God sends him. However, Cornelius also actively participates in Peter's call. Cornelius receives the first vision. Cornelius sends the servants to find Peter. Cornelius welcomes Peter into his house and listens intently to Peter's teaching. Peter, the evangelist in the story, *suffers* the call of God and the invitation of Cornelius. Peter goes, but his going is *in response* to the initiative, activity, and voice of others. Peter bears witness to the gospel of Jesus Christ as a *response* to the work of God and the questions, presence, and activity of those *outside the church*. And when we look closely, we see Luke consistently telling the story of God's mission with an emphasis on the initiative of those beyond the church. Peter's speech on the day of Pentecost comes in response to the genuine perplexity of the crowds (Acts 2). Peter and John witness to the gospel before the authorities because they are genuinely confused about what to do with these two "uneducated and ordinary men" who defied expectation (Acts 4:13). Philip baptizes the Ethiopian official in Acts 8 after the Ethiopian asks Philip to explain the words of the prophet Isaiah to him. I want to suggest that these are not accidental details in Luke's narrative; rather, they disclose a critical understanding of God's mission and the crisis it precipitates.[12]

In each of these stories, the church discovers something and is prodded into action by various elements of context. People and place, situation and need invite the church to go places it might not naturally go and to discover God at work in ways it might not expect. God meets the disciples as they witness in various contexts, for the mission of the church is the mission *of God*. Jesus' declaration in Acts 1:8 ("you will be my witnesses in Jerusalem, Judea, Samaria, and to the ends of the earth") is not an invitation to an all-night strategy session, but rather a literary foreshadowing. The disciples will know that the Spirit has come upon them when they find themselves witnessing in these places. It is a statement that only makes sense after the fact of God's Spirit coming in power and God leading the church into the world. In Acts 1:8, the church does not yet have a self-understanding that could lead it into Samaria or Rome. It takes Saul's methodical persecution in Jerusalem (going house to house) to spark Philip's foray into Samaria and his encounter with the Ethiopian. It takes several visions, Cornelius's initiative, and the surprising gift of the

---

[12] Lesslie Newbigin notes, "almost all proclamations of the gospel which are described in Acts are in response to questions asked by those outside the Church." See Lesslie Newbigin, *The Gospel in a Pluralist Society* (Grand Rapids: W.B. Eerdmans, 1989), 116.

Spirit for Cornelius and his family to provoke church leadership to consider the fact that "God has granted even the Gentiles repentance unto life" (Acts 11:18).

Philip, Peter, Paul, and others go into God's world as they are sent. Sometimes this sending looks like the promise and call of Abraham. God appears to Peter in a vision, Paul sees the man from Macedonia in a dream. Other times this sending looks like a surprising or traumatic disruption: Philip flees persecution; Peter finds himself in the house of a Gentile and confronted with a set of decisions he did not anticipate. In each case, the church discovers something regarding their own identity as God's sent people and the God who sends them. In each case, the church *suffers* some crisis of sending or interruption or the surprising initiative of an outsider before discovering God and God's leading in the encounter.

This is true not only in the book of Acts, but also as we look across the history of Christian mission.[13] Christianity is simultaneously local and global, in the sense that it does not stretch across the globe as a singular entity with a clear center or shared language, as is the case with Islam.[14] Although Islam is a truly global religion, Mecca remains a geographic and cultural center. This, of course, is due to the presumed untranslatability of the *Qur'an*, along with daily prayers facing Mecca and the Hajj. Everywhere Islam has expanded, so has the Arabic language and a reverence toward Mecca. However, Christian history remains more dynamic culturally and geographically. In the first centuries, the Christian story shifts geographical centers, from the Middle East and North Africa to Rome, then on to Northern Europe and now to the global South. Each of these movements changes fundamental characteristics of the faith. Christians in Victorian England have little in common with those who met

---

[13] See Andrew F. Walls, *The Missionary Movement in Christian History: Studies in the Transmission of Faith* (Maryknoll, NY: Orbis Books, 1996).

[14] See Lamin O. Sanneh, *Translating the Message: The Missionary Impact on Culture*, 2nd ed., Vol. 42 (Maryknoll, N.Y.: Orbis Books, 2009), 324.

in the temple in the first century. Modern Christians in Nigeria have little in common with those of Victorian England. All parties are drawn to wholly different frameworks for reading Scripture, their worship shaped by wholly different practices, their ethical priorities also remarkably diverse. This diversity underscores the mobility and cultural adaptability of the Christian faith. It is not a problem for the faith, but rather is its genius and its glory.[15]

Furthermore, the cultural diversity of the faith is not accidental, but rather the historical tapestry of God's people discovering new faithful responses to the gospel in new cultural, linguistic, and even generational contexts. In ever new ways, the Spirit enables the church to display new contextual embodiments of the Christian faith. Without this work, the faith fossilizes and eventually atrophies into a brittle image of itself. Christian cultural diversity does not develop from a generic or aesthetic preference for pluralism, but rather from centuries of faithful reflection as God's people suffer the crisis of God's call, God's world, God's mission in the name and hope of Jesus.

Conclusion: Mission as Crisis

God calls God's people within their worldly, creaturely existence to participate in very particular ways in God's mission in the world. The different levels of this basic Christian truth suggest crisis as constitutive of faith, for the faithful hear God's promise and learn to desire concretely what they (perhaps) only vaguely sensed. Through promise, they learn to desire "a better country, a heavenly one." This crisis of faith is not a

---

[15] By drawing attention to Christian cultural diversity, I do not mean to neglect Christianity's relationship to Israel through Jesus. Willie Jennings rightly cautions us against accounts of diversity and mobility that forget this history as one of Gentile inclusion in Israel's story. Christian diversity should theologically draw attention to the creation of God's new humanity through the cross of Christ (Eph. 2:11-22). See Willie James Jennings, *The Christian Imagination: Christian Theology and the Origins of Race* (New Haven: Yale University Press, 2010), 250-288.

singular event, as we might think of a crisis that leads to conversion, but it is an ongoing one that suggests discovery, mobility, mystery, and an unpredictable learning curve. In the life of Midtown, we see evidence of such crises expressed as the church seeks a faithful, perduring presence in response to the call of God to stay in the West End, along with their sense of being dislocated from the center of a dynamically changing neighborhood, and the invitation to discover new ways of shaping their community attentive to the people to whom God sends them.

Faith is forged in crisis because God is the living God. Just as Mark's gospel ends with fear and uncertainty,[16] so also God's surprising action in the world confounds our expectations and idolatrous designs. Crisis comes to God's people as a way of helping us to imagine afresh, to live creatively and boldly. Crisis invites risk and opportunity. But even more significantly, faith is forged in crisis because the living God calls God's people to participate in God's mission in the world. The angel at the tomb in Mark 16 instructs the disciples to go to Galilee, for Jesus had already gone on ahead of them. The living God is not static, but an active agent in the world. And God's people are called, in the midst of their worldly, embodied, creaturely lives, to participate in God's work. This is bound to be unsettling. Faith is forged in crisis because God calls and sends us like "lambs into the midst of wolves."

When considering Midtown's decision to stay in its neighborhood and Midtown's perduring presence, three different types of crises emerge that roughly correlate with what we explored above. Perduring presence creates crises of *call*, *cultivation*, and *context*, in which, like Peter and Cornelius, Midtown discovers a new shape and form of Christian

---

[16] The earliest versions of Mark's gospel end at verse 8, where the women flee the empty tomb in fear and tell no one. Some scholars see this abrupt and dark ending as a brilliant artistic choice on the part of Mark. It asks the reader – if the women are afraid and telling no one about the resurrected Christ, what will you do? It also begs the reader to go back to the beginning and read the gospel once again. Other scholars think that the real ending of Mark simply has been lost to history. Given Mark's fast-paced storytelling and the overall mood of his gospel, I agree with the first theory. See Donald Juel, *A Master of Surprise: Mark Interpreted* (Minneapolis: Fortress Press, 1994).

faithfulness. First, Midtown's perduring presence is discerned in relationship to God's mission. That is, the congregation's life in the neighborhood discloses God in some way. Chapters 3 and 4 explore perduring presence as a theological crisis, a crisis of call, whereby mission provides the possibility for Midtown to be evangelized again by the good news of the triune *missio Dei,* while also creating capacity to practice theological and missional discernment. Second, as the congregation extends itself outward into mission, it finds surprising partners in ministry and mission that offer different gifts, challenges, and possibilities to the church. Like Israel in exile, the public witness of the congregation is shaped by relationships in which Midtown does not have power or authority.[17] They depend upon a variety of partners to work within the neighborhood, which invites the congregation to reimagine its missionary vocation. We will consider this crisis in chapters 5 and 6. Finally, as the congregation encounters and learns to be welcomed by the stranger, it allows itself to be changed, challenged, and interrupted by the stranger. While the story of Gary's conversion suggests the church changing Gary, it overlooks the ways in which Gary has brought his own history, gifts, and perspectives into the life of the church. Midtown imagines itself a family, but its neighborhood ministries pose a challenge to this self-image. We address these questions in chapters 7 and 8.

At a very simple level, these three challenges demonstrate, each from a different angle, the ways in which neighborhood mission reflects back upon a congregation. The arrows in mission do not point in only one direction, but rather come back to shape the church sent out into the

---

[17] I hesitate to make a connection to the Exile here because the sense of vulnerability that Midtown faces is nothing like the horrific violence and disempowerment experienced by Israel – or any other exiled people, for that matter. However, the fact of God's presence and gift in the midst of vulnerability creates, I think, a strong enough image that I draw upon the exilic narratives...with caution. See also Scott Hagley, "Exiles on Main Street: Reframing Short-Term Mission," in *Cultivating Sent Communities: Missional Spiritual Formation*, ed. Dwight J. Zscheile (Grand Rapids: Eerdmans, 2012), 56-80.

neighborhood. Mission calls into question practices of intimacy and piety, benevolence and service, and theological reflection. As the church participates in the mission of God, it finds itself being shaped by that mission. This crisis of engagement with the neighborhood must be navigated through learning capacities of responsiveness. Before turning to these capacities for mission, however, I describe the three crises of mission – call, cultivation, and context – as they are reflected within the life of Midtown. While I offer a description of a single church, I think that such a description can function allegorically, to help us see different variants of these crises in the congregations and contexts within which we work.[18] We know from the "scandal of particularity" that the concrete and the particular can also be revelatory and disclosive. I am betting that Midtown's particularity, while perhaps not revelatory, can help us to see our own contexts more clearly, ask new questions, and perhaps imagine new futures in the name and hope of Christ.

---

[18] James Clifford argues persuasively that thick descriptions of particular cultures or contexts (ethnographic writing) can function allegorically, helping us to make connections in other areas of our life. See Clifford, "On Ethnographic Allegory", 98-121.

CHAPTER 2

LIVING AND LEARNING: ETHNOGRAPHY OF A CRISIS

See ... I send you out like lambs
Into the midst of wolves
(Luke 10:3)

She had become a "sleepwalker on a sidewalk."[1] In her book *On Looking,* Alexandra Horowitz describes an experience of waking up to the world of her dog walking route in New York City. Watching her two dogs dart between trees and fences, people and unseen points of interest led Horowitz to the gradual realization that her dogs experienced an entirely different one block walk than she did. She confesses, "I was paying so little attention to most of what was right before us."[2] This realization led her to explore the question of attention through the simple practice of walking her neighborhood with another person. She takes her first walk with her nineteen-month-old son, through whom she discovers the scope of the neighborhood and the exuberance of exploration. She later walks with a mindfulness researcher who, in the course of exploring the importance of attentiveness, casually steps over $60 left on the sidewalk. Horowitz's dog stops for the money, but the mindful humans initially miss it completely. One of her last walks is with a blind man, who alerts Horowitz to the aural and tactile world of the neighborhood. The book raises an important

---

[1] Alexandra Horowitz, *On Looking: A Walker's Guide to the Art of Observation* (New York: Scribner, 2014), 2.

[2] Ibid., 2.

question: What is attention? What does it mean to pay attention? How do we learn attentiveness?

On Looking demonstrates the relative and social nature of attention. For each of Horowitz's walks, her social context gives shape to what counts as worthy of attention. A city looks different when walking with a toddler than a scientist, for instance. What makes *On Looking* interesting is the fact that the eleven different walks she takes unveil such different insights into the same space. One leaves the book with a sense of the unremitting possibilities of discovery within a single city block. Eleven more walks with eleven more people would certainly disclose additional new and unforeseen discoveries. Experience provides an immeasurable surplus; we can only ever attend to our surroundings in fits and starts.

Horowitz's gradual awakening and her subsequent reenvisioning of her neighborhood is comparable to the theme of crisis reflected in the previous chapter. The biblical story records awakenings among God's people as a flattened and fossilized understanding of self. God becomes untenable in light of God's promise and call, one's experience in the world, or the surprising work of God outside the assumed boundaries of the community. While Horowitz's experience is neither theological nor characterized as a crisis, it does provide a picture of how disruptive experiences guide learning, and how the presence of others facilitates possible disruptive moments. Horowitz moves from a sleeper to one more fully awake because her dogs embrace the block in an entirely different way. She then learns to notice new things by inviting new people (and not only her dogs) to walk the neighborhood with her.

Horowitz provides a lighthearted anecdote for a significant insight from Midtown's experience in the West End. In the previous chapter, I suggest crisis as one element of our experience in mission. God calls us as creatures to participate in God's work in the world. The call, the conditions of the call and the place to which we are called all require that we build new capacities because God is living and active in the world ahead of us.

Mission precipitates a crisis because we must continually learn as we go. We do not sleepwalk into God's mission. In this chapter, we turn from biblical pictures of this crisis to Midtown's own learning curve in mission. As Horowitz discovered, strangers and outsiders play a significant role in Midtown's learning. Like the biblical narratives traced in the previous chapter, the role of such strangers carries theological possibility and agency, for the different disruptions faced by Midtown disclose key capacities for enabling Midtown to live faithfully as a sign of God's love, alive in the West End.

This chapter is organized into two different sections. First, I provide an ethnographic account of Midtown's crises in mission. Drawing from research conducted in 2009-2010, I recount the places of tension, surprise, and ambiguity, highlighting three different crises precipitated by Midtown's perduring presence in the neighborhood. The second part of the chapter proposes three critical capacities Midtown must learn in the midst of its ministry of presence. The crisis of *call* invites theological discernment, the crisis of *cultivation* invites intentional and improvisational discernment of public partnerships, and the crisis of *context* invites hospitality as a practice of contextualization.

An Ethnographic Account of Missional Crises

Ethnography is a form of qualitative research that comes from anthropology and aims to *interpret* culture in the writing of an essay.[3] It is an admittedly messy endeavor since "culture" is an amorphous, fluid, and contested set of meanings about what we do and what we mean. Furthermore, it often attends to what is assumed, to the pre-reflective,

---

[3] On ethnography as writing, see James Clifford and George E. Marcus, eds., *Writing Culture: The Politics and Poetics of Ethnography* (Berkley: University of California Press, 1986). For a picture of ethnography in the church or as part of pastoral ministry, see Mary Clark Moschella, *Ethnography as a Pastoral Practice: An Introduction* (Cleveland: Pilgrim Press, 2008).

since the most formative aspects of culture are the elements that participants engage unthinkingly, like the organization of a church worship space into rows and chairs facing a stage or the use of financial metaphors such as "invest" when talking about ministry. Because of this difficulty, ethnography requires several layers of attention, from participant observation and journaling/making field notes, to interviews and focus groups. My research engaged the congregation on all these levels with the addition of intentional feedback loops where observations, insights, and results of previous interviews and observations were given to focus groups to reflect upon. Three areas of tension became apparent as I explored the public witness of the congregation and sought to describe both Midtown's neighborhood engagement and the sense the congregation made of this engagement. In each of these areas, Midtown's own self-understanding and language remained disconnected from its practice. These areas, I suggest, provide insight into the critical capacities the congregation is learning for its perduring presence with the neighborhood.

Midtown as an Intimate Family: Crisis of Context

"You must be new here?" I heard this question so many times I checked to make sure I wasn't wearing a "visitor" badge or sitting in a "visitors" section. On most Sundays, Midtown has about 200 people in its worship gathering. Because the auditorium comfortably seats about 300, it feels neither crowded nor empty. I began to attend Midtown as a participant observer before I began the first round of congregational interviews. Originally, Midtown drew my attention through its history of intentional engagement in an urban neighborhood, but it caught me off guard with its warmth and intimacy that Sunday morning. It was certainly difficult to remain anonymous for long. Midtown may be a key partner with several public organizations, but it is also an intimate family that enjoys deep relationships and recognizes when a stranger is in their midst.

In fact, intimacy features prominently in Midtown's self-understanding and congregational aspiration. Interviews with a cross-section of congregants at the beginning of the research process invited members to share their hopes and anxieties, experiences of God, and how they would describe the church. In each of these questions, intimacy surfaced as a prevailing goal for one's relationship with God and the congregation. This was true both for those who were a part of the intimate family and for those who considered themselves to be strangers or outside the core membership of the church; for those who thought of themselves as close to God and those who did not. Congregation members used intimacy to make sense of their experience. They either praised the church for being a close, intimate family or expressed disappointment that they did not feel close to the congregation. The same dynamic shapes Midtown's experiences of God. God-encounters reported by interviewees prioritized immediate, personal, and interior encounters. They did not report an encounter with God through the church, through contact with a stranger, or while serving others. God revealed Godself[4] to them through interiority—in the heart.

At one level, this should not be surprising. Midtown's roots within North American evangelicalism in general and Pietism in particular suggest as much. A core feature of twentieth century Western evangelicalism has been a highly internalized conversion narrative where participants tell the story of Jesus as one's "personal Lord and Savior." While these narratives have helped to underscore the need for persons to respond to the gospel, it has also led to a challenge in how evangelicals both conceive of and relate to the church. As one book of essays suggests,

---

[4] When possible, I will use gender-neutral language to refer to God throughout the book. While the first-person of the Trinity is called "Father," and biblical texts use a masculine pronoun in referring to God, the biblical witness and theological tradition is consistently refuses a single gendered image of God, describing God in both masculine and feminine terms. I will follow this practice for both theological reasons and what has become expected, gender-neutral language across English writing and usage.

"evangelical ecclesiology" has become an oxymoron.[5] It is no great insight to suggest that evangelical experience values the personal over the communal, for the revival experiences that shaped evangelicalism insisted that membership to a church community and regular participation in Christian worship was not sufficient if one did not have a personal "I-Thou" encounter with God.

Midtown's leadership, however, is quick to point out their heritage as *pietistic* evangelicals. With this distinction, they mean to draw attention to the ways that their form of life draws from a particular evangelical renewal movement begun by Philip Jacob Spener and August Hermann Francke in Halle, Germany at the beginning of the eighteenth century.[6] Originating in the midst of a dry Lutheran scholasticism, the Pietism of Spener and Francke combined a religion of the heart with close and intentional community. In such a vision, conversion to Christ was imagined to be an inward experience reflected in outward change and life in community. This combination inspired John Wesley and the later trans-Atlantic revivals that gave shape to North American revivalism and evangelicalism.

This personal, experiential, and community component of pietistic Christianity has shaped segments of modern evangelicalism with what Roger Olson calls a "conversional piety." He describes this as "the experience of conversion to Christ by repentance and faith, resulting in justification, regeneration by the Holy Spirit, and an intimate, personal relationship with Christ marked by prayer, holiness of life, worship of God,

---

[5] John G. Stackhouse, ed., *Evangelical Ecclesiology: Reality Or Illusion?* (Grand Rapids: Baker Academic, 2003), 232.

[6] For an overview of Pietism research as it relates to North American congregations, see Jonathan Strom, "Problems and Promises of Pietism Research," *Church History* 71, no. 3 (2002), 536-54. Pietism traces its roots to the work of Philip Jacob Spener. See Philipp Jakob Spener, *Pia Desideria*, trans. Theodore G. Tappert (Philadelphia: Fortress Press, 1964).

and active participation in the church of God's people."[7] Conversional piety does not mean that the church and Christian living are unimportant, but simply that they lose some of their meaning without an ongoing authentic relationship with Jesus. Authentic faith requires both an immediate encounter with God and a conscious, personal response from the person— a response that cannot be made by the church or anyone else. In the words of Olson, there is a "mediated immediacy" to evangelical piety that makes faith "irreducibly *individual*" without being "individualistic or autonomous."[8] Intimacy with God and one another expresses concretely these particular strands of Midtown's tradition.

Our preferred categories for describing the world, however, rarely accommodate the breadth of our experience in the world. The same is true of Midtown's expectations of intimacy. While Midtown's aspirational and self-referential language speak within the grammar of intimacy and interiority, their participation in civil society suggests a much wider range of relational and theological goods. As mentioned in the introduction, Midtown collaborates with other congregations to provide emergency shelter for homeless families one month a year. This massive undertaking draws volunteers well beyond the church family. The ministry could not function apart from companionship with a host of strangers and outside organizations. While Midtown's public worship gatherings are the primary space for those in the "church family," the church hosts hundreds of families, kids, and youth throughout the week, many of whom will never attend Sunday worship. Through partnerships with local schools and universities, Midtown builds community in the neighborhood while also caring for a wide variety of physical and spiritual needs, cultivating space

---

[7] Roger Olson, "A Free Church Ecclesiology and Evangelical Spirituality: A Unique Compatibility," in *Evangelical Ecclesiology: Reality Or Illusion?*, ed. John G. Stackhouse (Grand Rapids: Baker Academic, 2003), 165.

[8] Ibid., 166.

for deeper relationships with God and one another. However, these ministries and these neighbors cannot be described in terms of intimacy, for they do not often have clear "conversion" narratives to report, nor do the children, families, and youth from these ministries "join" the church family in ways that match expectations of warmth and familiarity. Thus, the congregation implicitly references two different churches: one is the intimate family that meets on Sundays, while the other consists of neighborhood ministries that meet all week.

While this tension between experience and theology is certainly related to Midtown's appropriation of pietism, it also aligns with broader trends in North American society. In *Welcoming the Stranger*, Pat Keifert describes North America as "the intimate society," claiming that we have succumbed to "the ideology of intimacy." Keifert argues that we have reduced "the important and the real to only the private dimensions of our lives."[9] Following the argument of Richard Sennett, Keifert traces how this has come about through an approach to public life as "a revelation or expression of the self," where the world is a stage and public interaction thick with the possibility of shame.[10] Life among strangers is rarely identified as one of the conditions for the good life, but rather a threat. The good life, then, is found in "an enduring, profound human relationship of closeness and warmth."[11] We can see these themes played out in the popular romantic comedies released every year, as an individual focused on various pursuits discovers intimacy as the pearl of great price, racing through a crowded city to catch the beloved at an airport or train station

---

[9] Patrick R. Keifert, *Welcoming the Stranger: A Public Theology of Worship and Evangelism* (Minneapolis: Fortress Press, 1992), 15.

[10] Ibid., 20.

[11] Ibid., 24.

just in time.[12] We see the same focus on intimacy expressed in the assumption that a congregation should be described as an intimate family.

Keifert does not wish to denigrate close relationships within a congregation, nor is he advocating a life free from close personal relationships. Rather, he is concerned that life in the intimate society shapes the public nature of the church such that we "project" private images onto the church's public life and expect healthy congregations to behave like warm and trusting families.[13] While the experience of warmth and trust is not a problem for a congregation, Keifert worries that the exclusivity of "family" hinders the public witness of the church by excluding strangers, for how does one join a family? Only under rare and formal conditions, such as a wedding or adoption, does one join a family. Moreover, this encapsulates both the promise and problem of "family" as a metaphor for congregational life. They are a family of faith whose life intersects in vital ways with its neighborhood and city; and intimations of intimacy do not always account for the lived experience of the congregation's interaction with God, strangers, and the world.

The family metaphor does hold possibility and promise for Midtown, for the congregation welcomes strangers from the neighborhood like an anticipated guest at a family dinner. In an era where many churches offer gifts and provide "welcome centers," and special parking for newcomers on a Sunday morning, Midtown members simply make themselves available before, during, and after the worship gathering. These members have been doing this on Sundays and in partnership with

---

[12] Take, for example, the popular film *Jerry McGuire,* where an ambitious sports agent (played by Tom Cruise) strives for money and fame, only to find almost too late that the intimate relationships in his life are the true measure of success and happiness. In one of the final scenes in the movie, he rushes back to make amends with the woman he abandoned in his pursuit of worldly success (played by Rene Zellweger) to make an impassioned speech in front of her friends and support group. Often, these final scenes are preceded by a frantic travel scene to make one's way back to the beloved.

[13] Ibid., 24.

neighborhood organizations for a long time. Yet, it is difficult to find people who have been members of the church less than five years. While continuity is an asset, it also discloses a subtle barrier between the church family and the strangers from the neighborhood, raising the question "how does one join this family?" On Sunday mornings, the stage right portion of seats tends to be filled with older members and their adult children and grandchildren: the core members of the intimate family. Stage left tends to seat young people from the neighborhood: singles and young couples with less history in the church. Several groups from the neighborhood—a man who sometimes lived on the streets, some men and women from a live-in care facility—often occupy the back-left of the worship space. Each person was welcomed, but how does such welcome turn into belonging or membership? As the core membership of the church continues to age, this problem has become more and more apparent. Can this intimate family learn to welcome the stranger beyond the guest at a family dinner? How can we think of belonging and participation in a community marked by intimacy?

Midtown's participation in God's mission through welcoming and including neighbors and strangers into various congregational events and programs challenges these assumptions of family. It creates a crisis of boundaries for the church stemming from Midtown's established and perduring presence. We might say that Midtown's presence *in* the neighborhood puts two different goods in tension. When we join with the people God sends us to in mission, this can happen. After Peter enters the house of Cornelius and sits at his table, the church begins to rethink and reimagine who they are and what it means to belong. While not nearly as paradigmatic or dramatic, something similar happens at Midtown as it dwells in the neighborhood.

On the one hand, God makes Godself known through close personal relationships and within the interiority of the heart. On the other hand, the public life of the congregation depends upon relationships that may never achieve these goods, in partnership with agencies and people who do not join the congregation and remain, at one level, strangers. Can Midtown's relational expectations move beyond the intimate and account for its broadly based social engagements? Such questions underscore a crisis of cultivation, where Midtown's experience with and among strangers creates a formational challenge for the congregation. Newcomers at the edges of the intimate family raise the question: who are we becoming, and what does Christian faithfulness at this time and place look like? Such a crisis presents the possibility for building capacity, to which we will refer at the end of the chapter.

Heroic Missionaries: Crisis of Cultivation

At the corner of one interview sheet, a respondent scribbled, "no one has done more for the outreach of this church in recent years than Pastor Keith."[14] The interview did not ask for such an assessment, but apparently, someone felt so strongly about Keith's engagement in the neighborhood that she felt *something* must be said. In my experience with the church, I suspect that this statement is not much of an exaggeration. Keith's consistent involvement in the lives of young people and their families in the city has been remarkable and exemplary. He actively maintains a broad network of relationships in the neighborhood and serves as an advocate for many at-risk youth and their families. Many people in Keith's circle of care will never attend a Sunday morning gathering or give financially to the church, many will drop in-and-out of involvement in one

---

[14] The interview process followed the "applied ethnography" process developed by Church Innovations Institute. I trained a team of six interviewers to conduct interviews within the congregation, aiming for 24-30 interviews that would represent a cross-section of the congregation. With help from the church leadership, we divided the congregation into the "family," "inside stranger," and "outside stranger" (terms borrowed from Church Innovations Institute). Family members are those who have history and extended relational connections to the congregation. Inside strangers are those who attend and participate, but are not deeply connected relationally. Outside strangers are occasional or selective participants in the life of the congregation. Interviewers selected one-quarter of their interviewees from the family, one half from the inside stranger, and one quarter from the outside stranger. In total, we conducted 25 interviews, with 7 from the family, 12 inside strangers, and 6 outside strangers.

of Keith's many youth-oriented programs or activities, but each person knows Keith to be a trustworthy and dependable person and, through Keith, understands the church as a place of peace and care. The congregation maintains a great deal of pride in the ways that the youth ministry has "reached" young people in the neighborhood. Many congregants expressed gratitude for the fact that Keith fills the church gymnasium each week with students from the neighborhood. They love to tell stories like Gary's, of the neighborhood kids who have come to faith and joined Midtown as a part of Keith's ministry. As the church proclaims "God's Love, Alive in the West End." Keith serves as an exemplary, even heroic figure. While this is something to celebrate and a reason to honor Keith, a problematic tension also lurks in the shadows.

Keith's exemplary ministry draws our attention to the way that a *heroic missionary narrative* shapes the language and imagination of the church. Depending upon which ministry one refers to, the name changes while the story stays the same. The Midtown children's ministry features Sara, a mother of three and seminary student who lives near the church building and maintains a broad network of relationships with kids and their parents in the neighborhood. Sara, like Keith, is a trustworthy and tireless point of contact for families and kids between the church and the neighborhood. Anyone spending time around the tutoring or Wednesday night programs will notice Sara relationally at the center; she has cultivated relationships with the college student volunteers, teachers in the local school, parents, and children. As with Keith, neighborhood families are quite loyal to and appreciative of Sara.

Whenever focus groups in the church were asked about the ways in which the church relates to the neighborhood, Sara and Keith became the focus of conversation.[15] Their presence, energy, and programs were

---

[15] Focus groups provided two different sources of data for the research. Because the research attended to the dynamic between the congregation and community, most focus groups gathered congregational teams who engaged civil society and/or the neighborhood in

identified as an immediate point of contact between church and neighborhood. When asked how members in the focus group felt connected to their ministry and presence in the neighborhood, the answers were more varied. Some could tell about ways in which they have come alongside Sara or Keith, many others talked about the financial or prayer support that the church gives. Keith and Sara serve as heroic missionaries to the neighborhood, sent out by the rest of the church.[16]

Keith and Sara are exemplary figures, but the term "heroic missionary" means to draw attention to the role they play in the collective imagination of the congregation, for they are the "set apart" and "sent ones" funded and supported by the rest who stay behind. They are heroic in that what they do and accomplish is unique and courageous. And they are missionaries in that they are sent out from the church to cross specific boundaries in the name of Jesus. In understanding Keith and Sara in these roles, the congregation reflects an "imaginary"[17] shaped by the modern mission movement. While we will develop this theme more in a later chapter, some initial history may help clarify.

---

some way. Teams who provided tutoring, feeding programs, youth and children's programs, and the day care ministries engaged together around questions designed to tell and reflect upon their ministry together. This first kind of focus group helped me to attend to the lived theology of the congregation in relationship to mission. What did they think they were doing in relationship to the neighborhood? However, I also imagined the congregation as a co-author of the project, and so I also used a consistent Sunday School hour, as well as two different retreats over the course of several months, as venues in which anyone from the congregation could come and reflect with me on what I was learning from my research. This provided a "feedback loop" to reflect with me on what I was learning and the changing dynamics between the congregation and the neighborhood.

[16] There is an exception to this paradigm—the 'homelessness ministry' in September involves everyone and even partners from the neighborhood.

[17] "Imaginary" refers to a social, shared, and often pre-reflective 'image' of the way things are. It is like shared values, but embedded in history, language, culture, and story in a way that is often inexplicit. See Paul Ricoeur, "Imagination in Discourse and Action," in *From Text to Action: Essays in Hermeneutics II*, trans. Kathleen Blamey and John B. Thompson (Evanston: Northwestern University Press, 2007), 168-87.

In popular imagination, William Carey's *An Enquiry* marks the beginning of the modern Protestant missionary movement.[18] In this booklet, Carey catalogues what is known about non-Christian people groups in the world to suggest that modern technology and financing give the church no excuse but to go out and proclaim the gospel. Carey, a Baptist shoemaker, then proceeded to create what would become known as an independent "missionary society" that raised funds and sent Carey himself to India.[19] In Carey's book and formation of the missionary society, Carey acted apart from church hierarchy and policy. What had previously been an issue for theologians and pastors to debate—what is mission and what responsibility does the church at "home" have for evangelizing the various subjects of English empire—was not so much solved as worked around in a very practical and strategic way. Andrew Walls calls this one of "God's theological jokes" played on church leaders and theologians who take themselves too seriously, for they found themselves suddenly on the outside of a new initiative that they could not anticipate.[20] Soon after Carey went to India, other independent missionary societies began to pop up all around Europe in which *individuals* as well as churches could pledge financial and prayer support to send a missionary to a far-away land in the name and hope of Jesus.

Carey's innovation contributed to a century of furious missionary activity, sparking hope by the Edinburgh missionary conference of 1910

---

[18] Of course, Carey was a figure of his time and a participant in a broader movement, not the lone visionary he is sometimes presented to be. Bosch says "Whilst there is some validity to thus singling [Carey] out, it has to be remembered that he is only one of many similar figures from this period and as much a product as a shaper of the spirit of the time" (280). See Bosch, *Transforming Mission: Paradigm Shifts in Theology of Mission*, 630 The full title of Carey's book is *An Enquiry into the Obligation of Christians to Use Means for the Conversion of the Heathen.*

[19] Other missionary societies existed, such as the Society for the Propagation of the Gospel in Foreign Parts, but Carey participated in a move toward voluntary societies for mission organized independently from denominational polity.

[20] Walls, *The Missionary Movement in Christian History: Studies in the Transmission of Faith*, 246.

that the whole world could be evangelized in the next generation. The *missionary* was imagined to be an exemplary figure, a risk-taker who steps out in faith, leaves home and homeland, risks life and limb for the sake of the gospel. In the nineteenth and twentieth centuries, Christian publishing houses printed biographical sketches of missionaries telling about their adventures and their status as exemplary Christians.[21] So also, churches throughout North America began to hold "missionary conferences" that would celebrate the adventures and successes of those who were "sent out" from their congregation. The "missionary association" along with the biographies and congregational mission conferences all worked together to reinforce a particular arrangement where the few would heroically *go*, while the rest would faithfully *send* and *support* these global endeavors. While two world wars and encroaching secularization in the west slowed missionary activity and the work of missionary societies, Carey's basic model and argument still captures the evangelical imagination around the term "mission."

In the case of Midtown, this heroic missionary narrative has been carried over to their engagement with the neighborhood. Clearly, Keith and Sara are among the heroic few who go out into the neighborhood while many others understand their role as providing support for Keith and Sara financially or in prayer. While this arrangement effectively mobilizes gifted people for neighborhood engagement, it also blunts the impact various neighborhood partners have on the ministry of the church. Placing folks like Sara and Keith on the boundary of church and neighborhood buffers the church and the neighborhood in certain ways. The heroic missionary builds neighborhood partners and ministers to the congregation *on behalf of* the intimate family. Such an arrangement enables the congregation to

---

[21] "Heroes of the Christian Faith" is the title of a popular children's book series on my bookshelf at home. It focuses on the initiative of individual missionaries in Christian history.

remain connected to the neighborhood without being affected or changed by it. Furthermore, the modern missionary imagination constructs Midtown's relationship to the neighborhood as one of effective agency. Sara and Keith are effective change agents in the neighborhood. When the church makes an appeal for more funds to support Sara and Keith's ministry, it does so on the grounds of neighborhood change: please give so that we can extend our ministry into the neighborhood. The heroic missionary narrative imagines missions (and neighborhood mission) as a *heroic act* of *extension*. Midtown encourages, forms, and sends missionaries into the West End, but is not necessarily itself missional.[22] Within such logic, the called individual collects from the overflow of wealth, resources, knowledge, care, and grace of the congregation and then extends this outward to the mission site. Mission thus becomes an act of extending love, as an overflow from the congregation, mediated through the one called and sent.

The problem with imagining mission as an act of extension, however, is that it makes congregations and missionary societies susceptible to cultivating benefactor-client relationships. The wealth, so it seems, only flows one way in such models. So also, the "hero" necessarily becomes an agent of mission rather than a participant in mission. While it seems like a small distinction, the concrete embodiment of unequal relationships is illustrated historically between "young" and "mature" churches, or between "systematic" and "contextual" theologies. This distinction identifies the real danger with mission as an act of heroic extension. Midtown enacts this same risk, for its ministries in the neighborhood extend Midtown's life through Keith and Sara. In the end, Midtown's perduring presence is at risk, for the presence of a benefactor amidst clients undercuts the kind of relationships Midtown envisions as a

---

[22] That is, mission does not form the identity of the church in relationship to the neighborhood. Midtown sends people into the neighborhood, but largely envisions that sending as an extension of the church. Learning to live as a guest in the neighborhood, I argue, is a critical element of Midtown's shift toward a missional identity.

neighborhood church. Moreover, the thread connecting Midtown and the neighborhood is at risk whenever Keith or Sara move on or retire from their ministry.

The changing context of the neighborhood exposes the inadequacy of congregational identity and invites Midtown to reimagine its life, its membership, its participation in the neighborhood in new ways. This is a task of building partnerships, of discovering new companions in ministry. It is a move from mission as heroism to mission as ordinary and every day. However, it involves shaping a new imagination for mission that recognizes the relational means and ends of God's mission. Mission participates *with* God in joining ourselves *with* those to whom God sends us.

Losing (and Finding) the Story: Crisis of Call

"Tell a story of God's presence or activity in this ministry," I asked one of the children's ministry teams. It is a question that I asked throughout my research of a variety of groups both within and outside the church. As with most groups, the initial answer I received from the children's ministry was highly stylized and followed a predictable narrative structure. A child from the neighborhood started to come to the tutoring program, came to faith, and through a series of difficult and trying circumstances, has found himself/herself doing well in high school despite ongoing chaos in his family. God is present in this story because there has been clear, even measurable, transformation. The growth of this child into a mature young person is something to celebrate. But the story is also over five years old. So I focused the question: "Tell a story from the past month that tells you God is present and active in this ministry?" Awkward silence. Shifting chairs. Fiddling with notebooks. The leadership team was certain of God's presence and activity, but struggled to tell a story about it because they had few narrative forms for bearing witness to God's activity. If they did not hear a confession of faith from the child or see demonstrable changes in a child's life, they did not know how to describe God's presence. However, the ambiguity of day-to-day work with at-risk students in the neighborhood did not always fall into these narrative forms. Some days saw improvement; others did not. Sometimes, students showed improvement in school work but this improvement did not translate into spiritual interest or loyalty to the church. Still other times, students did not show measurable improvement and dropped out of the program all together. In what ways is God present and active in these types of situations?

When given time to wrestle with this question over several months, members of the church were able to draw upon other narrative forms for describing God's presence and activity within more ambiguous circumstances. During one particular meeting, the parable of the sower from the gospel of Mark generated fruitful theological description for the ministry team. The organic textures of the story—seeds and soil and growth—resonated with the patient and (sometimes) mystifying experience of ministry. When the group, through the parable, could imagine *God* as the profligate farmer, they began to re-describe their experiences of ambiguity and apparent failure to solicit clear stories of transformation. They began to talk about God freely pouring out gifts upon the neighborhood and the uneven way in which these gifts might be received or recognized. Suddenly, the question "where is God at work here" shifted from a question about success stories and the effectiveness of the ministry to stories of presence, of recognition, of continuing acts of care and surprising moments of love. It took some time for the *theological understanding* of the ministry team to catch up with their practice of ministry. Their obedience to the call of God toward their neighbor, their faithful welcome of families and children in the neighborhood, *practiced* a theological identity that was not yet articulated.

We often make sense of our world and ourselves retrospectively. Alistair MacIntyre says that "man [sic] is in his actions and practices, as well as in his fictions, is essentially a storytelling animal."[23] He means to emphasize that we live according to the stories we tell. Our stories organize, order, and provide a horizon (a direction and *telos*) for our lives. While we inherit these stories, our experience in the world can sometimes run up against them. Thus, we regularly work to fit, interpret, or narrate our experiences in terms of these stories. We *make sense* of our experiences in retrospect by *telling stories*. However, not all our inherited or preferred stories can adapt to our experiences, and so we must grapple for new ways to understand or interpret an experience. We can imagine how this works when, for instance, a child decides to reenact the story of Superman as though this is how the world works. He might don a red cape and jump off a chair, arms extended several times. Each time, reality "bites back" in such a way that the story might be interesting, but no longer a plausible image for the way things work. Such experiences also happen in communities of faith. In the middle of Midtown's neighborhood ministry, their inherited narratives of God's work focused on conversion and transformation narratives, but were not able to account for other theologically significant experiences. The research question made this inadequacy clear, and the ministry team discovered a new narrative framework and metaphor not only to describe their experience but also to claim a renewed theological identity.

Midtown's perduring presence in the neighborhood has opened the congregation not only to crises of companionship and cultivation, but also to a crisis of call. The crisis of context comes about because various ministries associated with Midtown have created vibrant community groups that participate with the church but not *in* the church. Midtown faces the challenge of integration with the neighborhood, which means discovering new forms of contextual Christian faithfulness. The existence

---

[23] Alasdair C. MacIntyre, *After Virtue: A Study in Moral Theory*, 3rd ed. (Notre Dame: University of Notre Dame Press, 2007), 217.

of two separate groups, however, points toward a deeper challenge of missional formation for Midtown. The congregation manages its relationship with the neighborhood by "sending" gifted persons as "heroic missionaries" into the neighborhood on its behalf. The crisis of context, then, points toward a deeper crisis of cultivation. How can Midtown members reimagine its life as *with* and not only *in* the West End?

These two crises draw attention to an even deeper challenge of theological identity. In responding to God's call to remain in the neighborhood and in dwelling with neighbors, Midtown's congregational life has been pushed and pulled in surprising directions. It is no longer in a Swedish Baptist neighborhood. It is not wealthy. It does not participate in cultural and social worlds that make old signifiers of success frequent or viable. Midtown's experience of God's call into mission offers an additional crisis for Midtown at the center of its identity. Who are we? And who/where is God in this changing and unstable world? As we go out into God's world and build partnerships and relationships beyond the church, we open ourselves to suffer the presence of others, to be shaped, challenged, and gifted by those beyond the boundaries of the church. When churches like Midtown build such relationships, such interactions may challenge and even give shape to the self-understanding and identity of the congregation.

The difficulty that the children's ministry team had in reporting stories of God's presence and activity in their daily acts of faithfulness underscores the fact that ongoing relationships with those in the neighborhood did not always fit into their prescribed vision for neighborhood outreach. As a result, certain settled elements of theological identity were open to challenge. For example, through the prodding reflection of the research process, the ministry team began to recognize their experience with tutoring not only as a means of evangelism but also as an invitation to holistic discipleship, an opportunity to create habits and practices for the flourishing of kids and families. However, this knowledge was learned in practice. It was embodied in the practice of mission before they could articulate it. Their initial narrative of revivalistic conversion needed to be challenged by their own experience for them to recognize other biblical metaphors (such as sowing seeds) for understanding their ministry.

Here we get to the core or root of Midtown's challenge: they are in a crisis of call, which presents itself as a theological challenge. They have difficulty reconciling their theological commitments with their experience in mission. Just as welcoming the stranger challenges their sense of an intimate family and the needs of the neighborhood call into question their sense as a "sending" organization for heroic missionaries, these challenges and the relational demands of working in their neighborhood give them very few stories of triumphant missionary success, and so they are not sure how to account for God's presence and activity in their midst. This is not to say that their ministries are "secularized," only that their theological understanding and articulation have not caught up with their experience in mission.

This is not only the experience of Midtown. Crisis is a common feature of Christian mission in general; and these crises often come back to theological understanding. In mission, we encounter God in new and surprising ways, as God leads us in disruptive movements of the Spirit through our welcome of the stranger and announcement of the reign of God. For example, in eighteenth and nineteenth century England, the experience of missionaries abroad began to subvert some of the class distinctions in the Anglican Church. As the Church of England began to respond to the missionary fervor of the era, they found that few clergy wanted to leave comfortable parish posts for life far away from home and in uncertain conditions, whereas the less-educated and the laity were moved by the call to global missions. The church hierarchy did not want to ordain less-educated folks from the working class, and yet they wanted to send missionaries and pastors across the globe. This new venture across new boundaries caused the church to question some long-held assumptions, and to rethink theologically the role of laypersons in ministry as well as class assumptions in relationship to clergy.[24]

Even more dramatically, we see this dynamic in the book of Acts. Acts traces the Christian movement from a Jewish sect meeting in the temple courts to an international and inclusive movement in which both Jews and Gentiles together demonstrate the gospel of the resurrected Christ. At critical points, the early church is challenged to rethink and reimagine key elements of their identity because of missionary engagement and relationship with the (Samaritan or Gentile) other. We see this with the ministry to the Grecian widows, Philip's preaching to the Ethiopian, and (most directly) Peter's encounter with Cornelius. Each event invites change in language for the church and some surprising theological shifts: Jesus is Messiah *and* Lord, the leadership of this movement is Hebraic *and* Hellenistic, God, indeed, *does not* show favoritism to Jew or Greek.

For the London Missionary Society, those who heard the call to mission were not always among the educated elite and within in the social class of the clergy. Low enthusiasm among educated clergy for mission and high enthusiasm among less educated classes challenged long-held assumptions about ordained ministry. The call of the Spirit upon laity and the global call to participate in mission created a crisis of identity within the Anglican Church, challenging class assumptions and paving the way for a more radicalized view of the priesthood of all believers. In *Translating the Message*, Lamin Sanneh reflects on the ways in which mission, and the act of translating the Scriptures into a new language, reflects back upon the missionary herself. He notices that Bible translation destigmatizes indigenous language and culture.[25] What he means by this is that when the

---

[24] Andrew Walls tells this story in *The Missionary Movement in Christian History: Studies in the Transmission of Faith*, 160-172.

[25] Sanneh, *Translating the Message: The Missionary Impact on Culture*, 324.

missionary searches the vernacular language for terms and categories through which to communicate the gospel, she must depend heavily upon trustworthy relationships with native speakers, to the extent where the translation of the gospel into a new language and culture is done in *partnership* with those that the missionary is working with. That which is "other" and "foreign" to the missionary now takes on new meaning as it is shaped into a means for communicating the gospel message. This foreign culture initially stigmatized as alien to the gospel is now turned toward Christ in surprising ways. This, Sanneh notes, affects the missionary and even the community sending the missionary by *relativizing* his or her own cultural expressions and understanding of the gospel.

These examples of mission precipitating a crisis might seem a bit farfetched for our contemporary setting. We are not translating Scriptural texts into the vernacular of West Africa peoples, nor are we working with Jewish purity codes, as Peter and his contemporaries were. It seems that the connection of a church to its neighborhood is far less dramatic than the examples given. This may be true, but crisis and mission are still linked. In *The Continuing Conversion of the Church,* Darrell Guder, wonders aloud why we in North America find evangelism so difficult. In tracing some of the sources we have recounted here, Guder suggests that since evangelism points toward an event of good news, that the church will only truly bear witness to it when the church itself encounters this good news. He says it this way: "evangelizing churches are churches that are being evangelized."[26] What he means by this is that there is an element of discovery in sharing the gospel. It is not information that we master and then dispassionately dole out in well-formed propositions, but a transformative reality among us, a public event—news that is good for the whole world. In the act of bearing witness in word and deed, we find that

---

[26] See Darrell L. Guder, *The Continuing Conversion of the Church* (Grand Rapids: Eerdmans, 2000), 24.

we discover new dimensions of the gospel among us. We don't stand over the gospel, but rather underneath it, for it is a mystery unfolding before us; a mystery that we discover in mission as we build bridges and bear witness to the Triune God. Like Guder's church being seized by the gospel before it preaches the gospel, like the crisis of class in the London Missionary Society or the relativizing experience of Bible translators, Midtown's faithful participation in God's mission in the neighborhood has begun to challenge and relativize certain assumptions they have held about church, ministry, and even God. In mission, they have both lost and begun to find their story.

Eat What is Set Before You: Three Capacities for Mission

Midtown's perduring presence in the neighborhood raises three different points of tension, each of which provides an opportunity for Midtown to learn something new. Like Horowitz's experience of gradual awakening, these points of tension arise precisely because Midtown remains present to a host of "others": the neighborhood, the stranger, and God. Midtown's experience thus challenges various theological and congregational assumptions. In Luke 10, Jesus sends the seventy out ahead of him as an advance team. They are to go emptyhanded to depend upon the hospitality of those to whom they are sent. If they are received into a home by a "person of peace," they should remain there and not move about from house to house. Their ministry in the town is one of faithful presence in response to the hospitality of the town, which means that they will eat what is set before them. It is after Jesus mentions the provision of shelter and food that he instructs the disciples to heal the sick and announce the reign of God.

Midtown's perduring presence follows this pattern. Midtown can tell stories of healing and the announcement of the gospel in the neighborhood. These remain the preferred stories of mission. However, Midtown's commitment to the West End and partnerships with persons of peace means that Midtown must also learn to eat what is set before them, to learn to learn to become guests in *being hosted* and welcomed by the neighborhood even as they seek to host and welcome the stranger. As David Bosch has said, crisis presents both opportunity and danger, and Midtown faces danger. Can it dwell in this neighborhood and join with various neighborhood partners in a way that is faithful to the call of God? This is a question Midtown must navigate, and it is a question that also presents incredible opportunity.

Imagine a pair sent by Jesus out ahead of him. They arrive one evening in a village, intending to discern places and people of hospitality. Jesus instructed them to remain with hospitable people, with all the concreteness that this implies. They are to remain with the people of peace in terms of proximity ("do not move about from house to house") while also sharing in whatever food and table fellowship they have to offer ("eat what is set before you"). They arrive in the village with passionate, powerful, strong intentions. They are instructed to heal the sick and to announce the nearness of God's reign. They are to bring good news and work for the wholeness and shalom of that village. Yet, these intentions and this activism are fixed firmly into the dynamic dance of developing mutual relationships. They may arrive in the village with a strategy for announcing their message, but the concrete conditions of their physical need (for shelter and food), and their intention to *remain,* invites the pair to *suffer* the intentions and concerns of the village even as they seek to proclaim and embody the good news of God's reign. It is not enough for the pair sent by Jesus to have a clear plan and intention for mission. In fact, Jesus has given them instructions that may thwart their preferred vision for such mission. Mission in this way requires them to build capacities responsive to the particular place in which they are located, to remain in one place and eat what is set before them. Similarly, Midtown's crises of companionship, cultivation, and call describe a similar process of responsiveness and learning required for us to remain among those to whom God calls us.

Conclusion

For this reason, crises represent not only challenges, but also opportunities for learning and building capacity. Like any relationship, perduring presence is an accomplishment, not a fact. It requires learning and adapting. At least three critical capacities for perduring presence emerge from the above ethnography. First, the crisis of *call* underscores the theological questions that rest underneath the following two crises. In its navigation of a new formation of congregational boundaries and in its ongoing adaptation to neighborhood life, settled theological certainties do not always align with Midtown's experience. In hearing the call of God to stay in the West End neighborhood, Midtown embarks on a journey with God that reshapes its understanding of congregation and God's mission. That is to say, Midtown's learning is also one of building theological capacity: what theological and identity forming practices does Midtown need to learn? We explore mission as *suffering-love* and practices of theological discernment in chapters 3 and 4.

Second, the crisis of *cultivation* emerges at precisely the place where Midtown is able to manage its boundaries between "congregation" and "neighborhood" without losing its presence in the neighborhood. Through its practice of sending gifted individuals to minister to the neighborhood on the church's behalf, the congregation is able to support and bless the neighborhood in a way that leaves the intimate family untouched. This arrangement presents risk to the congregation because these "heroic missionaries" bear the burden of Midtown's presence. It therefore creates a benefactor-client relationship with the neighborhood, whereby Midtown provides services that the neighbors draw upon. Within this crisis lies an opportunity for Midtown to cultivate practices and imagination for Christian formation attentive to issues of place and mission. Can Midtown learn to cultivate everyday missionaries for everyday neighborhood mission? We explore in chapters 5 and 6 Midtown's opportunity to minister *with* various West End partners by attending to dynamics of neighborhood and civil society flourishing.

Finally, the crisis of *context* notices that relationships in the community pose both a direct and indirect challenge to the implicit boundaries of a congregation. What does it mean to belong to the congregation when the "intimate family" is outnumbered by new families from the neighborhood? How is Midtown to think about mission when its ministries are only possible through a variety of partnerships beyond the congregation? However, in these questions, lie opportunities for reconfiguring Midtown's boundaries through the practice of hospitality. In the practice of hospitality, Midtown both enacts and discovers the gospel of Jesus Christ, while also creating the possibility for new Christian community at the boundaries of the congregation. Hospitality, I suggest, enables contextualization, which is taken up in Chapters 7 and 8.

PART II: THE CRISIS OF CALL

CHAPTER 3

SUFFERING THE CALL: ENCOUNTERING GOD ON THE WAY

At moments of wonder, it is easy to avoid small thinking, to entertain thoughts that span the universe, that capture both thunder and tinkle, thick and thin, the near and the far.
(From Life of Pi, by Yann Martel)[1]

Trumpets at the Tomb

The grey sky lightened over Burnaby, British Columbia, a sign that the sun was rising behind thick cloud cover so common in the Pacific Northwest. I was gathered with some members of my congregation on Burnaby Mountain, a ridge rising over 300 meters to provide a breathtaking view of the Vancouver metro area, mountains, and Vancouver Island. In silence, we made our way from a parking area out toward an open space where we could see the sleepy city wrapped in the heavy fog of spring. In hushed tones, we greeted each other with a declaration: "He is risen!" and responded to one another with an affirmation: "He is risen indeed!" Through prayer, liturgy and singing, we entered the story of Easter, anticipated the resurrection of the dead and proclaimed the good news over our city.

In the middle of our gathering, we huddled in small groups to pray for our city. It was then, as we prayed in tones just above a whisper, that we began hearing shouts and the rhythmic blast of a trumpet. One by one, groups sputtered in their prayers to glance over to another part of the mountain, where another group of people had assembled to watch the grey skies grow lighter and participate in the Easter story. However, their form of participation was remarkably different from ours. Their prayers were

---

[1] Yann Martel, *Life of Pi* (Toronto: Random House, 2001), 233.

shouts of joy and prophetic declarations over the city. Trumpets announced their presence and dancing attended their singing. We participated in, remembered, and celebrated the same story. We confessed the same reality. We expressed hope in the same future. We were gathered by the same Spirit. Yet, our practices and postures looked very different.

A neutral observer might not be able to connect the two groups. In fact, many Christians might not be able to see the common space shared by such different expressions and practices. It provided a fitting contrast, for the diversity on display that Easter Sunday in British Columbia anticipated the very promise of Easter and the fulfillment of Pentecost. Even more, it gave expression to the election of Abraham and the testimonies to and experiences of God in the Jewish Exile. In short, biblical faith resists attempts to frame it as a monolithic whole. While it is rooted in the family histories of people like Abraham and Moses and Hannah, while it finds expression in the cultural, political, and linguistic imaginaries of Israel, it can never be fully grasped, understood, or owned by any particular people, language, culture, or group. There is always a surplus of meaning, a critical moment, a further disclosure of God.

For the faithful throughout biblical and Christian history, such disclosures are decentering and disconcerting. Events like Isaiah's declaration that Cyrus, the Gentile warmongering emperor of Persia, would be Yahweh's servant in liberating Israel (Isa. 45:1-7), or the resurrection of a crucified Messiah, thrust theological uncertainty upon God's people. Acts of God and experiences in the world threaten some settled certainties for God's people, inviting them to articulate some renewed understanding of God's presence and activity in the world. This dynamic of surprise and reflection constitutes biblical faith. It also characterizes the ongoing experience of the congregation as it learns to participate in God's mission in God's world.

In the previous chapter, I suggested that Midtown's perduring presence in the neighborhood precipitates three different crises relating to

Midtown's sense of identity and agency as they learn to live as guests in the West End. The crises of context, cultivation, and call each contribute to a reconfiguration of Midtown's identity as a missional people and their imagined agency as participants in God's mission. Midtown's effective involvement in the neighborhood challenges assumptions of intimacy and piety in the life of the church, unveiling a crisis of context, which invites Midtown to reimagine congregational life in ways that are more porous. What role does the stranger, the outsider, the new, play in Christian life and community? The crisis of cultivation emerges as Midtown attempts to serve the needs of the neighborhood. The congregation imagines itself engaged in mission by extension, funding benevolent ministries through sending heroic missionaries into the neighborhood. However, its experience is much more ambiguous, inviting the congregation to cultivate partnerships in the neighborhood rather than meet needs. Both crises challenge prevailing notions of identity and agency, while also presenting opportunities for the congregation to develop critical capacities for participating in God's mission, for becoming better missiologists. First, they must be able to envision these crises as an invitation to knowing, understanding, and following God. What I mean to say is this: before we have the crisis of context and cultivation, we have a crisis of call

Thus, in this chapter I suggest that these crises are, at their core, *theological*. By "theological", I mean to say two things at once. First, these crises remain consistent with the story of God's people in Scripture and Christian history. Second, these crises provide the possibility for knowing God in new and surprising ways, for this is what we mean when we say that the Triune God is in relationship to the world through the *missio Dei*. Such theological framing of the crises shape the rest of what follows, for learning critical capacities for "eating what is set before" the congregation is not a strategy, but a journey of trust and faithfulness. We come to know God as we participate in *and suffer* God's mission in God's world.

The Faith of Abraham, Mission History, and the Global Church

The faith of Abraham, of Moses, and of Jesus is mobile and migratory. Jehu Hanciles, in his book *Beyond Christendom: Globalization, African Migration, and the Transformation of the West,* sets the recent migration of African Christians to North America within the broader picture of Christian mission and globalization. Hanciles's story weaves the wandering of Abraham, exilic Israel, the Gentile mission, and recent global migrations of Christians into a single, complex tapestry highlighting the tension between the local and the global, the particular and the universal. Hanciles suggests that Christianity is the "most universal of faiths" because it is the "the ultimate local religion" in that the Christian faith "locks diversity and unity in perennial tension: each living Christian community is a model of the whole and the whole is a reflection of the individual parts."[2]

Hanciles's argument leans heavily on Andrew Walls, who also understands biblical faith as holding the particular and the universal in creative tension. For Walls, processes of contextualization (when Christian faith takes root in a particular cultural setting) rather than migration disclose the tension between universality and particularity. In contextualization, Walls suggests both a "pilgrim" and an "indigenizing" principle at work.[3] The latter principle denotes the fact that the Christian faith makes its home in new cultures, languages, and practices in surprising ways. It is, as Hanciles says, the "ultimate local religion." Yet, this local, indigenous expression of Christian faith must always be stretched, challenged, critiqued by its participation in a broader community, a bigger story, a universal hope for the new creation. Thus, indigenous Christian communities cannot be completely at home within

---

[2] Hanciles, *Beyond Christendom: Globalization, African Migration, and the Transformation of the West,* 155.

[3] See Walls, *The Missionary Movement in Christian History: Studies in the Transmission of Faith,* 3-15,

their cultural setting, they are always, in some way, called out from that setting as pilgrims because of their connection with the global, catholic church mediated through Scripture, tradition, and relationships.

Let us take American Protestant Christianity as an example of this dynamic. The United States stands out among Western nations in the fact that the Constitution and Bill of Rights legally disestablished the link between church and state even for church polities forged in European contexts. This decision to separate church and state created an environment where the various faith traditions organized separately as denominations.[4] Because the government sanctions a *range* of acceptable religious expressions (the U.S. has never been as religiously free as we think), religious communities and individuals are free to organize themselves according to conscience, specialized concerns, or even to register a complaint against a broader movement. This relative freedom and disestablishment of the European form of the state church creates a volatile yet dynamic religious economy. Sociologists Roger Finke and Rodney Stark use the metaphor of economic competition to understand the rise and fall of denominations in the United States.[5] They suggest, perhaps counterintuitively, that this competitive religious market of denominations and religious movements is what has contributed to America's stubborn religiosity while other Western nations have slid into some version of secularism.

However, the emergence of denominations in the context of a 'religious marketplace' is only one feature of American Christianity. The emphasis on issues of conscience and the lack of government oversight has made the organization of denominational systems very difficult to

---

4 See Robert Wuthnow, *The Restructuring of American Religion:* (Princeton: Princeton University Press, 1988). Thanks to Craig Van Gelder for clarification on this point.

5 See Roger Finke and Rodney Stark, *The Churching of America, 1776-1990: Winners and Losers in our Religious Economy* (New Brunswick, NJ: Rutgers University Press, 1992).

maintain. Power is often asserted at the local level, where congregations can contemplate leaving one denomination for another, or even declare independence from all denominations. This is particularly true with "free church" traditions or homegrown American religious movements, but congregational defection is detectable even in connectional denominational systems inherited from Europe, such as the Episcopal or Presbyterian Church. The United States has cultivated a "de facto congregationalism," which means that church polity has a limited capacity to hold individual, local, communities of faith.[6] This is true for mainline as well as evangelical and Catholic churches.

One might say that these features of American Christianity— religious competition, voluntarism, independence of the local congregation—evince an indigenous form of American Christianity. In an essay entitled "The American Dimension of the Missionary Movement," Walls begins with a reflection from Kanzo Uchimura, a Japanese Christian on the form of American Christianity that he had encountered, where Uchimura questions whether Americans are fit to teach the Japanese about religion at all. Americans are resourceful, energetic, and creative; they are good with materiality, Uchimura says, but not necessarily with spirituality. Walls concludes: "it seems that the word *American* conveys, first of all, immense energy, resourcefulness, and inventiveness—a habit of identifying problems and solving them—and, as a result, first-rate technology." Such problem-solving orientation leads Uchimura to observe an uninhibited enthusiasm for "size and scale" in American endeavors, which he worries

---

[6] This is a phrase that comes from R. Stephen Warner's article on congregations in the United States. By this phrase, Warner means to draw attention to the fact that all religious communities are organized "more or less on the model of the reformed Protestant tradition of the congregation as a voluntary gathered community." See R. Stephen Warner, "The Place of the Congregation in the Contemporary American Religious Configuration," in *American Congregations: New Perspectives in the Study of Congregations*, eds. James P. Wind and James W. Lewis, Vol. 2, 1994), 54.

leads to a "somewhat stunted appreciation of certain dimensions of life, notably those related to the transcendent world."[7]

It is not difficult to recognize the features of a religious economy characterized by denominationalism and congregationalism in this summary. During the great missionary mobilization of the nineteenth century, individuals and congregations were encouraged to raise money, to organize and to take advantage of new communication and travel technologies for the sake of sending missionaries and social workers around the world and across the American frontier. The vibrancy and creativity required for the American religious economy helped nurture American missionary engagement and vice versa. For Walls, an indigenous American Christianity stands as one of the significant accomplishments of nineteenth century missions.[8]

The conditions of such mission: the reliance upon technology, the voluntary missionary society, and a vision of expansion, helped solidify "a specifically American Christianity, an expression of the Christian faith formed within and by American culture."[9] The American 'can-do' attitude becomes reflected in its religious life, which generates a great deal of activity, vibrancy, and fluidity, which mirrors other elements of American economic and social life. Generally speaking, this is the indigenizing principle at work. For those raised within American Christianity, the congregation as a voluntary association seems natural and normal; we assume that all sorts of technologies can be used for evangelism, worship,

---

[7] Walls, *The Missionary Movement in Christian History: Studies in the Transmission of Faith*, 222-223.

[8] I return to develop this theme more closely in chapter five.

[9] Ibid., 234 Walls continues to describe the unique dimensions of this form of Christianity: "vigorous expansionism; readiness of invention; a willingness to make the fullest use of contemporary technology; finance, organization, and business methods; a mental separation of the spiritual and the political realms combined with a conviction of the superlative excellence, if not the universal relevance, of the historic constitution and the values of the nation; and an approach to theology, evangelism, and church life in terms of addressing problems and finding solutions" (234-235).

and Christian formation without considering what is lost in such mediations; we tend to measure success in terms of expansion—buildings, budgets, and people in pews.

Walls does not offer criticism of American Christianity. As a missiologist, Walls argues for the necessity of such indigenization. The gospel of Jesus Christ, in the power of the Holy Spirit, makes itself at home in the language, culture, and practices of human communities it touches. However, Uchimura's critique lingers in the background. When American Christianity comes into contact with other expressions of the faith, whether it is through immigrants to the United States, as Hanciles argues, or through conversation with the global church (as Walls observes), certain elements of American Christianity can immediately be seen as problematic or incomplete or overly pragmatic. Certain assumptions, perhaps regarding expansion or the free use of technology or American exceptionalism, may be called into question or relativized. Eventually, these questions lead to a crisis of faith or identity. But they also might, as in the case of Uchimura, provide prophetic words for the church. Such prophetic words help to lead the church into deeper self-reflection and greater faithfulness. The view from outside, questions from strangers, and challenges from the global church, are *necessary* to unlock the church from its cultural captivity. This is what Walls identifies as the pilgrim principle.

In what follows, we build upon Walls and Hanciles to demonstrate that the indigenizing and pilgrim principles are not just part of Christian history, but also the very fabric of the biblical faith. We come to know God in the midst of diverse cultures, peoples, and languages in unique and surprising ways. We might say our faith *suffers* the concerns, situation, and initiative of those with whom we come into contact. In the first chapter, we explored biblical themes of crisis, that biblical faith is formed in various crises and demonstrates dynamic fluidity. In this chapter, we move past this observation of fluidity and mobility in the Christian faith to suggest theological dimensions to this suffering. The crises of call, cultivation, and context disclose the *missio Dei*. That is, we come to know God truly in suffering God's world in faith and hope.

For God so Loves the World...

Moments of disruption and dislocation shape our self-understanding in surprising ways because biblical faith is a mobile faith, a faith sustained in moments of renewal and risk, a faith that makes its home within the linguistic and cultural diversity of God's world. With the Scriptural tradition, we remember that "a wandering Aramean is [our] father;"[10] Abraham is the paradigm and example for our faith. Learning from the biblical story, we recognize that stasis and self-satisfaction are problematic. Because of this, questions of calling and identity faced by Midtown Church can be understood as a gift in that it creates a moment of dislocation and disruption that calls Midtown into a journey of faith and discovery.

But what is it that Midtown discovers? What is it that God's people discover when their sense of identity and agency is disrupted? It would be easy at this point to make a purely pragmatic observation, that such crises enable communities to adapt to new cultural or social settings. In many leadership and organizational models, crisis and failure create the necessary grounds for organizational adaptation and innovation. However, such crises in the church are not about organizational survival or effectiveness. The crises are an encounter with God. For in the invitation to trust, to risk, and to suffer, God's people discover God's presence and invitation in a fresh and surprising way. We should expect this every time

---

[10] A reference to Deuteronomy 26:5: "Then you shall declare before the Lord your God: "My father was a wandering Aramean, and he went down into Egypt with a few people and lived there and became a great nation, powerful and numerous." This particular phrasing is how Hanciles refers to the verse in chapter six of his book. See Hanciles, *Beyond Christendom: Globalization, African Migration, and the Transformation of the West,* 139.

we confess, "God is love" or recite the Scriptural affirmation "God so loved the world." Love, in a broken world, looks like trust, risk, and suffering. Love, in a broken world, looks like the cross and resurrection, like an invitation to come and share in the cup that Jesus drinks and the bread that Jesus breaks. In what follows, I sketch some theological implications for the crises noted above. Who is this God that we encounter in the crises of faith, world, and mission?

The Triune *Missio Dei*

Our faith is mobile and migratory because Christian faith is not in response to a static set of propositions, but rather formed by and in response to the triune life of God. Through Christ and in the Spirit, God calls us to participate in God's redemptive and reconciling work, which is always more than what we can accomplish or understand. Thus, we experience participation in God's life and presence as suffering: learning to respond to the work and initiative of God in others. In suffering the initiative of others and the conditions of our creaturely nature, God redeems, calls, and shapes us into Christlikeness. We do not elect God; God elects us. In this way, we can talk meaningfully about suffering the love of God.[11] Such suffering gives rise to faith because such suffering is a means of participation in the life of God as suffering-love: the Son receiving and responding to the sending of the Father, the Spirit receiving and responding to the sending of Father and Son for the sake of the world that God loves.

---

[11] By using the term "suffering" in relationship to God and God's love, I mean to emphasize something different than suffering as pain or sorrow, but rather suffering as being affected by another. We are not pure agents, able to select and control our environment, but rather, as Alistair MacIntyre says, "dependent rational animals." By using "suffering," I mean to draw attention to these features of human experience as also theologically significant. When we suffer the initiative and presence of others, we should be attentive to the presence and work of God, even in interruptions or surprises.

By now, the story of *missio Dei* is well known as the so-called "Copernican revolution" in missions.[12] While this metaphor may indulge in some hyperbole, the story of *missio Dei* does certainly disclose a massive shift in the social imaginary of mission, church, and theology. Before the 1950s, the term *missio,* Latin for "to send," was almost exclusively used in systematic theology to refer to the interior life of God, describing the relations between Father, Son, and Spirit in terms of procession and sending. The Father sends the Son, the Father and Son send the Spirit (in the Western tradition, anyway). In contrast, during the height of the modern missionary movement (1800-1914), *missions* referenced the sending activity of the church for global evangelization. As a result, theology and mission worked in separate spheres of concern. Theology settled the question of God, gospel, and the concern for evangelization. Missions worked out how, where, and what evangelization and church development might entail. Through years of great industry and activism, Western nations organized, supported, and sent missionaries by the thousands to colonial lands around the world. Colonialist power and assumptions, of course, accompanied and made possible this activism even if missionaries themselves proved to be critical of the colonialist enterprise.[13]

Two world wars and independence movements in the two-thirds world shattered this arrangement. The missionary movement suddenly appeared to be far more implicated in colonialism than Western Christians

---

[12] Craig Van Gelder, "How Missiology can Help Inform the Conversation about the Missional Church in Context," in *The Missional Church in Context: Helping Congregations Develop Contextual Ministry*, ed. Craig Van Gelder (Grand Rapids: Eerdmans, 2007), 12-43.

[13] Willie Jennings makes this case quite strongly in *The Christian Imagination.* Missionaries accompanied soldiers and merchants in re-making the world, and not always in ways that they intended or expected. I will highlight the story of Bishop William Colenso in chapter 7. See Willie James Jennings, *The Christian Imagination: Theology and the Origins of Race.*

were prepared to admit. Western theology and missions rightfully came under scrutiny, with mission agencies themselves asking why Christians should engage in mission at all. In fact, it was this anxiety—"why mission?"—that gave shape to the 1952 conference of the International Missionary Council (IMC) in Willingen, Germany where the critical theological concerns of the *missio Dei* came together.[14] The term *missio Dei* is credited to a German missiologist named Karl Hartenstein, who used the term to bring clarity to a crisis of funding for mission in the German church in 1934, suggesting *God* as the primary sending agent in mission rather than the church.[15] While Hartenstein's use of the term *missio Dei* was not a fully Trinitarian reference, he did offer a particular theological response to the crisis in missions: suggesting that mission has more to do with God's agency than ours.

Even though scholars and missiologists looked for a theological response to the malaise in global missions leading up to the Willingen conference, Hartenstein's phrase did not generate widespread enthusiasm. Instead, the American delegation prepared a report for Willingen, which offered a slightly different theological rationale for mission rooted in the doctrine of the Trinity. Rather than focus on God's mission as the sending of the Son and the Son sending the Church, they saw Trinity as a way to

---

[14] Technically, "why missions?" was not the theme of the conference. The conference was concerned with the missionary obligation of the church and produced a document written by Lesslie Newbigin called "The Missionary Calling of the Church." See account of the conference and archives at WCC webpage: "WCC Archives, Willingen IMC," accessed August 17, 2015, http://archives.wcc-coe.org/query/resultatliste.aspx. See also John Flett's account of the events leading up to the conference. John G. Flett, *The Witness of God: The Trinity, Missio Dei, Karl Barth, and the Nature of Christian Community* (Grand Rapids: Eerdmans, 2010), 123-162.

[15] Hartenstein writes: "[M]ission today is called to examine itself in every way and always anew before God, to determine whether it is what it ought to be: missio Dei, the sending of God, that is the sending which Christ the Lord commands to the Apostles: 'As the Father has sent me, so I send you' – and the response to the call passed along by the apostles to the church of all times on the basis of its Word: 'Go out into all the world.'" Karl Hartenstein, "Wozu Notigt Die Finanzlage Der Mission," *Evangelisches Missions-Magazin* 79 (1934), 217. Quoted in Flett, *The Witness of God: The Trinity, Missio Dei, Karl Barth, and the Nature of Christian Community*, 131.

emphasize the scope and breadth of God's work in the world beyond the proclamation of Jesus' name. They identified political, environmental, and economic realms where the Spirit of God is at work quite apart from the church.

John Flett quotes from the report to summarize: "With a proper Trinitarian reading, the missionary duty was not one of saving souls but one of 'the sensitive and total response of the Church to what the triune God has done and is doing in the world.'"[16] While the differences between Hartenstein and the American report are great, we see in them a sudden expanding of horizons for mission. If, as Hartenstein insists, missions is properly rooted in mission of God, then any such crisis must be understood theologically and not as one of strategy or even obedience. If, as the American Report notes, God's triune life as Father, Son, and Spirit expresses itself in the world in multiple ways, then the mission of God's people must be properly oriented toward the world, systems, politics, economics, and all this entails.

While the conference proceedings were considered a failure at the time, Lesslie Newbigin wrote the conference report in a theocentric and Trinitarian way, bringing trinity, mission, church, and world together. He begins with an explicitly Trinitarian statement: "the missionary movement of which we are a part has its source in the Triune God himself."[17] After some explanation, Newbigin continues with "There is no participation in Christ without participation in His mission in the world. That by which the

---

[16] Ibid., 141 The report can be seen here: "Why Missions? Report of Commission 1 on the Biblical and Theological Basis of Missions" Paul L. Lehmann Collection, Special Collections, Princeton Theological Seminary, Box 41.2, Princeton, NJ, 1952).

[17] Norman Goodall, ed., *Missions Under the Cross: Addresses Delivered at the Enlarged Meeting of the Committee of the International Missionary Council at Willingen, in Germany, 1952, with Statements Issued by the Meeting* (New York: Friendship Press, 1953), 189., as quoted in Flett, *The Witness of God: The Trinity, Missio Dei, Karl Barth, and the Nature of Christian Community*, 154-155.

Church receives its existence is that by which it is also given its world mission. 'As the Father has sent me, even so I send you.'"[18]

In the years after the conference, the expansive view of mission as *God's mission,* served to correct the vision of mission as a mere extension of the church or the responsibility of Christians. Soon *missio Dei* came to be used as shorthand for some combination of these emphases: mission is rooted in the life of God and directed by the agency of God; mission is concerned with the redemption, restoration, reconciliation of God's world. For some, this invited missioners to bypass the church completely.[19] For others, such as Lesslie Newbigin when he returned home from the mission field of India to the mission field of England, the *missio Dei* restored the church to its primary missionary calling. The resulting "missional church" conversation insists that the church is the church as it participates in the Triune God's mission in God's world. The life of the church exists to participate in the life of God in the world, to exist "for those who are not yet members" as a "hermeneutic of the gospel" indwelling their particular local context.[20] However, *missio Dei* is only moderately interesting as a historical idea. The reason for its present currency in congregational mission has to do with the way it clarifies human agency in mission as *participation* rather than *extension.* In mission, we participate in the suffering-love of God.[21]

Participation in the Triune Life

When Karl Hartenstein first used the term *missio Dei* to describe a theocentric view of mission, he did so with only minimal reference to the

---

[18] Ibid.

[19] This is not an entirely fair characterization of J.C. Hoekendijk, but it is the way his work has been perceived. See Johannes Christiaan Hoekendijk, *The Church Inside Out* (Philadelphia: Westminster Press, 1966), 212.

[20] Newbigin, *The Gospel in a Pluralist Society*, 232-233.

[21] See Jannie Swart et al., "Toward a Missional Theology of Participation: Ecumenical Reflections on Contributions to Trinity, Mission, and Church," *Missiology: An International Review* 37, no. 1 (2009), 75-87.

Trinity. For Hartenstein, *missio Dei* expressed the extension of Christ through the church into the world. The Father sends the Son; the Son sends the church: "As the Father has sent me, so I send you." In this formula, Hartenstein misses the work of the Spirit, both in the life of the Son and in the experience of the church in the world. As a result, we imagine mission in directional arrows, *from* one place or person or community *to* another, to *extend* the care of God. Mission becomes a progressive movement from Father to Son to church and to the world. The world is the target for God's mission. The church, in such a conception, is an *extension* of Christ, a body who receives the mission and then extends it into the world.

In popular usage, this is often what is meant by *missio Dei*. The material spawning the "missional church" conversation has focused on helping congregations focus their energy outward into the world.[22] The "externally-focused church" holds a particular interest for those wanting to know what "missional" looks like when it lands in actual congregations. Those writing the more practical and inspirational guides to the missional church, from Reggie McNeal to Ed Stetzer to Alan Hirsch, all utilize metaphors of extension into the world when describing the implications of the missional church. Alan Hirsh and Michael Frost make the theological roots of this metaphor clear in their well-received book *Re-Jesus: A Wild Messiah for a Missional Church*. In this book, they are working against what they perceive to be a lack of attention to issues of discipleship in this wave of missional energy in North America. Rightfully, they are convinced that only those communities formed around apprenticeship to Jesus will be capable of proclaiming the good news of the gospel in a post-Christendom context. To this end, the book does a great service and fits

---

[22] For a detailed and insightful mapping of the different ways in which "missional" is used, see Van Gelder and Zscheile, *The Missional Church in Perspective: Mapping Trends and Shaping the Conversation*, 186.

within the blossoming missional church literature that calls churches not only to outward focus, but also to discipleship. However, the Christology of *ReJesus* intentionally avoids the Trinitarian conversation behind *missio Dei* in favor of a more straightforward account of discipleship as obedience to and imitation of Jesus – the "wild" Messiah who upsets our expectations and settled certainties.[23]

ReJesus contributes meaningfully to the missional church conversation. However, it also embodies some of the limitations of a non-Trinitarian theocentric framing of mission. If discipleship is only obedient imitation, if mission is the extension of Christ's mission into the world, then the world contributes little, if anything, to discipleship, mission, and church. The world is the audience, the receptacle, the target for our obedient sending from Christ's church into God's world. Mission as the extension of Jesus into the world maintains the theological rationale that sustained the colonial project. The world, the "other," the "culture" remain passive recipients of the missional energy of the church, sent by Jesus into the world. Suffering in mission, then, can only be from persecution or the hard-heartedness of the world. Suffering such as we see with Midtown, or as we see in relationship to the response of faith in God's world and God's mission, remains beyond the imagination within the straight-line logic of mission as a series of sendings. The question of the contribution of the world, of the integrity of the world *as the world that God loves* remains abstract and unsettled. To answer these questions, we need to return to our understanding of God. *Missio Dei* transforms our understanding of

---

[23] Michael Frost and Alan Hirsch, *ReJesus: A Wild Messiah for a Missional Church* (Peabody, MA: Hendrickson, 2009), 120-121. Frost and Hirsch do give attention to the doctrine of the Trinity early in the book to underscore the fact that a renewed vision of Jesus will enable God's people to experience God as the *missio Dei*. However, later in the book they defend their choice to avoid Trinitarian discussion in hopes of keeping the conversation accessible.

God, church, and world precisely in its Trinitarian framing. For the *triune missio Dei* is a field of ek-static love.[24]

One of the famous biblical texts on love, 1 John 4:16, says, "God is love, and those who abide in love abide in God, and God abides in them." What does this mean: "God is love?" At face value, this text provides a picture of reciprocity and indwelling. The one abiding in love also abides in God while God also abides in them. This image of mutuality, of God indwelling the person while the person dwells in God under this banner of love provokes feelings of warmth, of intimacy, of trust and dependence. One pictures a variety of idyllic scenes: a family, snuggled under blankets, sipping hot chocolate and enjoying the warmth of a fire while snow silently pads the ground outside. Under the warmth of the roof is safety and belonging, a realm of intimate familial love where parents and children abide with and alongside one another. The parent is not a parent without the child, the child a son or daughter in relationship to the parent. They belong to and identify with one another. In addition, while these relations can be fraught with broken promises and saturated in disappointment, we can picture what was lost.

We intuitively understand such love, even if only as a hoped-for future, as a tangible realm of relationship. It is easy, then, to turn to this text and place upon it the expectations of intimacy, warmth, and safety: love as a relational realm similar to the warm home on a snowy night, excluding all that is dangerous, cold, and alienating. Similarly, this is what we then picture when it comes to the Triune life: God as Father, Son, and Spirit *is* this relational realm of warmth and safety cut off from what is alienating and hostile. The straight-line logic of mission as extension

---

[24] Johannes Blauw, uses the framework of "ek-stasis" to talk about the trajectory of God's mission in the Bible. He suggests that in Paul's ministry, the center of the people of God is turned outward into an ek-static ministry. See Johannes Blauw, *The Missionary Nature of the Church: A Survey of the Biblical Theology of Mission* (New York: McGraw-Hill, 1962), 182.

depends upon such an image of God. From the absolute safety and security of hearth and home, God sends the Son (and, by extension, the church) into the cold, brutal world to bring others around the fireplace to share in the hot chocolate and realm of love. Extended reflection on the Trinity makes little sense in such a framework, for it serves only as the origin of the mission but not a guiding image for understanding mission itself.

However, if we look more closely at 1 John 4, we see that the vision of love in relationship to God works *against* romantic notions connecting intimacy and safety. The section begins in verse 7 with the encouragement to love one another, since love marks those who know God and where God is present. The section ends with a more direct statement: "The commandment we have from him is this: those who love God must love their brothers and sisters" (4:21). The concrete other, the person in front of us, focuses our theological reflection in this text. That is, the demands placed upon us by our "brother and sister" whom we might be tempted, at times, to hate, whom we must suffer and who confronts us with his or her (at times) wearying presence, this person and these demands are the conditions for encountering the love of God. If we overlook the brother or sister, if we despise the concrete 'other' in our presence, if we "refuse to help" a neighbor in need (3:17), then we do not know or participate in the love of God. For we love "because he first loved us" (4:19). Love is not the intimacy of a nuclear family safe at home around the fireplace, but rather the response of the family to an uninvited knock at the door or even the dependence of the family on a neighbor or stranger because they are in need and unable to heat their own house. The love of God, the love in which we abide, is formed in response to the presence of another. It is not safe but risky. It is not only about intimacy, but also hospitality.

The love of God invites participation in God's love while in the midst of a world of others. We participate in the love of God in acts of responsiveness, in hospitality and risk in a world that makes a variety of demands upon us (as the author of 1 John says, how can we ignore the needs of a brother or sister and say we love God?). "God is love" invites us to consider a family finding joy, hope, and comfort in the midst of the cold evening, receiving the welcome of an unexpected stranger or shoveling the walk of a neighbor. We participate in the love of God in God's world with and among those persons God has placed before us and around us. So what does this tell us about God?

At the very least, it underscores the importance of Trinity for knowing God; for love describes the Triune life of God, which is made public and hospitably open in the midst of God's world.[25] It is a love rendered visible in Rublev's icon of the Trinity, with Father, Son, and Spirit sitting at a table with the cup of suffering in the middle, an opening at the table inviting the pilgrim, the saint, the mystic, and the human creature to this table of fellowship, love, and hope. 1 John continues in verse 13 to appeal to the gift of the Holy Spirit as evidence of our participation in the love of God. The Spirit, given to us, enables us to testify to the goodness of the Father in sending the Son for the sake of the world. The experience of the Spirit, who enables us to see God's work and to live in the world in a way that testifies to the fact that Jesus is Lord, affirms our participation in the love of God. We know God's love because God sent the Son; we testify to this love because God has given us the Spirit; we experience and participate in this love as we learn to see and respond in love to those others God has given us.

We can make several observations in connecting our confession "God is love" with Trinitarian reflection. First, God's revelation bears a distinctly Trinitarian shape. The Catholic theologian Karl Rahner's axiom on Trinitarian theology states: "the 'economic' Trinity is the 'immanent'

---

[25] Wolfhart Pannenberg, *Systematic Theology*, Vol. 1 (Grand Rapids: Eerdmans, 1991), 422-48.

Trinity and the 'immanent' Trinity is the 'economic' Trinity."[26] In this well-known statement, Rahner emphasizes the fact that before we can even contemplate the Trinity "in itself" (called the "immanent" Trinity), we have the experience of grace, the salvific encounter with the Triune God (called the "economic" Trinity, the experience of God "for us" as Catherine LaCugna says).[27] The gospel, Rahner insists, is that the God we experience in our salvation is the one, true God who exists as Father, Son, and Spirit. We participate in the Trinity before we have a doctrine of the Trinity. We experience the Triune life even as we bear witness or begin to understand it.

Second, the Trinity connects our theology to the world, and vice versa. We began this section with a critique of mission that thinks in straight-line-logic, as though the world is a target for those sent by God or an extension of the work of Christ. This imaginary envisions theological work as an activity prior to our sending into the world, and it often fails to recognize the relationship between experience in the world and knowledge of God. It envisions a more homogeneous practice of Christianity and tends to export certain cultural assumptions along with Christianity.[28] However, with the Trinity, we see that our experience in the world, the experience of responding to the presence of a concrete neighbor or a brother or sister in need, reveals the triune life of God. The God we come to know as we abide in love for God and neighbor is One whose life consists of the mutuality and ek-static self-giving of love.

Third, God's life as Trinity unveils relationship (and suffering-love) at the center of all creation. The German theologian Wolfhart

---

[26] Karl Rahner, *The Trinity*, trans. Joseph Donceel (New York: Crossroad, 1997), 22. The italics are Rahner's.

[27] See Catherine Mowry LaCugna, *God for Us: The Trinity and Christian Life*, 1st ed. (San Francisco: HarperSanFrancisco, 1991).

[28] For a more extensive critique and the way in which a doctrine of the Trinity helps reimagine mission, see Swart et al., "Toward a Missional Theology of Participation: Ecumenical Reflections on Contributions to Trinity, Mission, and Church," 75-87.

Pannenberg talks about Trinitarian theology as our experience of God's life in terms of "reciprocal self-distinctions" that are irreducible and yet singular in unity.[29] What Pannenberg means by this is that Father, Son, and Spirit all testify to the unity of God in their reciprocity. The Spirit is sent by Father and Son and always points back to the Son (1John 4:13-14). The Son, who is only the Son in relationship to the Father, is sent by the Father into the world to give the gift of the Spirit and to bear witness to the Kingdom of the Father. The Father sends the Son and Spirit and raises the Son in the power of the Spirit to be the Lord, the savior of the world. Father, Son, and Spirit are distinguished from one another in a way that honors and points back to one another. Here is a unity of mutuality and reciprocity. Here is a picture of divine joy and love, into which we participate by the work of Christ in the Holy Spirit. We abide in God and God in us.

However, it is not divine love left to itself, it is divine love expressed within a broader field of actors as the story of salvation unfolds. Robert Jenson works similar terrain to Pannenberg, but emphasizes the narrative of salvation more explicitly. For Jenson, Father, Son, and Spirit are characters within the divine drama of God with God's creatures, where God directs the story of God and God's people and then solicits in the Spirit a response from creation. The story culminates in death and resurrection, where the deity and character of God are put to the test in human history. Jenson says:

> The crucifixion put it up to the Father: Would he stand to this alleged Son? To this candidate to be his own self-identifying Word? Would he be a God who, for example, hosts publicans and sinners, who justifies the ungodly? The Resurrection was the Father's Yes. We might say: the Resurrection settled that the

---

[29] Pannenberg, *Systematic Theology*, 308.

Crucifixion's sort of God is indeed the one God; the Crucifixion settled what sort of God it is who establishes his deity by the Resurrection.[30]

The "reciprocal self-distinctions" of Father, Son, and Spirit create a field of love that envelops not only the Three who are one, but also all those welcomed by and included in the work of Father, Son, and Spirit.

Four, the love of God, the love that is Father, Son, and Spirit is finally shown through the story of God and God's people to be an ek-static love. It is a love that extends outward for the sake of the world. It is a love present in the historical narratives of Israel and the crucified Messiah. It is a love alive with participation. It is this love, the reciprocity of Father and Son and Spirit that seeks out, invites, and enables our participation in the real world, which we know as the Triune *missio Dei*. It is, finally, this Trinitarian understanding of the *missio Dei* that brings the necessity of suffering—suffering the world, suffering the other, suffering the call of God—into our discernment of God's mission.

The God who bears

In the movie *The Princess Bride,* the "Dread Pirate Roberts," in the process of kidnapping a princess, grows weary of her complaining about love and loss. "Life is pain, princess, anyone who tells you differently is selling something," he sneers. Drawing from the wisdom of the "Dread Pirate Roberts," we might say, "love is suffering," or, "to love is to suffer." In a broken world, love and suffering are inseparable. I remember holding each of my daughters minutes after they were born in the hospital, counting tiny fingers and toes, watching tenuous first breaths and eyes clenched shut against hospital lights. Suddenly, the immense joy and promise of the moment unveiled my vulnerability. Within seconds, my life became intertwined with the tepid breathing and uncertain future of a

---

[30] Robert W. Jenson, *Systematic Theology*, Vol. 1 (New York: Oxford University Press, 1997), 189.

newborn that didn't even have a name other than "daughter" and "beloved." The same is true of marriage vows, of deep friendship, of the interdependence we create with our neighbors and strangers. To love is to open oneself to the other in a way that multiplies our vulnerability. Love creates a field of reciprocity where we each suffer the other: the insecurities, hopes, fears, pain, joy, initiative, hairbrained ideas, and gifts. My life, happiness, and wellbeing now also depend upon that of my daughter alongside a host of others with whom I work, live, and depend. I suffer these networks of people as I learn to live as a participant in the love of God. My life is better, richer, and riskier because of it. All this to say, we cannot understand the triune *missio Dei* as a field of ek-static love without considering what difference the cross makes for God and for mission.

In a broken and fragmented world, we confess that God is love. In addition, because of this, participation in the *missio Dei* necessarily invites risk and suffering. We know the love of God because the Father sent the Son. This sending is not a mere extension of God into the world, but rather a dynamic interplay of Father, Son, and Spirit in a way that includes, welcomes, and gifts the world with participation in this love. The life of God expresses and reveals itself within the events of human history and the cross in particular.

Jürgen Moltmann argues in *The Crucified God* "the death of Jesus on the cross is the *centre* of all Christian theology."[31] It is a statement that can seem unremarkable until we consider its implications. Moltmann continues, suggesting that the doctrine of God, the incarnation, theological anthropology, and political theology each take their cue from the cross. For when we consider the cross, we see that God became human in Christ not according to our ideal for humanity, but rather "he became the kind of man

---

[31] Jürgen Moltmann, *The Crucified God: The Cross of Christ as the Foundation and Criticism of Christian Theology* (Minneapolis: Fortress Press, 1993), 205.

we do not want to be: an outcast, accursed, crucified."[32] Moltmann argues that the crucified Christ reveals the "image of God," for "Here he himself [God] is love with all his being."[33] For Moltmann, this means that the cross is a Trinitarian event, an event of humiliation, loss, and abandonment between Father and Son and Spirit. In such an event, Moltmann suggests, God suffers human sin and the fragmentation of fallen creation. God suffers our godlessness and godforsakenness as Jesus cries out "my God, my God, why have you forsaken me." This event enacts the love of God in visual and visceral form; God's greatness is God's love, which is not an idealistic or distant love, but a love that "become[s] a curse" for those living under the curse of sin and death (Galatians 3:13). When we say that God sent the Son, the cross stands as a correction to any hint of triumphalism, of the world as simple target or receptacle for the divine message. The cross demonstrates that the *way* and *intent* of this sending is one of humble identification. This is the glory of God in mission: God's humble identification with sinful humanity because God is love. Moreover, as Galatians 3:13 suggests, this identification with us in the cross is also the means of our salvation. Kathryn Tanner writes, "If the powers of the Word are to reach humanity suffering under the forces of sin and death ... the Word must take on humanity as we know it in all its horrors if the powers of the Word are to be translated to humanity in a saving way."[34]

The centrality of the cross for understanding God and world, then, shapes our vision of mission in at least two ways. First, it discloses the sending act of the triune *missio Dei* as solidarity with a sinful world. The missionary God we know in Jesus Christ is one whose glory and power is enacted in loving solidarity with the sinner. Mission takes on the relational

---

[32] Ibid., 205.

[33] Ibid., 205.

[34] Kathryn Tanner, *Christ the Key* (New York: Cambridge University Press, 2010), 257.

tinge of a preposition like *with* rather than *for*.[35] The Triune God is *with* us, and all this entails. Second, the cross invites us to consider the *way* of participation in the mission of God as our participation in suffering love. For this reason, Dietrich Bonhoeffer says that suffering is the "identifying mark" of a Christian.[36] He says, "God is a God who bears. The Son of God bore our flesh. He, therefore, bore the cross. He bore all our sins and attained reconciliation by his bearing. That is why disciples are called to bear what is put upon them. Bearing constitutes being a Christian."[37] We participate in the triune *missio Dei* as we participate in God's suffering love in the world, as we learn to bear with and for one another, considering the neighbor that we can see as we consider the God that we do not always see. Mission, then, is our participation in the life of faith in God's world. Because it participates in the love of God for God's world, it takes the shape of suffering love. That is why mission precipitates a crisis in the life of the church. It is not an extension of our relative warmth and safety out into the world, but rather the risky solidarity with God in solidarity with the sin and dysfunction of our world. Moreover, as we learn to engage the risk, as we enter the crisis, we come to know this God in surprising and ever deeper ways.

Conclusion

When Jesus sent the seventy two-by-two ahead of him, he sent them empty-handed like lambs into the midst of wolves with the simple instruction to depend upon the hospitality of those in the villages where they were sent. He told them to dwell with the people of peace who welcomed the missionaries, to eat what was set before them, to heal the

---

[35] See Samuel Wells, *A Nazareth Manifesto: Being with God* (Malden: Wiley Blackwell, 2015). The crisis of cultivation brings this theme to the fore. See chapters five and six.

[36] Dietrich Bonhoeffer, *Discipleship*, Vol. 4 (Minneapolis: Fortress Press, 2001), 89.

[37] Ibid., 90-91.

sick, and to announce that the Kingdom of God had come near. These instructions confront most of our perceptions and practices when it comes to mission. Jesus invites the disciples into acts of dependence, encouraging them to suffer the hospitality, culture, food, ideas of the neighbor while demonstrating the healing power of God and the nearness of God's Kingdom. By doing so, Jesus provokes a crisis of faith, of encounter with the world as the disciples participate in God's mission. In such a crisis, they not only prove effective in casting out demons and healing the sick, but they discover *God* in God's world, coming back to Jesus praising God.

Midtown, and congregations in North America like Midtown, enter into their own crises of mission. The days of extending God's love from the relative comfort and safety of congregational benevolence are gone. We are in a moment of crisis, the crisis of call, cultivation, and context. This crisis is not the exception to effective Christian mission, but rather the rule, the way, the means. The real suffering of the congregation is its call into mission, its invitation to participate in the triune *missio Dei*. We have sketched some of the theological presuppositions for this argument, and now need to consider the more immediate and practical implications. How might we make sense of God's call to mission in the midst of such suffering and crisis? We do so by learning to practice missional discernment and by cultivating an improvisational, sensemaking approach to congregational leadership.

CHAPTER 4
FAITH DISCLOSED: DISCERNING GOD'S CALL

I still have a prayer
because I love what I cannot control
(From "Rabbit Will Run" by Iron and Wine)

Everything You Know is Wrong

The Irish rock band U2's "Zoo TV" tour of the early 1990s overwhelmed and disoriented stadium audiences all across the world. The stage featured a bank of televisions constantly channel surfing before landing on video confessionals or saturating the audience with discordant images, words, and sounds. The tour gave an ironic twist to the earnest activism of U2 during the 1980s, making not-so-gentle mockery of pop culture in the process. The show warned early of its intent to disorient, with one television flashing the phrase "everything you know is wrong." The music, the theatrics, the constant distraction and media saturation of televisions all worked together to disorient audiences while the band hoped to create some sort of authentic rock-n-roll experience on the other side of ironic detachment. While Zoo TV was, in the end, just a rock show, it can illustrate a deeper sense of discordance and malaise in our churches. What if everything we know is wrong?

Alan Roxburgh uses the anthropological term "liminality" to describe the present disorientation that many congregations (including Midtown) feel in North America.[1] He borrows the term "liminality" from

---

[1] Alan J. Roxburgh, *The Missionary Congregation, Leadership & Liminality* (Harrisburg, PA: Trinity Press International, 1997), 71.

Victor Turner, whose work focused on rituals around rites of passage (for example a boy crossing the threshold into manhood) in a variety of people groups. In Turner's work, a robust rite of passage suspends the identity and social norms for a boy, sending him away from the village without the protection of parents or elders to complete a particular task. While in the wilderness, the child's sense of order and identity is suspended and uncertain. He is "betwixt-and-between" an old sense of identity, place, and agency and a new one while seeking to complete the task given him before returning to the village.[2] The old has gone, but the new has not yet arrived. He is in a liminal state, enduring a threshold experience in a way that suspends belief, order, and identity.

Roxburgh's point is simple. Social and cultural forces have collided in such a way that not only does the church find itself at the margins, but also the conceptual frameworks of "center" and "margin" are no longer adequate. We are in an era of discontinuous change, which means that rapid shifts in values, technologies, and practices seem to occur with little or no warning. Organizations, including churches, simply find themselves unable to predict or prepare for the future. Discontinuous cultural change, along with the disestablishment of the church (post-Christendom), has placed congregations in what Roxburgh calls a liminal space; the old has gone, but what is the new? How will we know when it arrives? And how might we live with this unbearable tension?

Perhaps liminality is a gift to the church in North America. Like a rite of passage, the church has opportunity to rediscover our missional identity, our vocation to participate in the mission of God in neighborhoods across the continent. When we set out to participate in God's mission, we enter and learn to navigate this liminal state. The first two chapters explored the experience of Midtown Baptist Church in this regard. Certainly, the social forces named above do buffet Midtown, but

---

[2] Ibid., 32.

these social forces are perhaps less significant and disruptive than Midtown's own response to God's mission. The faithful, perduring presence of the church in the neighborhood creates challenges, even crises, for the congregation as it learns to participate with various neighborhood partners in a particular context. The previous chapter explored a theological rationale for Midtown's crisis of call, understanding God's mission in relationship to suffering love. Suffering names the ways in which relational fields of love and care shape us to know and love God. We come to know God by participating in love; which means dwelling with and among those to whom God sends us in solidarity.[3] It is in being sent into God's world, suffering the disorientation of God's call and the uncertain dynamics of a broken world, that we know, love, and dwell with the *missio Dei*. That is to say, the love of God creates its own liminal space.

But what does it look like to live into such a space? If mission provokes a theological crisis, what does faithful theological work look like? Surely *everything* we know is not wrong! In what follows, we explore these questions, suggesting that the theological crisis precipitated by the call of God into the neighborhood provides opportunity for congregations to develop specific capacities for leadership and theological reflection. In mission, we discover the means for making sense of God's voice, leading, and call. The crisis of call invites the congregation to know God in a new way, to suffer God's call and love in God's world. Such an invitation requires a discipline or a practice. In this chapter, we explore *theological* and *missional* discernment as a practice for navigating the crisis of call.

Who Am I to Stand in the Way of God? Discernment in Mission

Acts chapter 11 looks like many church council meetings gone wrong as a question quickly turns into an accusation. The council calls

---

[3] This idea will be developed more completely in chapter six as we explore the crisis of cultivation.

Peter to account for troubling rumors, namely, that Peter shared table fellowship with a Gentile named Cornelius. Luke doesn't tell us how the story originally broke in the Jerusalem church, but it appears that news of Peter's adventure had already caused some concern. Perhaps the rumor mill churned ahead of the meeting, whispering hushed concern that Peter spent time at the table of an "unclean" Gentile, that an unclean one had become like them in accepting "the Word of God" (11:1). The church asks Peter a question that doubles as an accusation: "Why did you go to uncircumcised men and eat with them?" We can all recognize the urgency of the question. The boundaries of the fragile faith community had been breached in a substantial way. Peter's action called to question certain fundamental assumptions regarding their identity as God's people. His actions must be explained.

Peter answers with a story, explaining to them step-by-step (11:4) what happened in a way that makes theological sense of the event. This is, of course, the second time Luke tells the story of Peter and Cornelius. In Acts 10, Luke records the story as it is happening. In Acts 11, he tells the story in Peter's voice before the Jerusalem church. By retelling the story, Luke presents a picture of leadership and theological discernment in the early church. Before the Jerusalem community, Peter begins where Acts 10 does, reporting to the church his experience of a strange vision while praying, where a sheet from heaven descends to display a host of unclean animals while a voice instructs Peter to do the unthinkable: "kill and eat" (11:7). Peter emphasizes that his response to the vision was *exactly* how the Jerusalem church initially responds to Peter's culinary adventure. "Surely not, Lord, for nothing unclean or impure has ever entered my mouth" (11:8)! But Peter receives a rebuke that the church is just now coming to terms with, where the voice says "do not call anything impure what I have made clean" (11:9). After this happens three times, Peter describes a knock on the front door and a visit from Cornelius's servants. Like the Jerusalem community, Peter is uncertain about going to the home of a Gentile even after the threefold vision, but the Spirit instructs him to go, so he does.

In Luke's telling, Peter now leads the community to learn with him, to discern together God's presence and activity in their midst. Peter reports that after arriving at the house of Cornelius, the Holy Spirit fell upon Cornelius right as Peter began to speak. Although Acts 10 describes a full-fledged conversation between Peter and Cornelius complete with Peter's announcement of the gospel, Peter's story minimizes any role his preaching or teaching might have had. Instead, he emphasizes the mighty act of God, for the Spirit fell on Cornelius "as it had fallen on us at the beginning" (11:15). Peter ends his story by inviting the congregation to discern with him: "who was I that I could hinder God?" (11:17). Luke gives no insight into the ensuing conversation, jumping instead to the punch line. After hearing the story, the congregation turns from condemnation to doxological bewilderment: "So then God has given even to the Gentiles the repentance that leads to life" (11:18). We cannot call impure what God has made clean.

Luke's use of this story demonstrates something crucial about both the work of theology and the task of missional leadership. Theologically, Luke's storytelling highlights the interrelationship between mission and theology, in that Peter is changed as well as Cornelius. Like the seventy in Luke 10, the church learns something about itself and God only as they go out and participate in God's mission. As a story about leadership, Peter demonstrates the hermeneutical and reflective dimensions of leadership for our liminal and dynamic situation. Peter helps the community reflect on a surprising turn of events, an experience of mission, and then the community exercises discernment together with a declaration of God's activity in their midst. We will take each part in turn. By clarifying the relationship between theology and discernment, we will be able to better understand the theological task in our present uncertainty. In addition, by articulating the dimensions of leadership for our era of discontinuous change, we can see the way in which the theological challenge we face is one in the same with our present leadership challenge.

Paying Theological Attention

In Luke's second account of Peter and Cornelius, Peter arrives at a startling and surprising theological conclusion: God has given even to the Gentiles repentance unto life. Certainly, first century Judaism expected some kind of eschatological witness, that their election would bless the Gentiles and draw some of them into worship of God, but the early church does not anticipate Gentile inclusion in *this* way.[4] The surprising work of God in their midst requires careful attention by the community. Did they hear and experience this right? Should Peter be condemned? Has he violated the Scriptural witness? What is God up to in this event? These questions frame the theological dimension of leadership, highlighting the importance of learning to pay theological attention.

Peter demonstrates leadership in the midst of these questions, helping the community to make theological sense of the concrete situation in which they find themselves. His story tests one particular interpretation of the events with the community and awaits their response, placing the event within the historical and theological tradition by drawing upon the words of Jesus and the previous experience of the community with the Holy Spirit.[5] He does not only repeat inherited theological formulations, nor does he simply "apply" doctrine to a situation. Rather, he engages

---

[4] There is some debate in scholarly literature about the nature of "mission" and/or proselytizing within First Century Judaism. See Eckhard J. Schnabel, *Early Christian Mission*, Vol. 1 (Downers Grove: InterVarsity Press, 2004).

[5] Peter quotes Jesus in verse 16, remembering that Jesus said "John baptized with water, but you will be baptized with the Holy Spirit," and Peter also remembers the experience of the community in their own baptism of the Holy Spirit. He is making a connection between Cornelius, the experience of the church community, and the living tradition of Jesus' own teaching. He is saying, in effect, "I'm convinced that this was the work of the Holy Spirit."

contextual, "sensemaking"[6] work that begins by attending to God's presence and activity in the world. In mission and through Peter's theological leadership, the Jerusalem community comes to know and understand God in a deeper way. Mission, the concrete engagement with one's neighbor for the sake of the gospel, is the occasion and the impetus for theological leadership. The missionary encounter thus gifts the church in at least two important ways: it provides the impetus for learning and leading theological discernment while also gifting the church with renewed theological understanding. We learn new leadership capacities and we understand God more truly. Before moving on to consider leadership capacities, more needs to be said about the theological gifts given in the crises provoked by mission.

Discernment Gives Us the Scriptures

In considering the conditions that gave rise to the New Testament, Martin Kähler famously said, "Mission is the mother of theology."[7] Kähler draws attention to the fact that New Testament writers did not write theological tomes from the relative safety or leisure afforded a scholar. Rather, they wrote in the midst of an "emergency situation"[8] in which they were "*forced* to theologize" because of the church's "missionary encounter with the world."[9] Even though we are no longer adding texts to the canon, we are still forced to theologize by our new missionary encounters with the

---

[6] By using the term "sensemaking," I am referring to social science literature that attends to the processes and the social structures generated by the ongoing human act of making sense. For an overview, see Karl E. Weick, Sensemaking in Organizations (Thousand Oaks: Sage Publications, 1995).

[7] Martin Kähler, *Schriften Zur Christologie Und Mission* (Munich: Chr. Kaiser Verlag, 1971), 190. Translated by and quoted in Bosch, *Transforming Mission: Paradigm Shifts in Theology of Mission*, 16.

[8] Ibid, 16.

[9] Ibid, 16.

world. Luke's testimony in Luke-Acts can provide guidance for the ongoing theological work of congregational leadership.

In *Scripture and Discernment*, Luke Timothy Johnson draws from the Luke-Acts narrative to suggest ways in which Scriptural texts and spiritual experience inform one another in theological discernment. Luke-Acts connects the story of the early church to the ministry of Jesus, focusing especially upon the unexpected success of the Gentile mission and the rejection of Jesus by Jewish leadership.[10] Drawing upon prophetic imagery and echoes of the Hebrew Scriptures, Luke's theological storytelling interprets historical events in light of the broader biblical story.[11] He pays attention to the life of Jesus while also inhabiting the hopes, images, and stories of the Hebrew Bible. However, this does not mean that Luke writes shoddy history, for he reflects the real grappling in the early church with a set of unexpected events—a crucified Messiah and a growing Gentile movement. As a first-century history, Luke "investigates" and writes for a (presumed) benefactor so that he might "know the truth" (Lk. 1:1-4). However, Luke is also an *interested* interpreter of these events, approaching them with an expectation that they reveal something about the God of Abraham, Isaac, and Jacob, assuming that these events are in continuity with the unfolding of God's story in the Hebrew Scriptures. The Lukan community thus makes sense of its own life in terms of the biblical story and the God identified in and with this story. As such, Luke shares with the biblical tradition a concern for concrete history. For God is not

---

[10] See Luke Timothy Johnson, *Scripture & Discernment: Decision-Making in the Church* (Nashville: Abingdon Press, 1996), 166. What follows is a general reading of Luke-Acts found in a variety of scholars. My reliance upon L.T. Johnson is in focusing on the Acts 15 narrative as a picture of discernment that discloses both the theological work of the church and the practice of discernment in real-life dimensions.

[11] Luke draws upon the prophet Isaiah in several critical moments, with Simeon and Anna (Jesus as "a light to the nations"), at the Nazareth synagogue (Isaiah 61), when Phillip is with the Ethiopian official (Isaiah 53), and many others. Each of these stories draws critical connections between biblical hopes and expectations and the particular person/event being described.

only accessible in the inner depths, but also revealed in the plight of a people and a renewed creation.

This is also the way in which other biblical writers seem to work. Scripture attends in content and form to the stories of particular persons and communities, seeking to tell these stories through the lens and in the language of the broader biblical story. This act of biblical and theological storytelling is an exercise in discernment. Luke, as well as Mark, Matthew and John, seeks to tell the story *and* make sense of it in light of the broader biblical story. We see Peter engaging in precisely this kind of storytelling as he shares with the Jerusalem church. Peter makes a clear connection with the disciples' own experience of the Spirit ("the Spirit fell on them just as upon us at the beginning") and with the words of Jesus ("then I remembered the word of the Lord 'John baptized with water but you will be baptized with the Holy Spirit'"). Such discernment as attentive storytelling to real-world events marks an important feature of the Christian faith. It is the task that our biblical authors took up for the sake of the church. Furthermore, it is required if we are to confess faith in the living God as an active Subject in our world and everyday experience.[12]

However, a second feature that rests in the background is also equally as critical to understanding the emergence and work of the biblical texts. When Luke, John, Mark and Matthew wrote their texts, the broader church community tested them. We now know of many other textual options that emerged in the second century and beyond that trace the life of Jesus. Likely, a document like Q circulated with sayings of Jesus. We now also have other documents like the gospel of Thomas. However, the

---

[12] L.T. Johnson makes the theological importance of discernment a core part of his work. He says "Living faith seeks to understand the Living One to whom it responds. It thereby also seeks to understand itself and the implications of being so called and gifted. So understood, theology is essentially an ecclesial activity. The theological task is implied by the very life of faith itself. Every Christian is called to the act of discernment of God's activity in the world and within the community . . . The church is the place within which the activity called theology makes sense, as all the faithful seek articulation and understanding of their common life in the Spirit." Ibid., 51.

church together discerned these four stories as inspired, authoritative, and authorizing narratives for the church. The church, through reflection, engagement, and use said "yes" to these specific texts, affirming that God was speaking and revealing Godself in a way that required careful attention. The work of the early church in writing and collecting such texts is certainly a unique part of our history. However, this kind of work did not stop once the canon was decided or the NT texts written. The work of discernment, modeled for us in the New Testament, remains a primary task for the Christian community as we seek to act and live faithfully in God's world, with all the unexpected events that come our way.

A Picture of Theological Discernment

Acts 10-11 did not solve the Gentile problem. Big shifts in identity take time to settle within a community. We should not be surprised, then, when Acts 15 reports the convening of a full-blown church council to address the same questions raised by Peter's visit with Cornelius. Increasing numbers of Gentile conversions dampened the initial joy of Cornelius's inclusion into the early church. We have limited information on the council, but it seems that certain camps required Gentiles to abide by certain Jewish boundary markers in obedience to the Torah. Others suggested that since God has accepted the Gentiles without these boundary markers, they should be received into the church as Gentiles and not become Jewish proselytes. The nature of the Church and the shape of the Gentile mission hung in the balance. The experience of the church in the world provoked a massive identity crisis; the surprising gift of the Holy Spirit given to the Gentiles created difficult ground for discussion. What do we do when God acts outside our given expectations? Luke records the debate, highlighting a particular speech from James, which again interprets recent church experience within the broader story of God's people. James shows great concern for the Jewish Scriptures, the experience of the faithful, and the Gentiles in their midst. He has listened to the conversation with care, and he risks an assertion. The listening, storytelling, and conversation of discernment must lead to such a risk: James risks, stating what he believes God is up to in their midst.

As Luke tells it, James's assertion brought clarity to the group. A sense of peace rested with the council and in their letter to the Gentile believers, they described their decision as one that "seems good to the Holy Spirit and to us" (15:28). Having discerned together God's leading, the council takes action simultaneously instructing Jews to welcome Gentiles and encouraging Gentiles to avoid certain practices that will make Jewish-Gentile fellowship impossible.

Following L.T. Johnson, I suggest Acts 15 as a picture of discernment in the church. While the story does not give us a method for discernment, it does help us to see particular practices and capacities that are necessary for discernment. Johnson focuses on four such capacities. First, discernment creates the capacity for perceiving God's presence and activity in one's life, enabling us to "articulate … experiences in a narrative of faith."[13] Peter models this in Acts 11, where he narrates his experience as a narrative of faith, a narrative of God's work in the world, as though it may reveal something about God. Such storytelling is necessary for the work of discernment. Second, discernment requires from us and creates in us the capacity to listen to the narratives of faith given by others. The Jerusalem comunity listened to Peter; the Jerusalem council *listened* to the testimonies of Gentile conversions. Before a declaration was made, the council heard testimonies of God at work. This is not to say that all testimonies must be affirmed immediately, but it does encourage in us a posture that is open to the narratives of faith offered by others. We cannot discern if we do not listen. Third, such listening is done with an ear for "the

---

[13] Ibid., 109.

word of God that they [the narratives of faith] might express."[14] The council listened with a particular question or lens. The council was listening for what these stories might express regarding the word and leading of God. Finally, such storytelling and listening leads to a decision, an articulated risk regarding what the community believes God is saying or doing in their midst. Such a decision is done in humility, with the expectation of future testing, weighing, listening, and discerning.

Over the course of Christian history, a wide variety of methods and approaches to discernment has developed. Ignatian spirituality works with some form of "The Spiritual Exercises," as a basis for discernment retreats.[15] In more recent years, several different groups have begun working out processes for communal spiritual discernment, imagining such discernment as a regular process for making decisions at church council meetings.[16] Still other groups have worked out conversation models for discernment.[17] We can and should learn from each of these models. However, in what follows, I explore a way of building habits and creating practices for congregations to develop *capacities* for discernment, for whichever model we use. I suggest that three habits are essential for discernment: habits of attention, habits of risk, and habits of reflective action.

---

[14] Ibid., 109.

[15] For an introduction to this approach, see Thomas H. Green, *Weeds among the Wheat: Discernment, Where Prayer & Action Meet* (Notre Dame: Ave Maria Press, 1984), 204.

[16] One of the best and most thorough processes for the practice of discernment when facing big questions in a congregation comes from Danny Morris and Charles Olson. See Danny E. Morris and Charles M. Olsen, *Discerning God's Will Together: A Spiritual Practice for the Church*, Rev. ed. (Herndon, VA: Alban Institute, 2012), 145.

[17] Church Innovations Institute has developed a conversation model for discernment in congregations, which is one of their "six disruptive practices" for missional church and a key part of their "Partnership for a Missional Church" process. See "Spiritual Discernment for Thriving in Change," Church Innovations Institute, , accessed September 8, 2015, http://www.churchinnovations.org/events/recent-events/spiritual-discernment/. See also Patrick R. Keifert, *We are here Now: A New Missional Era* (St. Paul: Church Innovations Institute, 2011).

Paying Attention

A 2015 commercial for the Škoda Fabia begins with the statement, "To test just how much attention the attention-stealing design the new Škoda Fabia actually steals, we left one parked on this ordinary road in West London."[18] The video shows a blue car parked on a street as people and cars pass. The voiceover continues, pointing out the various features of the car and wondering if things like the wheels or design of the lights will stop people in their tracks or invite a crowd to gather. The viewer watches the car and the commercial, waiting for something to happen. But nothing does. No crowds gather. Nobody stops to look. Nobody on the empty street pays the car any notice. After highlighting the features of the car, the narrator admits that the car has not exactly attracted the attention he had hoped. Then he asks us—the viewers—whether the car has stolen *our* attention. Did *we* notice that the entire street has changed before our eyes? The rest of the commercial walks backwards to all the changes on the street—awnings appear, a van changes to a taxi, a car into a bicycle, a building even changes color. Apparently, the narrator suggests, the car does captivate the attention, to the extent where we notice little else.

It is an effective commercial, a classic misdirection. The narrator and flashing video focus the viewer on all the things that are *not* happening so that we miss the things occurring right before our eyes. Misdirection works by controlling attention. The data available to our five senses are so overwhelming, we have developed an amazing capacity for attention, to separate figure from ground, so that we might see and hear in a way that filters out noise and enables us to move through the world. We all naturally know how to do it. When in a close or intense conversation with a friend in a crowded, noisy restaurant, we intuitively use our bodies and other senses

---

[18] See "The New ŠKODA Fabia Attention Test," YouTube, , accessed August 20, 2015, https://www.youtube.com/watch?v=qpPYdMs97eE.

to aid in our focus. We lean closer, we read lips, and we listen for context cues to piece together what is being said. In such situations, we can have someone in the room yell "fire" or have someone on the other side of the restaurant waving their hands at us, and we may miss it. Our whole body and mind become fixed on this conversation, this next word. Our capacity for paying attention is remarkable. Misdirection works by taking advantage of our need to separate figure from ground by suggesting we fix our attention on one thing—a bump or a magic wand or a car parked on the street—so that we will miss what is taking place in plain sight: our wallet being taken or a street changing before our eyes.

Discernment begins by admitting our propensity for misdirection. The Škoda commercial works by focusing our attention on what is *not* happening; therefore, we miss what *is* happening before our eyes. The same is often true as we seek to make sense of God's presence, leading, and work in our midst. In the course of congregational life, we establish certain fixed narratives for understanding our congregation and our world. These narratives differ by congregation, but they are also marked by a shared history. In the case of Midtown, the progressive politics, largess, and history of benevolence has led to a well-established assumption that Midtown provides something substantial for the neighborhood, as mediator and example of God's love. After all, their sign says "God's love, alive in the West End." Furthermore, Midtown works with certain assumptions regarding intimacy and piety: they imagine the church as an intimate family and God's work as primarily the work of interior transformation. The philosopher Charles Taylor calls such assumptions operating within a community "social imaginaries."[19] Social imaginaries operate in all communities that share history and practice. They help make congregational life coherent and meaningful. But they can also become

---

[19] Charles C. Taylor, *Modern Social Imaginaries* (Durham: Duke University Press, 2004). For Taylor, a social imaginary describes the confluence and dynamic relationship between both ideas and practices, the social imaginary as "what enables, through making sense of, the practices of a society" (2).

distracting at best or idolatrous at worst. They can become the means of misdirection, where the congregation misses something taking place in their midst because their attention remains fixed elsewhere.

The first habit for discernment, then, is the practice of paying attention to our experience and to the 'other' through theological storytelling. Listening and telling stories create the capacity to notice surprising and disruptive events in one another's lives. Like the old-time art of sharing testimonies, we must learn to imagine our lives as a site for God's work, the experience of the day as a place for God's leading and action and speech. Within our modern social imaginary, we tend to live agnostic lives; we rarely imagine God as an acting subject in our world.[20] Why? Because we have settled assumptions about how God speaks (a sermon? The Bible? Through 'experts'? Exclusively through emotional experiences?), and miss the multitude of other ways in which God's grace moves us, provides for us, forms us, rescues us. We begin to practice discernment when we help people pay theological attention to experience.

It is, admittedly, a difficult and dangerous practice. We don't always do it well. And, like the old-time practice of giving testimonies, it can leave us open to emotionalism, formulaic answers, and bad theology. But it is worth the risk. How else will we learn to imagine our lives as lived with God? How else will we learn to shift our attention to God in our midst? Thankfully, the Christian tradition bestows spiritual practices upon us such as "*examen*" to guide us in this process. "*Examen*" is an Ignatian exercise that guides us to reflect upon our experience and the condition of our heart. It teaches us to slow down and develop capacities for sensing the promptings and guidance of the Holy Spirit. Practicing the *examen* can help congregations to learn not only how to attend to our experiences theologically, but also to narrate our stories of faith.

---

[20] See Craig M. Gay, *The Way of the (Modern) World, Or, Why it's Tempting to Live as if God Doesn't Exist* (Grand Rapids: Eerdmans, 1998), 338.

Besides attending to our own lives, theological storytelling also invites the stories and experiences of others outside the community. Organizations develop limited feedback loops for the sake of simplicity and maintaining identity. We have ways of valuing the feedback and opinions of those that support the status quo and rejecting or minimizing those that do not. On the one hand, such practices keep organizations running smoothly. On the other hand, they can lead to high levels of dysfunction and provincialism. In the case of the church, such practices can keep the prophetic voice marginalized, protecting the status quo from the new work in our midst. Luke Timothy Johnson claims that as we learn to narrate our own story, we must also listen to the stories of others with generosity and goodwill. Habits develop new capacities. Theological storytelling helps us develop confidence in God and shapes our theological imagination for mission. However, habits develop through practice. Some questions that can help frame habitual theological storytelling are:

- Where did you encounter welcome or hospitality from a stranger?
- What gifts were you given today?
- What surprises did you encounter? What did you hear from God?
- Where did you experience loneliness or encounter pain or disappointment?
- Where did you see injustice?
- What do you wish you heard from God today?

Risky Speech

In Luke 10, the seventy are instructed to announce, "The Kingdom of God has come near" whether or not the town receives them.[21] If they are

---

[21] The instructions are slightly different. If the town receives them, they will say that the Kingdom of God has come near to you. If they are rejected, they are to say "yet know this, the Kingdom of God has come near" as they wipe the dust off their feet. This, I think, has significant implications for how we envision hospitality in relationship to mission, which I will explore in chapters seven and eight.

welcomed, they bear witness to the nearness of God's reign. If they are rejected, they do the same. It is a remarkable instruction. God's reign is near. Those sent by God into God's world bear witness regardless of the circumstances of their reception. The piercing reality of God's reign does not depend upon the welcome of the town. As the seventy dwell among the townspeople, eat what is set before them, and heal the sick, they also risk *interpreting* the events unfolding in their ministry. Community meals and healing are evidences of God's reign, which the seventy announce whenever they recognize it. In dwelling among the townspeople, the seventy engage in risky speech: they name what they think God is up to at that time and in that place. "Yet know this, the Kingdom of God has come near."

Attention to our experience and context is not an end in itself, for theological attentiveness prepares us to risk theological speech: "So God has given repentance even to the Gentiles." Paying attention to God's work and presence equips us to bear witness to God's work with our words. Peter risks theological speech as he recounts his encounter with Cornelius: "who was I to stand in the way of God?" James risks theological speech in Acts 15. Paul risks theological speech whenever he says "therefore" and draws the questions and experience of the congregation into critical conversation with broader theological topics. We attend in order to make sense of God's work in the world, and we risk speech in order to test what we have experienced.

Just like the practice of paying attention, such speech opens the door to abuse. Some of us come from traditions where such risk invited license to speak on behalf of God, where theological speech entailed the condemnation of others or the promotion of a personal agenda. At least four different questions can help us to weigh and attend to the statements we risk. These questions are not "foundations" or "methods" that deliver us to truth. But they can function like guardrails. First, we should test the coherence and plausibility of theological speech with the Scriptural narrative: is this statement coherent or plausible within the biblical story? N.T. Wright tells a story about a Shakespearean troupe that discovers a new play written by Shakespeare but without a fifth act.[22] If they decide to perform the play, they must study the narrative, language and character development in order to write a fifth act that remains plausible within the existing character development and coherent within the narrative arc. Wright insists that our work with the biblical text in the midst of Christian community functions in somewhat the same way. We seek to live lives faithful to the call and word of God, and this means paying attention to things like plausibility and coherence.

Second, we should explore our own motivations for such speech: does this statement advance my will to power, fame, or wealth? The Ignatian tradition of spiritual discernment insists that power, fame, and wealth disable and confuse our ability to hear from the Spirit.[23] The *Spiritual Exercises* of Ignatius of Loyola test all decisions against our desire for power, success, and fame. Ignatius reminds us that theological speech can be used to advance our own agenda, to reinforce inequalities, and to marginalize possible rivals. We cannot always trust ourselves, and so we might simplify Ignatius's test to ask, is this statement about me or maintaining my vested interest in the status quo? Third, we should consider the effect of our theological speech. What does this speech accomplish? Does this statement build up the people of God? In *Scripture and Discernment,* Johnson emphasizes the exhortative nature of discernment. In exercising discernment, the church generates words that

---

[22] See N. T. Wright, "How can the Bible be Authoritative?" *Vox Evangelica* 21 (1991), 7-32.

[23] While Ignatius insists that "consolation" can only be offered by the gift of the Spirit, we often experience "false consolation," or experiences of peace or rest that end up undermining the work of the Spirit because they are self-serving and/or self-justifying. Ignatius provides a masterful account of our ability to mislead ourselves with pious language and intentions. Asking questions around wealth, fame, or power can be insightful. See Green, *Weeds among the Wheat: Discernment, Where Prayer & Action Meet,* 134-141.

build up the church. The first fruit of the Spirit – love – should help us test whether our theological speech is of the Spirit.

Finally, we should test our speech with the whole church community. What do my brothers and sisters in Christ think about my interpretation? Theological speech risks humility. When the Jerusalem church confronts Peter over his meal with Cornelius, Peter risks an interpretation of the event ("Who am I to stand in the way of God?") and invites a response from the church. With humility, he *tests* his statement with the community. After hearing his story and his interpretation, the church affirms his statement and concludes with Peter: "God has granted the Gentiles repentance that leads to life." When we risk theological speech, we must remember that it is never the final word. Rather, it is a first word, meant to be tested, weighed, and debated. It is a word that opens a conversation where we might be able together to recognize the nearness of God's reign in new words or new ways.

We attempt to make sense of what we see and hear by making statements regarding what we think God is up to, what we think God might be asking us to do, or where he might be calling us to go. These statements are risky, but they are made in the context of community and meant to be tested, to be weighed by God's people.

Risky statements might begin with:

- I think God said...
- I think God invites us to...
- I think God is doing...
- I think God is calling us to...
- I think God will surprise us with...

Act and Reflect

"But we don't need *talk*...we are practical people, we need to know *what to do*." Those suspicious of missional discernment often reply with some kind of plea for the "practical." This is a valid concern. Congregations grow weary of planning processes and conversations full of good intention but short on action. Often, when congregations feel vulnerable or find themselves in moments of transition like Midtown, the desire for strategic and practical action can overwhelm all other concerns. Such congregations become susceptible to any number of technological "fixes" to what ails them: new Sunday school curriculum, better coffee in the foyer on Sunday mornings, flashier graphics on the PowerPoint slides, etc. It is difficult to invest in practices of attention and risky conversation when anxiety regarding the future of the congregation hovers in the background. Surely, we should *do* something!

This anxiety regarding action underscores the importance of the final discernment capacity. As we learn to practice discernment by telling and listening to stories and risking theological speech with our community, we must test what we hear with experimental action. Listening, storytelling, and risking speech help us attend theologically to our life in the world. As practices of the church, they help us to live in the world in ways habitually attentive to God's Spirit. However, discernment without action is like creating an itinerary and packing a suitcase without ever leaving on a trip. The process is simply incomplete without changed action in the world. Attentiveness and theological speech enable the church to take new risks, to test new steps in new directions. Our storytelling and conversation enables us to walk by faith into what Patrick Keifert calls "God's preferred and promised future" for our congregation.[24] Taking action based on what we hear brings theological discernment back to the beginning, and is the means by which our congregations form new missional identities in response to God's promise and call. It does not happen without taking steps of faith, without experiments and action.

---

[24] Keifert, *We are here Now: A New Missional Era*, 23.

Think about how language acquisition forms in children. From birth, they are immersed in a language-rich environment, where language accompanies certain sights, smells, presences, and feelings. The child develops a capacity for visual and aural attention, focusing on some things and not others, alongside an awareness of his or her own noise-making abilities. Early on, the child learns to focus on the face of the parent and to cry. Soon, attentiveness expands to other people and objects, to movement and color; the sound-making repertoire expands to babble, cooing, and other sounds as the child attempts to mimic and experiment with sounds. During the whole first year, the child listens and makes his or her own noise; learning the world of language and communication at a remarkable rate.

Thus, language acquisition depends on feedback loops between experimental action and response. The child makes noise and gauges response in an infinitely exhausting and energizing cycle. I remember when my daughter looked at me and said "dadadadadada," I smiled and picked her up, praised her superior intelligence and tried to get her to say it again: "dad." Her babbling and listening construed a kind of experimental action in the world that solicited a favorable response from me. Children do not immediately utter sentences after spending time studying. Rather, they listen, imitate, and take action in a way that attends carefully to the social feedback that such actions elicit. In missional discernment, the listening/attending of the church moves from speech to experimental action in the world, in hope of a similar discovery. We hope to learn the way of God's children in God's dynamic and good world.

Language acquisition provides a particularly acute picture of our process for learning to discern God's presence and call in our lives.[25] We

---

[25] Alan Roxburgh uses "language house" to talk about the kind of learning that the church must do in our new missional era. The mission of God invites a whole new way of living, speaking, imagining, etc. See Alan J. Roxburgh, *Missional: Joining God in the Neighborhood* (Grand Rapids: Baker Books, 2011), 196.

are not necessarily learning a completely new language, for ongoing discernment in the congregation most often leads to small and incremental change. However, the analogy works in that it emphasizes the way in which discernment requires us to act and reflect in order to learn.

Paying attention, risky speech, and experimental action do not constitute a *method* for discernment, but rather the core competencies nurtured by missional discernment and in turn making missional discernment possible. By learning to do each of these, congregations will be better prepared to exercise discernment as an ongoing practice. They will also be better able to live in the midst of the crises that mission precipitates. We do not immediately acquire such competencies; rather, we cultivate an environment in which we learn to do these things together. The rest of this book describes such an environment by clarifying the ways people and place surprise, disturb, and provoke the church into new understanding and action. The remainder of this chapter explores the role of the leader and the exercise of leadership for creating discernment capacities, whereas the next two chapters (the crisis of cultivation) suggest a public and improvisational approach to leadership and relationships with the community. The final two chapters (the crisis of context) suggest that engagement with the hospitality tradition is a critical element of learning to participate in God's mission, enabling the congregation to "eat" what God sets before them.

Adaptive Theological Leadership for Our Missional Era

Church leadership books, manuals, and models multiply every month, and for good reason. Leadership in this new missional era, particularly around dynamic urban contexts, requires us to rethink some standard metaphors for leadership. For decades, church leadership materials mirrored business literature, sharing in the proliferation of the "leadership industry."[26] We have focused money and attention on principles for leadership, on ministry effectiveness, on the creation of management systems for church staff. We have moved from the pastor as a CEO to the pastor as servant-leader, from the pastor as a five-minute manager to the pastor as a spiritual director. In these metaphors, we have mirrored the leadership industry in both content and focus. What this means is that we have assumed that attention should be given to *the leader* when talking about leadership. We assume that if we can get the leader to function in a certain way, according to a certain metaphor, that the congregation will become healthier, more missional, and more effective.

However, this hasn't always been the case in the church or in the broader world. A recent book by leadership guru Barbara Kellerman calls the whole enterprise into question. In *The End of Leadership,* she confesses, "the tireless teaching of leadership has brought us no closer to leadership nirvana," and wonders what, if any, "major, meaningful, measurable" improvement to the human condition the leadership industry has brought.[27] According to Kellerman, we face a crisis of leadership, marked by underperforming leaders and an increased suspicion regarding leadership itself. It is not hard to find evidence for Kellerman's argument. In politics, business, and congregations we talk about transformative leadership, but rarely experience it. Kellerman moves past leadership angst, however, and suggests that we cannot understand the crisis in leadership or teach leadership in the 21st century without also paying attention to broader considerations of context and "followership." For Kellerman, the leadership crisis discloses the problem with isolating the leader from community and context. She argues that we should think more broadly and longterm, forming people for civics and followership as well as

---

[26] Barbara Kellerman, *The End of Leadership* (New York: Harper Collins, 2012).

[27] Ibid., loc. 50.

leadership practice. Such constitutes a curriculum of leadership for "the common good."[28]

I suggest above that the mission of God precipitates a crisis for congregations. As we hear the call of God, as we seek to live in God's world, as we participate in the mission of God, our self-understanding risks destabilization. Like the Spirit coming with a "sound like a violent wind," mobility and concomitant uncertainty come with the God-encounter. Such destabilization invites and teaches the church to practice discernment as a way of learning to attend to God's world and our experience, to risk making theological sense of this experience, and then to test our discernment in action. Congregations in mission have the opportunity to develop this capacity, but such formation requires a particular kind of leadership focused on some of the shifts that Kellerman suggests. In such a setting, the leader becomes both a facilitator and participant in a group process that is both *public* and *adaptive*.[29] In the next couple of pages, I sketch the shape of such leadership for the sake of learning capacities of missional discernment. In emphasizing the public nature of leadership and the adaptive nature of missional leadership, I suggest that congregational leadership must work diligently to cultivate the above habits of discernment in a way that attends very carefully to the intersection of the congregation and the world.

Public: Attention to the Interruption(s)

The 2006 film *Water* opens with a seven-year-old widow named Chuyia (which means 'little mouse') preparing to live in an ashram in accordance with certain Hindu traditions as practiced in 1938 India. Upon arrival, Chuyia embodies her namesake by biting the aged matriarch of the community on the foot and evading capture by the rest of the house. The

---

[28] Ibid., 190-194.

[29] The language of process in thinking about leadership, rather than position or task, comes from Peter Northouse. See Peter Guy Northouse, *Leadership: Theory and Practice*, Seventh Edition ed. (Thousand Oaks: SAGE Publications, 2015).

'little mouse' clearly disrupts the predictable life of the aging widow community; Chuyia's childish tantrums, her resistance to the practices and patterns of the community, her unwillingness to accept the given traditions and boundaries in Hindu society, and probing questions find a distant echo and moral depth in the voice of Gandhi at various points in the film. Chuyia is disruptive. Yet her disruption is like that of Gandhi, who is also at this time challenging various social practices for the sake of compassion and understanding. In the film, the audience begins to understand that Chuyia's disruptive presence, then, is not merely an annoyance, but a living testimony that suggests an alternative story regarding the treatment of widows. Her presence in the community as a child shouts to the entire community "seven year olds should *not ever* be widows!" Thus, the 'little mouse' interrupts the practices and self-understanding of the ashram in such a way that the plight of widows can be seen and recognized anew by various characters in the film. In the end, key figures in the film begin to challenge assumptions about patriarchy, child brides, and the humiliation suffered by widows in that society. The interruption of the "little mouse" creates the possibility for a new future for the Ashram and those that are willing to pay attention.

Christian communities, like the ashram, regularly play host to various Chuyia's—'little mice' or outsiders at the fringe of our communities—who tend to interrupt community practices and threaten the cohesion of the stories we tell ourselves. Sometimes, these "little mice" are genuine outsiders or marginalized people in our community who appear as a surprise – a stranger who comes into a worship gathering and pulls out a kazoo to participate in singing.[30] But mostly, the public life of our congregation provides multiple avenues for "little mice" to come in and chew away at our assumptions and self-satisfaction. If we are to learn

---

[30] This happened on one occasion during worship in Vancouver several years ago.

capacities for missional discernment, we can exercise leadership in the congregation by creating space for unexpected voices and experiences that arise from our context. How is it that our life in the world surprises us? What failures or unexpected results have we encountered? What strangers have we encountered? What did they say? What did they do? Leadership for a new missional era must imagine its role much more publicly – to facilitate space for hearing and attending to those in the broader community and not only the church. Especially, we must attend to the unexpected, the 'little mice' that we might want to pretend are not there.

For example, a group of young adults in Midtown decided to develop an open plot of land next to the church into a garden. They envisioned families in the neighborhood longing for fresh produce and cultivated green space in the middle of concrete, cars and crumbling infrastructure. The group tilled the land and planted a garden, with children in the neighborhood eyeing them suspiciously. While the group hoped for some parental participation, very few volunteered in the garden. Fewer still expressed gratitude when the first harvest of carrots, lettuce, and kale was passed around. Neighborhood children did not help with the harvest as hoped, and many refused to try the fresh vegetables.

At first, the group expressed frustration with the response. Why didn't their neighbors participate? Did they have any idea what these young adults were doing for the neighborhood and how hard they worked? However, upon reflection and in conversation the following winter with some families on the street, the group began to recognize how they assumed a benefactor-client relationship with the neighborhood. They entered the project assuming the neighborhood as a place of need, and they engaged in the project without first reflecting upon their own racial and socio-economic prejudices. They began to talk about going forward with partners in the neighborhood and finding ways to listen to and support families rather than to provide a garden. Their public life provided a robust challenge to certain assumptions the group (and the church) made about themselves and the neighborhood.

The story they told themselves regarding the resources of the church (benefactor) and the needs of the neighborhood (client) was called into question when the neighborhood refused to play the role of client. To continue the metaphor, the lack of enthusiasm in the neighborhood subtly chewed away at the rationale for the project and led to serious self-reflection. Whenever and wherever congregations act as a "public," that is, wherever congregational life creates room for strangers in a way that seeks the peace and wellbeing of the neighborhood or city, the congregation opens itself to self-criticism, disruption, and surprise. When we exercise leadership for the sake of God's mission in such settings, we learn to cultivate sensitivity toward the surprises and disruptions in our midst. We learn to embrace our presence in the neighborhood as a guest and not only a host. This is harder to do than most think.

As a group of young adults finishing undergraduate degrees (some in social work), the Midtown gardeners proved themselves exceptionally sensitive to the surprising lack of involvement. They did not need to react this way. Temptation certainly pulled in the other direction. The group could have reinforced rhetorical (and real) boundaries between "us" and "them" in a way that blamed the client for not acting like a "good" client. On the other hand, the group might have decided the lack of interest could be explained as ineffective marketing on behalf of the group. Either of those responses would have resulted in a failure for the group to learn, and would have allowed the group to function under the same classist and (perhaps) racist assumptions. Instead, as they gave attention to the little surprises and disruptions in their plan and listened to the side comments made in the neighborhood, they began to notice gifts and opportunities they initially missed. The disruption of neighborhood indifference forced the gardeners to make room for new voices and concerns. It forced them to ask questions of their neighbors, and it led to both repentance and a renewed vision. The next year, the garden re-launched with a much more cooperative and public spirit.

Chapter 3 already highlighted the relationship between mission and suffering-love. Because God is love and our participation in God is a participation in love, we must understand suffering the other as what it means to participate in mission. As God sends us into the world, we are shaped *as we also* participate in God's trustworthy work. In bearing with God's world, we come to know God; in being sent, we come to know the sender; in loving, we participate in the love of Father, Son, and Spirit. This framing of mission helps us to understand how it is that the church experiences tension in its local and catholic identity, how it is that mission calls us out from ethnocentrism. We are called and gifted to live the gospel in a particular place and time, yet we never exhaust the meaning or practice of the gospel. For these reasons, congregational leadership attends to the real ways in which the congregation suffers the disruptions, interruptions, and surprises of the neighborhood, particularly the surprises. Leadership in mission resists the temptation to build the walls higher and reinforce the stories we have always told ourselves. Instead, missional leadership trusts the God who sends us out into these public spaces to learn the shape of faithful witness in our time.

PART III: CRISES OF CULTIVATION AND CONTEXT

CHAPTER 5

HEROES AND HOPE

we are feeding each other
from a tree
at the corner of Christian and 9th
strangers maybe
never again.
(From "to the fig tree on 9th and Christian" in Catalog of Unabashed
Gratitude by Ross Gay)

Introduction

On most Sundays at Midtown, two figures occupy the second row in the center-right section of the sanctuary. Edith and Evelyn, sisters, widows, in their late 80s, can be seen hunched over and standing side-by-side often with an arm raised as the worship band leads the congregation. Whenever the worship leader gives opportunity for the congregation to speak during the gathering, one of them rises to the moment and shares a prayer request or encouragement for the congregation. They are articulate and energetic. During the "greeting" or "pass the peace" time of the service, they go out of their way to seek out new people in their part of the sanctuary despite the fact that they need to move slowly and deliberately. Edith and Evelyn are visible saints in Midtown, a picture of longevity in ministry, of faithfulness extended over the span of an entire life. They are part of a visible core of the church connected by deep bonds of longevity and kinship, a core whose membership in the church goes back decades and even generations.

Edith and Evelyn are not only pictures of Midtown family; their stories are also exemplary of Midtown sainthood. Members of the church use Edith and Evelyn as a picture of a life well lived. They grew up in the church and confessed faith in Jesus at an early age. Edith married a man who worked at the local Bible college and Evelyn married a professor. Both tell stories of hardship and sacrifice, raising children, and serving in ministry. In the early fifties, both women started a preschool through the church in response to needs they observed.[1] As exemplary figures in the congregation, they articulate a distinct vision of a personal faith in Jesus that somehow engages the world and serves the neighbor, demonstrating the end or *telos* toward which the church prays and serves.

In congregational lore, Edith and Evelyn provide coherence and connection between past and present. Both women express their faith commitment through compassionate activism, emphasizing piety alongside sacrificial hospitality and compassionate work for justice. Evelyn's reasons for starting the preschool helped inform the transition to a daycare, as the church recognized the need for low cost, high quality, all day childcare. When congregants speak of the enthusiastic activity taking place throughout the week at Midtown Baptist, they think of Edith and Evelyn and say, "we've always been engaged in the West End neighborhood." The church remains as active as ever, but now provides a broad range of programs throughout the week such as tutoring, a food pantry, youth group, children's ministry, and the daycare. In fact, every day of the week college students mingle with small groups of school-age children over math problems and read assignments with them while families pass through the foyer for the food pantry and parents pick up children from the childcare center. Although many who attend these programs rarely attend a Sunday service, the congregation continues to connect piety with compassion, faith with social action. Now, instead of folks like Edith and Evelyn leading the charge, Midtown has Sara and Keith.

---

[1] In the 1990s, Pastor Robert helped the preschool reconfigure into a daycare in order to provide low-cost, high-quality childcare for the neighborhood.

I introduced Sara and Keith in the second chapter. A seminary student with a social work background, Sara lives in the West End neighborhood and has spent the past five years developing a multifaceted children's ministry for local families and children. Keith began his role as the youth pastor twenty years previously and brought into Midtown a vision for youth ministry that focuses on neighborhood rather than "church" youth. One does not need to walk with Keith through the neighborhood for long without realizing that he is well known and connected. He has become a consistent presence for West End families and youth. Like Edith and Evelyn, Sara and Keith are upheld as exemplary members of Midtown. The congregation is immensely proud of them, for they connect the congregation to the city and fulfill congregational ideals for urban ministry. By building bridges into the neighborhood, Sara and Keith have not only developed programs that care for the West End, they have formed vibrant communities outside the boundaries of Sunday morning worship. Through Sara and Keith, the church envisions its presence in the West End as one of compassion and benevolence, where the faith of the church cultivates neighborhood-changing social action. The West End knows Midtown because many folks know Sara and Keith.

However, the reliance upon exemplary figures for connecting to the neighborhood carries some risks. First, it presents a pragmatic risk. What happens when Sara or Keith move on or if the church runs out of money to fund these fulltime positions? Second, and more significantly, it buffers the rest of the congregation from the people and concerns of its immediate context. Edith, Evelyn, Sara, and Keith are those persons uniquely gifted and called to extend the peace and love of the church. As I mentioned in the second chapter, they are the "heroic missionaries" sent on behalf of the community: they are exceptional individuals sent from the church into the neighborhood. Singular points of connection to the neighborhood, the heroic missionaries occupy a space between the life and mission of the congregation. In the best case, these individuals invite the whole church to participate in boundary-breaking behavior. But such an arrangement can also cultivate distance and passivity: *they* go on *our* behalf.

The previous chapter outlined three habits necessary for missional discernment in relationship to congregational call: attending to surprise and disruption, risking theological speech, and facilitating experimental action. These habits assume the congregation's lived experience as critical for discernment. It is in our encounters with the people to whom God sends us and in the contexts in which we find ourselves that we *discover* the shape of God's mission and the particular dimensions of God's call for our community. This can be upsetting to the status quo, as with Peter in the house of Cornelius or the seventy on the road ahead of Jesus. For this reason, participating in God's mission in God's world evokes several crisis moments for the congregation. As God's called and sent people, congregations work out their identity through dwelling in the places God sends them and joining themselves to the people there.

The next two chapters explore the challenge brought to Midtown's identity through its relationship with the people to whom God sends the congregation, which I call the crisis of cultivation. This crisis appears in the ministries of Keith and Sara, whose heroic missionary action on behalf of the congregation raises particular questions about the congregation itself and the nature of mission.

The crisis of cultivation, for Midtown, comes into focus in the gap between Midtown's heroic missionary imagination and its actual experience. Cultivation names a crisis in two different ways. First, Sara and Keith's work in cultivating community partnerships privileges presence over benevolence, which introduces a disruptive force in the life of Midtown by working against the predominant missionary imagination. Sara and Keith facilitate a healing *presence* with the neighborhood, but Midtown yearns for dramatic transformation of the neighborhood through benevolent action. Second, the gap between expectation and reality invites the congregation to reconsider its vision for mission and ministry; the implausibility of the heroic missionary narrative invites the congregation to cultivate a new missionary imagination and practice, which aims for *presence* before *benevolence*. While the particular shape of this crisis is unique to Midtown, the wider implications are not. Midtown works with images for mission that have guided congregations in the West for generations; their crisis of cultivation identifies problematic dimensions of the wider missionary imagination.[2] Thus, the following chapter explores Midtown's crisis of cultivation, attending to the gap between its expectations and experience to show how the dominant imagination for mission buffers the congregation from the people and communities to which they are called.

Heroism, Hope, and the World-Changing Missionary

Midtown aims for neighborhood transformation through benevolent action and evangelistic fervor. When considering mission and ministry, the church hopes to change lives and change the neighborhood. In fact, when reporting on different ministries in church meetings and on Sunday mornings, stories of change and transformation are highlighted as a means of accountability and inspiration. A ministry succeeds when one can point toward quantitative difference in the neighborhood. This is not

---

[2] In using a term like "imagination," I am referring to what Paul Ricoeur calls "social imagination" and Charles Taylor calls a "social imaginary." A social imaginary refers to unspoken, yet shared values and perspectives, largely taken for granted and actively practiced within the life of the congregation in the stories they tell, the congregational structures they maintain, and the relationships they form. It is social, in that the imaginary is constituted historically and cultivated relationally. It is not "located" within someone's mind, but formed and placed in the structures, stories, and practices of a community. It is an "imaginary" because, while it is manifest in the life of the congregation and reflected in its ideas and values, it cannot be reduced to either practice or values. It is, rather, a socially-shared 'image' of the way things are, which orients and shapes congregational life. It is both cultivated and disclosed in the stories, structures, and practices of the congregation. In this case, the "modern missionary imagination" is manifested most directly in the narrative, structure, and practice of the "heroic missionary." See Ricoeur, "Imagination in Discourse and Action", 168-87. See also Taylor, *Modern Social Imaginaries*.

an unusual perspective. The modern missionary movement, with its appropriation of the Great Commission and the example of the Apostle Paul, intends world-change and transformation: hoping to "turn the whole world upside down" like Paul does in Acts 17. Midtown intends to turn, perhaps not the world, but at least the West End, upside down with the hope of the gospel and a desire for justice. But what if something else is taking place? What if neighborhood change misdirects Midtown's attention from the actual shape of its relationships with neighbors and neighborhood?

Missionary Imagination and Experience

One Sunday in Lent, worship began with a brief dramatic reading. The congregation had been studying global poverty and considering a Christian response through a study guide published by World Vision. With the worship band playing softly, a voice from off-stage read from a script. A wealthy businessman travelled to Port Au Prince, Haiti and rented a car while on the way to important meetings. Driving through the city, he noticed a man with a spray bottle and squeegee at an intersection. Even though he was on the way to a meeting, the wealthy man pulled off to the side of the road and invited the window washer not only to wash the windshield, but to clean out his entire car. At the end, he paid the window washer generously for his work. As the wealthy man got into his car to drive off, the window washer asked him, "Sir, are you Jesus?"

The use of this narrative in worship unveils several important elements of Midtown's imaginary when it comes to mission. In the context of a conversation on global poverty, the story underscores the importance that heroic, individual action plays in effecting change. The direct and personal action of the wealthy man is implicitly celebrated and given Christological shape. The wealthy man *extends* the love and benevolence of Christ to the window washer; we in the audience assume our own place as the Christ-figure in relationship to need around us. We are to "go and do likewise," by giving of ourselves and our resources for the wellbeing of others.[3] World-change, it suggests, comes about through individual agency.

Not surprisingly, the children's and youth ministry teams reflect a similar narrative in their own accounting of neighborhood ministry. When the teams talk about successes, or particular moments when they are certain of God's work in their midst, they reference individual initiative as an *extension* of the church. While it might seem that these stories highlight the achievements of certain people, they tend to emphasize, instead, the fact that congregational connection to the neighborhood is mediated by a few individuals because of certain structural and financial exigencies. Structurally, the church funds plenty of services for the neighborhood: after school care, daycare, youth group, tutoring, homeless shelter, food bank, a meal program, and many others. However, these services do not necessarily build connections between church members and the neighborhood. The whole church gives generously to fund these programs, and many members have familiarity with them, but they cannot be staffed or run exclusively by those in the church because the congregation is already stretched thin. As with many congregations established decades ago, Midtown has its own matrix of boards and committees, small groups, and worship planning, which draw members into the life of the church and leave little extra time for providing services to the neighborhood. In addition, the sheer number of initiatives outpaces the membership of an already active congregation. Thus, its commitment to the neighborhood is expressed financially, in funding programs and paying staff.

Financially, Midtown incentivizes individuals to take benevolent action on behalf of the congregation. Like the wealthy man in the dramatic reading, Keith, Sara, and their leadership teams express a personal

---

[3] Of course, this is not the only way to think about such encounters. Matthew 25 also encourages us to serve those in need, but not as a Christ figure. We serve those in need because, in doing so, we serve Christ.

overflow of church care toward the neighborhood. They are sent to provide guidance, witness, and material goods on behalf of the church. Again, this can be seen in church practice and language. Practically, the congregation has several funding sources devoted to neighborhood benevolence, and congregants are expected to give a tithe and an offering to support such ministry. Midtown's stewardship committee keeps a close eye on congregational giving and energy. The two, they assume, are related. The generosity of the congregation enables an impressive array of ministries in the neighborhood.[4] Midtown's ministry in the neighborhood depends in no small way upon congregants continuing to give sacrificially. These structural and financial pressures place Sara and Keith in the position of mediator between congregation and neighborhood; they are the heroes who mediate the space between church and world for the sake of bringing good news and transformation. They are the man in Haiti, playing a Christological role in relationship to needy neighbors on behalf of the church.

However, a closer look at the work of Midtown's heroes displays tension between Midtown's missionary imagination and the experience of Sara and Keith. According to the leadership teams, the everyday ministry of tutoring, day care, youth and family ministry generates a dismaying number of transformational moments. While the congregation receives the occasional, highly stylized story of life change, those engaged in these ministries also report setbacks and the crushing heartbreak that sometimes follows an initial success story. It is not always clear to those working in the West End on a regular basis whether they *are* changing

---

[4] For this reason, for example, one will regularly find a stewardship insert in many Sunday bulletins, with a ministry highlighted and 2 Corinthians 8:9 underneath: "for you know the grace of our Lord Jesus Christ, that though he was rich, yet for your sake he became poor, so that through his poverty you might become rich." The implications of an insert like this are clear. Generous giving makes possible generous ministry in and to the West End neighborhood. Moreover, such generosity finds its model and rationale in the self-sacrificial life of Christ. The insert exhorts the congregation—like the Corinthian community Paul addresses—to bring riches to others by giving up their own.

individual lives, much less the world. When pressed beyond the stylized stories shared on Sunday mornings, everyday reflection on ministry tends toward agrarian metaphors: they sow seeds, provide water, or cultivate soil in this dynamic urban environment. Additionally, the individual agency of Midtown's heroes is, in actual fact, much more cooperative and dependent upon networks and partnerships than envisioned by Midtown's imagination and rhetoric.

For example, both Sara and Keith rely heavily upon volunteer networks and expertise well beyond Midtown. Both draw student volunteers from several local colleges who may or may not attend church. Keith even includes parental volunteers in his ministry without requiring a confession of faith. Reflecting on his recruitment of volunteers and his reliance upon people of goodwill in the neighborhood for providing programming and care for students, Keith continually asks himself, "How much information does a person need to come and work with kids?" Keith recognizes the broad relational matrix within which he works, in which students, parents, and volunteers are all on a possibly messy and indirect spiritual journey. So he receives volunteer leaders who have not yet "worked out their commitment to the church," but who are committed to kids and the common good. "My job is not only to mentor or foster relationship with my students," Keith says, "but to mentor and foster relationship with my staff," for "we are tutoring our staff and not only our kids . . . this whole thing is discipleship, it really is."[5] This sense of reliance upon the 'other' and the 'stranger,' then, offers a different vision of Keith's ministry, where he evaluates his own ministry in terms of the relationships he has fostered and not necessarily the change he has effectively caused. He recognizes his role in terms closer to presence than world-change. It is a practice of ministry carried by his volunteer staff, as one volunteer ministry leader described the youth ministry: "we [just] show up every

---

[5] Interview with a ministry leader by the author, March 10, 2009.

Wednesday" to provide unconditional "respect and love." They practice perduring presence at least one night a week.

The practice of presence means that hosts of strangers who share similar concerns for the neighborhood participate with Midtown in providing care, hope, and opportunity for young people in the West End. For Sara and Keith, such partnerships are essential for ministry survival. As extensions of Midtown sent with particular resources, they recognize the need to draw support from wider networks than the congregation. The fact that such partnerships are necessary for programming means that such partnerships tend to be described in pragmatic terms. In doing so, they miss opportunities to draw themes from biblical and theological sources that could articulate such presence *as* their participation in God's mission. They imagine these partnerships as a means to some other end, as a means to a benevolent missionary activism; thus, they miss recognizing companionship *with* their neighbors as participation in God's mission. This is because Midtown's structural and financial commitments to the neighborhood reflect a missionary imagination that has been shaped by nearly two centuries of American missionary work, which brings together an Enlightenment belief in progress with an evangelical understanding of missionary obedience and the enthusiastic energy of frontier religion, a cocktail of influences that makes the heroic missionary a significant trope for American congregationalism. This broader modern missionary imagination functions as a means of misdirection for the church, keeping it from paying attention to the gifts of God presented in these various partnerships. Before exploring a way forward, I sketch the basic features of this modern missionary imagination as an expression of Enlightenment progress, evangelical fervor, and entrepreneurial activism. Such a sketch is not unique to Midtown, but shapes the vision and imagination for mission in congregations across the United States.

Understanding the [Modern] Missionary Imagination

When Kenneth Scott Latourette wrote his seven-volume series on the history of mission entitled *A History of the Expansion of Christianity,* it certainly seemed as though *expansion* best described the modern experience of Christian mission.[6] Completed in 1945, Latourette anticipated the toll that two World Wars would play on the missionary movement, but his overall tone remained optimistic. The Christian church had expanded from Jerusalem to the Middle East and North Africa, to Rome and Europe, and then to the whole world. Certainly, it would continue to expand.[7] We know now that this phase of the missionary movement marked, not the triumph of European Christendom, but rather its last gasp.[8] Latourette may have predicted a coming world Christianity, but he did not anticipate that it would be accompanied by a chastened and uncertain church in Europe and North America. Even as the West enters post-Christendom, *expansion* still characterizes the modern missionary imagination.

Beginning in the late eighteenth century with William Carey's publication of *An Enquiry,* the "modern missionary movement" describes the reshaping of both church and world through the rapid expansion of missionary activity around the globe.[9] Up until the First World War, the story was one of expansion and possibility. Latourette calls these years the

---

[6] *A History of the Expansion of Christianity* is a seven volume series published between 1937-1945. For decades, it was an authoritative interpretation of mission history.

[7] Thus, he entitled his last volume *Advance Through Storm: 1914 and After.* See Kenneth Scott Latourette, *Advance through Storm,* Vol. 7 (New York: Harper & Brothers, 1945).

[8] I refer here to a persuasive argument made by Jehu Hanciles in a chapter entitled: "The Birth and Bankruptcy of Christendom." Hanciles argues that while Christendom gave birth to the modern missions movement, it was ill equipped for the new world the missionary movement created, thus hastening the dissolution of Christendom. See Hanciles, *Beyond Christendom: Globalization, African Migration, and the Transformation of the West,* 430.

[9] As mentioned earlier, William Carey stands as a particularly vivid example of a broader movement that took place during his time. He is not a solitary figure who initiates the modern missions movement, but rather a well-known early participant.

"great century of missions," a story he slowly unravels over two volumes.[10] Even though the events of the Twentieth Century brought crisis to Western missions, our missionary imagination remains tethered to the expansive, world-changing intention of the "great century" in a variety of ways. A few of these elements are drawn out in what follows, beginning with Enlightenment and evangelical sources of the missionary movement before considering the way it shaped congregational mission in the United States.

Mission and Enlightenment

After decades of war between Catholics and Protestants, a new intellectual order took root in European philosophy based on universal doubt and the exercise of reason. In this new intellectual order, called the Enlightenment, lie the fallow seeds of the modern missionary movement. [11] By most accounts, the Enlightenment begins with the quest of a French philosopher named Rene Descartes to find a rational and universal grounding for knowledge. [12] Seeking a secure foundation for philosophical knowledge in *Meditations on First Philosophy,* first published in 1641, Descartes begins with a strategy of universal doubt to clear his thinking of received tradition, presuppositions, and superstition. Stripping away body and world, Descartes develops a rational grounding for knowledge in the

---

[10] Latourette dates the "great century" from 1800-1914. See Kenneth Scott Latourette, *The Great Century: Europe and the United States*, Vol. 4 (New York: Harper & Brothers, 1941). See also Kenneth Scott Latourette, *The Great Century: The Americas , Australasia, and Africa*, Vol. 5 (New York: Harper & Brothers, 1943).

[11] David Bosch calls the modern missionary movement "a child of the Enlightenment." See David Jacobus Bosch, *Transforming Mission: Paradigm Shifts in Theology of Mission*, Vol. 16 (Maryknoll: Orbis Books, 1991), 274.

[12] Stephen Toulmin provides a particularly vivid intellectual account of the Enlightenment. Toulmin argues that Descartes grew up during a time when French society seemed on the verge of unraveling. Alongside the seemingly permanent conflict between Catholics and Protestants, the early decades of the seventeenth century featured famines, exceptionally cold winters, and general economic malaise. Social, spiritual, and political unrest ruled the day. Searching for a way to adjudicate between different claims, Descartes's philosophy seeks a rigorous and universal foundation for knowledge. Thus, in a time of anxiety and discord, Descartes searches for a means of security and unity. See Stephen Edelston Toulmin, *Cosmopolis: The Hidden Agenda of Modernity* (New York: Free Press, 1990).

certainty of conscious thought: *cogito ergo sum*—I think, therefore I am. The thinking, rational mind becomes its own foundation for truthfully knowing the world. Thus marks the initiation of the "age of Reason," where careful rational thinking is assumed to produce trustworthy knowledge. Amid the deep anxieties of European life, such confidence offered both optimism and the assumption of rational control. The rational, thinking self becomes the hope and agent of a better world, offering the development of knowledge and technologies to facilitate human mastery of the cosmos.

Such a philosophy would have died on the vine if it were not so successful. Advances in science and technology, alongside European global dominance offered credibility to this optimistic mastery of the world.[13] If knowledge can be reasonably built upon a certain foundation, then we can expect real moral, technological, and scientific progress. Captured in the term "Enlightenment" is the wager that human beings are progressing through history by gaining knowledge and controlling our environment. Indeed, European technological and scientific advances felt like human progress. Problems certainly seemed solvable, and we began to feel "buffered" from our creaturely dependencies and vulnerabilities, imagining the human creature as entirely of her own making, master of her own universe in some way.[14] All of this falls under the rubric of an optimistic belief in progress: we became masters of our environment and our world, which is progressing toward a better future.

---

[13] Bosch, *Transforming Mission: Paradigm Shifts in Theology of Mission*, 271.

[14] The optimism unleashed by the Enlightenment, however, stands in stark contrast to human experience in other times. In pre-modern times, for example, our experience of the world was "porous" in the sense that we understood ourselves to be subject to a variety of forces. We were subject to tradition, to family station, to spirits, and to nature. But with Enlightenment rationality and increasing trust in the scientific method, these forces became explainable and, at times, manageable. Charles Taylor makes a distinction between previous "porous" understandings of selfhood and the modern sense of the "buffered self." He says: "The buffered self is essentially the self which is aware of the possibility of disengagement. And disengagement is frequently carried out in relationship to one's whole surroundings, natural and social" (42). The difference between the "buffered" and "porous" self is in our sense of sociality and belonging to one another and to the earth. See Charles Taylor, *A Secular Age* (Cambridge: Belknap Press, 2007), 27-42.

Of course, some conservative mission theologians and missionaries were suspicious of modern philosophies and practices that challenged biblical authority. Yet the same intellectual forces that shaped politics, science, and morality also shaped religious expression. The "Great Century" of missions drew upon the free choice of individuals and an optimistic, problem-solving mastery of the world. As demonstrated in William Carey's *An Enquiry* and the creation of the success of the voluntary missionary society, Enlightenment instrumentality, problem-solving rationality, and optimism are marshaled for evangelical renewal and world evangelism.

Mission Obligation and Means

In the first section of *An Enquiry* William Carey writes: "Our Lord Jesus Christ, a little before his departure, commissioned his apostles to *Go, and teach all nations* . . . This commission was as extensive as possible, and laid them under obligation . . . [15] Carey, of course, refers to Matthew 28:18-20 as the commission that puts the apostles under obligation to go and teach. Moreover, while Carey acknowledges the obedience of the early church in this regard, he suggests that his own church has not necessarily taken up the charge to preach the gospel throughout the world with the same "zeal and perseverance with which the primitive Christians went about it."[16] From this observation, Carey builds a case for global missions as *obedience* to the command of Jesus in Matthew 28. Carey's case is relatively simple. If "going into all the world" was already completed in the apostolic era, then shouldn't we also be done baptizing and teaching? Jesus clearly connects going, baptizing, and teaching, so how can the astute interpreter separate them? Similarly, if going and preaching the gospel was only meant for the apostles, then what

---

[15] "An Enquiry into the Obligations of Christians," Hodder and Stoughton, http://www.wmcarey.edu/carey/enquiry/anenquiry.pdf (accessed May 18, 2017).

[16] Ibid.

do we make of Jesus' promise to be with the disciples "until the end of the age"? Carey's contemporaries, shaped by decades of evangelical renewal, echoed and agreed with this reading, establishing Matthew 28:18-20 as one of the critical texts for the modern missionary movement.[17]

The fact that such an argument is now unsurprising signals the enduring influence of Carey's tract. Among Carey's peers, it was not at all obvious that the "Great Commission" was a command for the modern-day church. Throughout church history, a variety of interpretations had been offered, with ancient sources suggesting the apostles divided the world among themselves.[18] For a variety of reasons, early Protestant Reformers showed little interest in amending this interpretation. However, decades of evangelical revival and an increased global consciousness created the right conditions for a general acceptance of Carey's reappraisal of Matthew 28.

Assuming obedience to the Great Commission, however, has shaped our missionary imagination in particular ways. While it shares certain theological features with other sending texts such as Acts 1:6-8,[19] it is unique by placing mission in the imperative mood. Recording Jesus' final instructions in the book of Matthew, the Great Commission connects the bestowal of Jesus' authority upon the apostles with the imperative to "go and make disciples" and the promise of Christ's presence. Unlike Acts 1:6-8, Jesus' sending is not paired with the promise of the Holy Spirit or the ascension of Christ, although Jesus' promised presence fulfills a similar role. In Carey's thinking, the *command* to go, coupled with the technological means to reach across the globe, created a moral obligation to use whatever means necessary for preaching the gospel. Obedience

---

[17] Again, Carey is representative in this regard, but not the only missionary to draw from Matthew 28.

[18] David Jacobus Bosch, "The Structure of Mission: An Exposition of Matthew 28:16-20," in *The Study of Evangelism: Exploring a Missional Practice of the Church*, eds. Paul W. Chilcote and Laceye C. Warner (Grand Rapids: Eerdmans, 2008), 218.

[19] Both texts pair sending language with the bestowal of authority and the promise of Jesus' power and presence.

demands *going*. Carey was not the first, nor the last to make this case. But he does mark a significant transition where this imagination for mission took hold of the Protestant church in ways that continue up to the present day.

First, by highlighting these particular verses and giving it a name like "The Great Commission," the text becomes "easily degraded to a mere slogan" in a way that simply reinforces preconceived notions of mission.[20] The command to *go* and *preach the gospel* was picked up by Carey's contemporaries and leveraged for action. Contemporary calls to mission, such as the Lausanne Covenant in 1974, maintain a focus on mission as obedience to Christ's command: "We believe the Gospel is God's good news for the whole world, and we are determined by his grace to obey Christ's commission to proclaim it to all mankind and to make disciples of every nation."[21] The problem with emphasizing obedience to a command is not necessarily that it places mission in the imperative mood, but rather the fact that it pulls Matthew 28:18-20 out of its context and interprets it as current missionary practice. Depending upon the group, the "Great Commission" will prioritize proclamation evangelism over social justice, a firm distinction between evangelism, church participation, and discipleship, or even offer implicit support for the "homogeneous unit principle" (as the meaning of "all nations" in 28:20).[22] Lost in highlighting the Great Commission is the broad, variegated textures of mission throughout the book of Matthew and the Scriptures, an oversight that has

---

[20] Bosch, *Transforming Mission: Paradigm Shifts in Theology of Mission*, 56.

[21] John Stott, ed., *Making Christ Known: Historic Mission Documents from the Lausanne Movement, 1974-1989* (Grand Rapids: Eerdmans, 1996), 7.

[22] Bosch, "The Structure of Mission: An Exposition of Matthew 28:16-20," 73-92.

been addressed by many recent books that outline a "missional hermeneutic" for reading Christian history and Scripture.[23]

Second, the way in which the Great Commission functions apart from the broader biblical context has led to an emphasis on mission as *going* to the nations, rather than *making disciples*. The "go ye therefore" of the King James Version holds popular sway in missionary literature and imagination in the English-speaking world. David Bosch insists that the "go" of the Great Commission reinforces the distinction made between missions abroad and evangelism at home.[24] Often missed in popular representations of Matthew 28 is that the grammatical structure of the text highlights "making disciples" rather than "going." "Go," "baptize," and "teach" appear in participial form and modify the main verb "make disciples." As such, Matthew 28 draws the broader themes of the gospel of Matthew together, connecting the announcement of the Kingdom of Heaven with the way of discipleship.[25] Rather than fit the invitation to "make disciples" into whatever present concerns we have for proclamation evangelism or social justice, the centrality of this theme in the book of Matthew should invite us to carefully parse out the variety of things that discipleship means throughout the gospel.

Third, Carey's appropriation of the text gives moral force to his argument, suggesting the *obligation* of the church to send missionaries into the far reaches of the British Empire. Focusing on the imperative to *go*

---

[23] See Christopher J. H. Wright, *The Mission of God: Unlocking the Bible's Grand Narrative* (Downers Grove: IVP Academic, 2006). See also Michael W. Goheen, *A Light to the Nations: The Missional Church and the Biblical Story* (Grand Rapids: Baker Academic, 2011).

[24] Bosch, "The Structure of Mission: An Exposition of Matthew 28:16-20," 73-92.

[25] Scholars often point to the fact that Matthew groups Jesus' teaching into five different sections, which signifies the five books of the Torah. The announcement of the Kingdom opens up a way of life, which Jesus articulates throughout the gospel. How differently would some of our debates between evangelism and social justice, church growth and discipleship be if we saw "go, teach, and baptize" as modifying the imperative to "make disciples"?

reinforces Carey's argument for the church to *use any and all means available* to obey God's command. Obedience to a command lends itself to instrumentality. This brings the evangelical fervor of the missionary movement into direct partnership with Enlightenment habits. In the modern world, technological innovation conditions missionary zeal.

The Voluntary Missionary Society and the American Congregation

In 1837, an American Missiologist named Rufus Anderson wrote an essay entitled "The Time for the World's Conversion Come."[26] In the essay, Anderson recognized the seeds planted by Carey and others coming to harvest in the immanent conversion of the world. Listing reasons for his enthusiasm, Anderson points toward the voluntary association and the social/political/economic conditions that allow the voluntary association to flourish. He extols the unique virtues of the modern "Protestant form of association"—an association that is "free, open, responsible, embracing all classes" and "is among the great results of the progress of Christian civilization in the 'fullness of time' for the world's conversion."[27] For Anderson, the right social conditions now match the right technologies. The progressive, expansive, problem-solving, and individualist ethos of the Enlightenment, nurtured by democratic governance and liberal market economics, found its natural religious expression in the voluntary mission society.

Anderson writes as an American missiologist nearly half a century after Carey's proposal to "use means" for world evangelization. The "Protestant form" of association to which he refers is the voluntary

---

[26] Rufus Anderson, "The Time for the World's Conversion Come," in *To Advance the Gospel: Selections from the Writings of Rufus Anderson*, ed. R. Pierce Beaver (Grand Rapids: Eerdmans, 1967), 59-76.

[27] Ibid. Quoted in Walls, *The Missionary Movement in Christian History: Studies in the Transmission of Faith*, 223.

missionary society (VMS), which Carey popularized and operationalized in his writing and ministry. [28] Assuming voluntarism and drawing from the business sector, Carey sought an efficient way to organize people around three basic movements: "identify the task to be done; find appropriate means of carrying it out; unite and organize a group of likeminded people for the purpose."[29] In the United States, the voluntary society became a natural organizational form for Protestants, facilitating home mission on the frontier alongside mission overseas.[30] According to Andrew Walls, the United States perfected the VMS, as rapid industrialization and territorial growth cultivated conditions for a unique American materiality, where "entrepreneurial activity, efficient organization, and conspicuous financing" became the hallmark of both American business and voluntarism over an ever expanding territory.[31] All sorts of entrepreneurial experiments, subjected to the whims of competition, thrived and failed along the American frontier, including religious ones.

Before the Revolutionary War, the field preaching of George Whitefield and the First Great Awakening demonstrated "the immense market opportunity" for religious organizations beyond the boundaries of traditional congregational structures. [32] According to Roger Finke and

---

[28] Other missionary societies were in existence before Carey. For example, the Society for the Propagation of the Gospel in Foreign Parts (SPG) began in 1701 to enable the Anglican Church to extend its ministry throughout the English empire. However, it struggled to gain momentum and, sometimes, workers for mission. A contemporary with Carey, the London Missionary Society, began in 1795 and organized evangelical Anglicans for mission. Carey, however, heightened the voluntary nature of such societies, envisioning and creating a society organized for mission apart from the structures of a denominational polity. See Ibid., 160-172.

[29] Ibid., 229.

[30] Of course, it is not that territory was expanding, but rather that voluntary mission societies organized people and resources to follow America's colonial expansion across the continent during the "great century" of missions.

[31] Ibid., 230.

[32] "First, Whitefield demonstrated the immense market opportunity for more robust, less secularized religion. In doing so, he provided the model for itinerancy. . . .Second, it was not the 'mainline' denominations of the colonies that gathered the primary fruits of Whitefield's awakening of religious sentiments . . . Many of those brought shivering and

Rodney Stark, American independence and the formal disestablishment of religion created a competitive religious economy that rewarded entrepreneurial activity. That is, the revivals of the First Great Awakening offered a script for evangelism and renewal presented in competition with mainline ecclesial bodies. Into the nineteenth century, as the United States extended its reach across the continent, the lack of institutional presence on the frontier simply exacerbated these conditions. Unlike in Europe, overseas mission in the United States provided a "continuation and extension of home missions," such that American Christianity bears distinct similarities with the modern missionary movement.[33] Congregations function as voluntary associations, and congregations organize local mission similarly.

It is not difficult to see how the religious economy described by Finke and Stark created ideal conditions for denominations with their agencies and voluntary religious associations. While developed in Europe, the VMS found its natural home in the United States in two ways: (1) as denominational boards and agencies, and (2) as independent mission societies that eventually became para-church organizations.[34] American political, economic, and ecclesial conditions made it possible for people to raise capital and freely organize around a common purpose. Religious disestablishment along with the political habits of a nascent democracy created the right political conditions and capacities for voluntary religious associations. So also, the robust American economy, with consumer and capitalist practices that create a surplus of wealth (and economic

---

trembling to salvation by Whitefield ended up in Baptist congregations." See Finke and Stark, *The Churching of America, 1776-1990: Winners and Losers in our Religious Economy*, 53.

[33] Ibid., 227.

[34] See Craig Van Gelder, "An Ecclesial Geno-Project: Unpacking the DNA of Denominations and Denominationalism," in *The Missional Church and Denominations: Helping Congregations Develop a Missional Identity*, ed. Craig Van Gelder (Grand Rapids: Eerdmans, 2008), 12-45.

inequality) and the personal freedom to distribute capital, inculcated the means and expertise for religious fundraising. In the end, the ecclesial dynamism of the frontier thinned religious commitments so that persons imagined themselves free to associate for religious purposes. A large number of congregations in the American context are almost indistinguishable from the voluntary association. Denominations with both congregational and connectional polities operate in a broadly voluntarist context. Thus, the VMS (or voluntary religious association) discloses a structural feature of the modern missionary imagination that continues to shape the work and witness of congregations such as Midtown. The natural "Protestant form of association," reinforces the voluntary, individual agency of mission "manifestly free of old institutions."[35]

Midtown and the Modern Missionary Imagination

Over the past couple pages, I have sketched what I call the "modern missionary imagination" by drawing attention to certain features of the missionary movement in Christian history that have shaped the practices and assumptions of congregations like Midtown. In particular, I have highlighted the way particular interpretations of mission texts that imagine mission as obedient activism have found resonance within Enlightenment understandings of personhood and progress to create an entrepreneurial and improvisational technology—the voluntary association—for carrying out the tasks of mission. Within this imaginary, the church engages in Christian mission in obedience to Christ by devising efficient means for sending persons across boundaries in the name and hope of Jesus. The imperative for mission leads us to the question of "how": How do we reach *those* people or effect change in *that* context? The voluntary nature of such effort means that we organize by shared concerns

---

[35] Walls, *The Missionary Movement in Christian History: Studies in the Transmission of Faith*, 228.

and into an efficient division of labor. Some will participate by giving money and others will participate by being sent. The emphasis on obedient, strategic, world-changing action means, in the end, that the imaginary, and the structures that sustain it, are created primarily for one-way traffic. Enlightenment assumptions regarding progress and improvement, alongside the voluntary and entrepreneurial energy ordered by the VMS, delivers goods (a message or benevolent care) from one group of people to another. It is not necessarily designed for cooperation, partnership, or mutual learning between groups.

In the United States, this form of organization shaped not only overseas missions, but also evangelism and church planting across the continent. The American religious economy has favored flexible and focused voluntary associations, such that many commentators acknowledge a *de facto* voluntarism within American churches.[36] This means that when congregations like Midtown desire to reach out to their neighbors, they naturally do so by constructing mechanisms that efficiently and strategically provide services for others. The activist, progressive, and instrumental aspects of the modern missionary imagination prioritize sending well-resourced emissaries from the congregation to *do something* on behalf of the congregation.

Maintaining this connection to the "other" beyond the boundaries of the congregation depends entirely upon the benevolence and resourcefulness of the church to raise money and create programs for the neighborhood. Midtown is especially generous in this regard. Sara and Keith are gifted urban missionaries, and the church has enjoyed a long history of generous giving on behalf of its middle-class congregation. Through Sara, Keith, and the programs they have spun off, the congregation provides a dizzying array of services and support to its

---

[36] See Warner, "The Place of the Congregation in the Contemporary American Religious Configuration," 54-99.

neighbors, displaying God's love for the West End neighborhood. However, in mission history and in congregations, such arrangements mask the relational complexities of mission. As suggested earlier, heroic missionaries and the structures that send them are inevitably shaped by the people and the places they are sent. The mission of God is not a project that can be completed or extended. The operative missionary imaginary is at odds with the experience of the church.

Earlier in the chapter, I described Sara and Keith's ministry as dependent in crucial ways upon gifts and partnerships within the neighborhood. According to Sara and Keith, such partnerships provide resources necessary to continue their respective ministries. I pointed out the gap between their practice in mission and their missionary imagination. By exploring the historical, theological, and philosophical dimensions of the modern missionary imagination, my interest is to clarify the reasons for this gap between practice and imagination. The structures, assumptions, and rationale for missionary engagement assume benevolent activism on the part of the missionary. If Midtown pays attention to these partnerships, it will then need to reimagine the shape of its mission and ministry in the West End, from mission as heroic action to mission as faithful, perduring presence. In the final part of this chapter, I turn to recent work by James Davison Hunter to suggest on both practical and theological grounds an understanding of mission as faithful Christian presence with a particular people. Ministry in the West End often feels like taking one step forward and another two steps back. I want to suggest that this might be a good thing, a gracious gift from God that allows Midtown to recognize an entirely different framework for mission. What if we do not participate in God's mission to change the world?

Why We Cannot Change the World:

Or, Mission as Perduring Presence

Surveying the work of religious communities seeking to shape political and economic systems, James Davison Hunter observes in *To Change the World* a yawning gap between intention and reality. Why, for all our effort at bringing change to the late-modern world, do we appear to be so ineffective? While assuming Christian responsibility for witnessing to "God's restorative purposes over all of life," Hunter suggests Christians should be engaged in the world and pursuing "God's restorative purposes over all of life." However, the means utilized and the ends sought by Christians who engage their world should be reconsidered.[37] Exploring this problem, he constructs *To Change the World* around three essays that address Christian public engagement. The first essay exposes a flawed or untrustworthy social imaginary regarding culture and culture change. Hunter draws from leading conservative and liberal figures to show that both groups intend to shape culture by winning hearts and minds to their cause. Imagining culture as the collective values and ideas of a population, Christians on the right and the left aim to educate and convert individuals to their cause. If Christians can bring about moral or spiritual renewal, cultural change will follow. Hunter finds this argument flawed for two reasons: (1) it misunderstands culture and cultural change; and (2) it falsely assumes that Christians are responsible for the moral and spiritual renewal of their context—that we are world-changers.

Both flaws are interrelated. Drawing from decades of cultural studies, Hunter offers a dynamic understanding of culture and culture change. Rightly, he argues that culture cannot be reduced to ideas or "worldview," because it is not an object whose boundaries can be properly

---

[37] James Davison Hunter, *To Change the World: The Irony, Tragedy, and Possibility of Christianity in the Late Modern World* (New York: Oxford University Press, 2010), 4.

named and fixed. Even though culture carries particular ideas and ideals (for instance, freedom in the American context), these ideas and ideals are never fixed or only available as ideas. Instead, they are embodied in practices, transmitted in narratives, and improvised continually. For example, we cannot understand "freedom" in the American context as a fixed idea. If we are to understand what people mean by "freedom," we will need to pay attention to social practices, narratives, and symbols which point toward "freedom." Watching a military flyover at an NFL game, reading the Declaration of Independence, visiting a Tea Party rally, or a Black Lives Matter gathering will all draw from American ideals of "freedom" but to very different ends. The complexity of culture leads Hunter to conclude that most attempts to change the world by Christians fail because we remain relatively naïve to cultural production and formation. For example, when congregations structure their worship with all the cultural signifiers of a rock concert or pep rally, with dimmed lights and theatre seating, they may do so to meet people on their own terms and to provide a culturally relevant space for the gospel message. However, such popular worship practices fail to recognize the ways cultural practices also carry meaning. A confession of faith made at a church rock show may have imported into the message of grace and freedom in Christ something different from what the church intends. The stylish way in which the church intends to change "culture," may in fact work the other way around, as the church borrows the language and cultural practices of a setting. In a word: cultural change is far more complex than congregations imagine.

The complexity of cultural change leads from Hunter's first concern to his second. Because we are shaped within cultural contexts even as we hope to shape them, cultural change is notoriously difficult to predict or instigate. In addition, when cultural change happens, it is often done indirectly through overlapping, dense networks of elites. That is, cultural change doesn't usually happen by winning hearts and minds from the bottom up, so to speak, but rather through improvisational engagement from the outside in among networks of people working at the margins of elite media, governmental, educational, and economic institutions. While a valid aspiration, Hunter concludes that culture-change is too amorphous a goal for the church.

After exploring different options for Christian cultural engagement, Hunter describes the Christian public vocation as "faithful presence within" the places, networks, and social spaces in which God places us.[38] The Christian vocation to remain faithfully present within various cultural contexts recognizes and seeks to participate in God's faithful presence among and within us. In Christ, God has made Godself present with us. Through Christ, God redeems, restores, and reconciles the world. *Shalom* is the work and promise of God. Rather than seek to change the world, Hunter suggests on (mostly) practical grounds, that we would be far more effective by seeking a means to live faithfully within the world. While Hunter's thesis has already generated insightful engagement from those writing on missional church and the church in the new parish, the project neglects strong theological or missiological rationale for "faithful presence within."[39] Furthermore, Hunter's vision of the incarnation operates at a high level of abstraction, as a rationale for a social agenda he has already decided. Nonetheless, I think "faithful presence" deserves attention missiologically. The problem with investing significant effort and strategy into changing one's neighborhood is not because change is complex and difficult, but rather it misunderstands the way in which the congregation participates in God's mission. It mixes the means and the ends.

---

[38] Ibid., 238-254.

[39] See David E. Fitch, *Faithful Presence: Seven Disciplines that Shape the Church for Mission* (Downers Grove: IVP Books, 2016). See also Paul Sparks, Tim Soerens and Dwight J. Friesen, *The New Parish : How Neighborhood Churches are Transforming Mission, Discipleship and Community* (Downers Grove: InterVarsity Press, 2014).

With Hunter, I suggest the congregation participates in God's mission by cultivating a particular kind of enduring presence within the neighborhood. Presence—understood as availability *to*, dwelling *among*, and solidarity *with*—is both the means and the ends of congregational mission. To develop this thesis, the next chapter draws upon three different conversations. First, I explore theological dimensions of God's mission as restoration of relationship. Second, I consider the public and practical dimensions of this missiological insight to argue for companionship with other civil society actors as one of the primary dimensions of missionary presence. Finally, I explore the leadership dimensions of such engagement. We now turn from crisis to cultivation.

CHAPTER 6

CULTIVATING MISSIONAL PARTNERSHIPS

When you pass through the waters, I will be with you;
and through the rivers, they shall not overwhelm you;
when you walk through fire you shall not be burned,
and the flame shall not consume you.
(Isaiah 43:2)

Introduction

A short story by George Saunders called "The Tenth of December" drops us into the middle of two different heroic fantasies.[1] We first meet a boy, lost in a self-made world, rescuing imaginary people from an imaginary menace. The boy has followed his personal epic deep into an actual forest, where he is alone and unsupervised. Next, we meet an old man named Eber, who has also wandered away from home. He is terminally ill and has decided to commit suicide to save his family the final burden of caring for a suffering old man. Like the hero in a Greek tragedy, Eber embraces his fate with rational stoicism. He sneaks from the house when his wife is away and trudges through the snow to a lonely bench near a frozen pond. He slips out of his coat, leaves it on the bench, and shuffles around the pond toward a hill. Eber climbs the hill until his body gives out and he wraps himself around a tree, short of the rock he had hoped to reach. Gripping the tree, Eber turns to look over the pond and consider his fate.

---

[1] George Saunders, "The Tenth of December," in *The Tenth of December* (New York: Random House, 2013), 215-49.

Meanwhile, the boy stumbles upon an isolated bench alongside a frozen pond. He notices a winter jacket that has been hastily dropped on the bench, tracks through the snow, and what looks like a shivering old man in short sleeves off in the distance. He grabs the coat and starts to run toward the man, taking the shortest distance across the frozen pond. A *real* crisis confronts him! A *real* person requires assistance! The hero is on his way!

Leaning against a tree, a deep, uncontrollable shiver seizes Eber; death is now inevitable. His thoughts turn toward his family, his illness, his fear of losing all dignity. He steels his nerve for what must inexorably come, but he cannot keep the sea of doubt from seeping into his consciousness. Is this really happening? Should he perhaps go back? But he is so tired. He is so cold.

Eber notices a chubby kid running across the pond, carrying his coat. He worries that the boy will find him dead. Worries how this might scar the child. Then he sees the child prodding the ice with his toy gun, before it gives way and the boy is thrashing in churning, black water. Without thinking, Eber gets up and stumbles down the hill to find the child collapsed on the shore, his jeans frozen and skin already white. Eber scans the scene for help. Seeing his own coat dry and on the ice, Eber ventures out on his hands and knees to pull the coat onto dry land. He undresses the boy, giving him his shirt and pants, boots, hat, mittens, and coat. Now in his underwear, Eber makes the child stand up, prodding him forward like a cattle rancher through the woods and back to the road. The child slowly becomes aware that a strange old man in his underwear seems to be following him, and he runs on ahead. Eber now stops, nearly naked in the snow, and his thoughts turn back to his family. He now sees the foolishness of his stoic deed:

He was offing himself. Offing himself, he'd involved a kid. Who was wandering the woods hypothermic. Offing himself two weeks before Christmas. Molly's favorite holiday. Molly had a valve thing, a panic thing, this business might . . . This was not – this was not him. This was not something he would have done. Not something he would ever do. Except he – he'd done it. He was doing it. It was in progress. If he didn't get moving, it would – it would be accomplished. It would be done. *This very day you will be with me in the kingdom of . . .* He had to fight. But couldn't seem to keep his eyes open. He tried to send some last thoughts to Molly. Sweetie, forgive me . . . Forget this part. Forget I ended thisly. You know me. You know I didn't mean this.[2]

Miraculously, the child's mother finds Eber, forces him awake and into a warm house, where he is given another chance to recognize the way gifts come even as we feel power, control, and life slowly slipping away. Soon Eber hears the voice of Molly, his wife, and he sees her concern, her anger, her embarrassment, as she approaches him, welcoming him in this "stranger's house."[3]

A story that begins with two individuals exercising solitary power ends with these same individuals utterly dependent upon one another and others. While they each imagine themselves acting unilaterally on behalf of others, their true acts of heroism flower in shared vulnerability. The boy's foolish trek across the ice rescues Eber from his isolation and resignation. In giving the boy his clothes, Eber is *giving* rather than *taking* his own life. In giving his life, he is able to recognize the glimmers of the good within the dependencies that will characterize his last days. Eber saves the boy, and the boy saves Eber, but only through their interdependence.

Midtown finds itself in a version of the Saunders story, where a particular vision of heroism has been subverted by experience. The previous chapter highlighted the impressive work of the youth minister

---

[2] Ibid., 245-46.

[3] Ibid., 251.

Keith and the children's minister Sara. Both leaders engage the neighborhood with such persistence and faithfulness, both leaders are so effective at cultivating relationships and trust, that they are held both in a place of awe and pride for the congregation. The church is pretty convinced that "Nobody has done more for this church than Keith." They are heroic missionaries. Practicing the social imaginary of the modern missionary movement, Midtown has created structures for funding and sending the few into the West End neighborhood on behalf of the whole church. By doing so, they intend to provide material and educational support for their neighbors and to share the gospel. They hope to express God's love to their neighbors, to help their neighbors thrive and flourish. As a congregation committed to the city, this concern for the wellbeing of others shapes their work to a profound extent. Through sending local mission workers, generous giving, supportive structures, and fervent prayer, they hope to change the neighborhood.

However, like Eber and the young boy, a crisis lurks within their noble intentions for two reasons. First, as mentioned in the previous chapter, Midtown has not had the kind of widespread effect on the neighborhood for which it has hoped. While its ministries can name many highlights and success stories, these rarely fit into Midtown's expectations. Those touched by the gospel do not immediately join the church or put their lives back together. Those brought up to grade level in the tutoring program do not always show interest in Christian discipleship. Second, the ministry of folks like Keith and Sara is in fact effective because of their willingness to develop partnerships in the community. The longevity of Keith and Sara's ministry depends upon the rest of the church understanding and sharing in these partnerships rather than outsourcing them to heroic others.

The success of Midtown's engagement with the neighborhood has made both problems seem imminent. The church is full most days with kids and young people from families that do not attend the church. They are there because they know and love Keith and Sara. However, they do not necessarily know or connect more broadly with Midtown. Furthermore, the church is an ordinary urban congregation shaped by the same demographic trends as other congregations after the years of the "great recession." Older, more established members provide the highest percentage of giving to the church budget. Younger members tend to give less and face less immediate opportunity for well-paying careers. The result is a trend of decreased giving even when the church is growing numerically. Therefore, while ministries and programs that connect with the neighborhood are wildly successful in terms of numbers, the sheer volume of activity may not be sustainable financially. How will Midtown continue to connect with the neighborhood if they have to cut programs or if they are unable to pay a full salary to send someone out into the neighborhood?

"The Tenth of December," however, flips heroism on its head. The boy and the old man have an opportunity to save one another through mutual interdependence. The initial picture of heroism that drives the story fades entirely from view and a picture of embodied solidarity is put in its place: an old man giving his own clothes to a hypothermic boy, two strangers linked in a shared struggle against the elements. Midtown finds itself in a similar moment, in which its own understanding of neighborhood mission and its dependence upon exemplary individuals are now challenged by its circumstances. Midtown's presence in the neighborhood has cultivated companions in ministry, which both provide opportunity and threaten the congregation's sense of agency and power. They have maintained a presence in the neighborhood through the partnerships with universities, other churches, schools, and social workers cultivated by their heroic missionaries. These are strong relationships, but they do not always *look* or *feel* like mission for the congregation. Cultivating relationships is not seen as an end for missionary engagement.

The crisis of cultivation meets the church precisely at this place where the modern missionary imagination crashes against the necessary interdependencies that make perduring presence possible.

This chapter charts a path from the heroic missionary narrative toward a theology and practice of public companionship.[4] I argue that faithful Christian witness in late-modern democracies will require that congregations learn to discern healthy partnerships with others in the community. Faithful Christian witness will cultivate trustworthy public companions within civil society, enabling connectivity and community. I begin by reconsidering the common ways in which agency, change, and mission are uncritically connected, arguing for mission practice as solidarity with a people. Next, drawing from civil society theory, I suggest *companionship* as a guiding metaphor for congregations in discerning the shape of their public witness. Finally, I consider the leadership framework necessary for such a practice, offering theories of improvisational leadership for cultivating the kinds of relationships needed for discerning public companions.

If Not a Hero, Then What?

The end of the last chapter raised questions about our missionary intentions to change the world. Following James Davison Hunter's analysis, I suggest that his use of "faithful presence within" clarifies the missionary vocation of the church. We are not heroic world-changers, but faithful witnesses to the gospel within a particular context and among a particular people. But how does "faithful presence" clarify our missionary vocation? In chapter 3, I developed a theology of mission attentive to the suffering love of God in relationship to the world. The church participates

---

4 My use of the phrase "public companionship" learns from Gary Simpson's work on civil society and the missional church, where he offers a vision of the congregation as a "prophetic/moral public companion" to civil society. See Gary M. Simpson, *Critical Social Theory: Prophetic Reason, Civil Society, and Christian Imagination* (Minneapolis: Fortress Press, 2002); Gary M. Simpson, "Civil Society and Congregations as Public Moral Companions," *Word & World* 15, no. 4 (Fall 1995), 420-27.

in the triune *missio Dei* by learning to respond to and with the activity of God in the world. In what follows, I extend this discussion to consider solidarity as descriptive of God's saving work in Jesus Christ and one way the church receives and witnesses the gospel.

The fact that God's mission is not *ours* to fulfill implies suffering and responsiveness at some level. In mission, God invites the church into relationships that will confront, thwart, challenge, and ultimately enrich the life of the church. When we say, "God is love," we mean that Father, Son, and Spirit exist in perfect, mutual, interdependent joy. We also mean that we know this love in the person of Jesus Christ and the gift of the Holy Spirit. The Trinity, together with Chalcedonian Christology (the doctrine of two natures: Christ as fully human and fully divine), holds together differentiation and unity in the doctrine of God and in God's relationship with the world. The two natures of Christ make the name "Emmanuel"— God with us—meaningful; they also point toward the Trinitarian dimensions of our faith in Christ, for the earthly life of Jesus is one that points toward the Father and is lived in the power of the Spirit.[5] As Son, Jesus reveals the perichoretic communion of Father, Son, and Spirit. As the son of Mary, Jesus fulfills the human vocation as a partner, a servant of Yahweh-God in the power of the Spirit. God, then, is *with us* in a double sense: in the presence of Christ and the gift of the Spirit; in the Word-made-flesh and creaturely life taken up into the Word.

The Trinitarian dimensions of Jesus' ministry direct attention to relational clusters of metaphors we use to communicate God's saving work. Through Christ and in the Spirit, Paul assures us, we call God "Abba Father." For the author of Ephesians, the cross of Christ breaks down the

---

[5] Both Wolfhart Pannenberg and Stanley Grenz make the connection between Jesus' as the *imago Dei* and his fulfillment of the human vocation as co-gardener with God. See Stanley J. Grenz, *The Social God and the Relational Self: A Trinitarian Theology of the Imago Dei* (Louisville: Westminster John Knox Press, 2001). See also: Wolfhart Pannenberg, *Jesus, God and Man*, 2nd ed. (Philadelphia: Westminster Press, 1977).

dividing wall of hostility between Jew and Gentile, creating "one new humanity" in the place of the two. In the Luke-Acts narratives, the Spirit who rests upon Jesus initiates physical healings that restore community and communion. The ministry of Jesus takes creaturely life into the Triune life of God and all this entails, inviting us into communion with God, with one another, and with the gift of our embodied, creaturely existence. Yet, in each of these pictures, the human person maintains her integrity as a person. God *with us* heals and saves without overcoming us. In Christ, we are brought into a differentiated communion with God and one another through the work of the Spirit. This is *God with us;* and it discloses the significant relational elements of God's mission.[6] The word *with* offers a critical insight into the gospel and the vision of mission as participation in the suffering-love of God, both as the way of mission and the hope of the church.[7] *With,* I suggest, offers a way to conceptualize mission-as-suffering-love, where the church in the world learns to be *with* the God who is *with us.*[8]

If we look for it, the language of solidarity stretches throughout the biblical story. In addressing both the Exile and the Exodus, God's word comes to Israel in the language of relationship: "I will be your God and you will be my people."[9] The cry of dereliction on the cross "my God my God, why have you forsaken me," expresses the horror of abandonment. The promise given by Jesus to one of the thieves "today you will be *with me*"

---

[6] This is a critical piece of Michael Welker's argument in *God the Spirit,* 141.

[7] Samuel Wells's important book *The Nazareth Manifesto* provides an important framework for this chapter. See Wells, *A Nazareth Manifesto: Being with God,*

[8] Samuel Wells asks whether God's saving work addresses us in our mortality or isolation. Tracing key biblical themes, he argues for the latter. Wells develops this point by tracing the contours of the biblical narrative, from God with Israel in the wilderness to God with Shadrach, Meshach, and Abednego in the furnace, to Jesus' baptism and even his Nazareth years as a carpenter before his public ministry.

[9] Robert Jenson develops his systematic theology around the notion of God's identification with God's people. God is known as "the God of" Abraham, Isaac, and Jacob. God is the God of the Exodus and the Resurrection. See Jenson, *Systematic Theology.*

situates a promise of life within a dynamic of relationship.[10] Throughout the Scriptures, God "comes down" and addresses us in our loneliness and alienation; God has surely not abandoned the creation. Rather, in the life, death, and resurrection of Jesus Christ, God definitively makes a home with humanity and brings to fulfillment the promises made in Exodus and Exile. The gospel itself witnesses God's solidarity with a sinful and suffering creation.

We don't always connect solidarity with salvation. Western substitutionary atonement theories have preferred the language of exchange to describe God's saving work in Jesus Christ.[11] While this certainly is one way of conceptualizing God's saving work, it has never been the only one in Christian history. Yes, the New Testament offers us language of exchange in talking about Jesus' work; Jesus bears our sin and death on the cross so that we might receive his life through the Spirit. Yet, our theological traditions have rarely been content with substitutionary language alone for thinking about the gospel and the work of Christ. For one, substitutionary visions of the atonement tend to overshadow the breadth of Jesus' life and ministry. Is the gospel only what happened at the cross? Is it only about a singular moment of satisfaction for human guilt? What of the incarnation? What of Jesus' baptism and teaching?

Second, the cross provides a rich cluster of images for interpreting the life and ministry of Jesus. In Christian history, the cross matters as a social location and not only an instrument for death. It matters for

---

[10] Wells, *A Nazareth Manifesto: Being with God.*

[11] Of course, our most common metaphor used for the Atonement is substitution, often in the mode of Anselm's model. But recent scholarship on the Atonement demonstrates a range of metaphors throughout Christian history. Tracing the diversity of atonement theories, Hans Boersma argues for the importance of describing the atonement with the help of multiple metaphors rather than only one. By suggesting a term like "solidarity," I share Boersma's assessment that we should use clusters of metaphors in describing God's saving work in Jesus Christ. See Hans Boersma, *Violence, Hospitality, and the Cross: Reappropriating the Atonement Tradition* (Grand Rapids: Baker Academic, 2004).

Christian reflection that Jesus dies "outside the city gate" (Heb. 13:12), abandoned by friends, tortured by the state, and rejected by religious authorities. If Jesus died in his sleep or through a carpentry accident, we would not have the same gospel.[12] On the cross, Jesus goes to the place of godforsakenness, to hell on earth; he bears in his flesh the full extent of human experience east of Eden. Thus, the cross makes tangible God's connection to a broken and sinful creation. On the cross, the Triune God embraces human sin, rebellion, and abandonment in its entirety.[13] Father, Son, and Spirit bear the consequences of sinful rebellion, taking human alienation into the life of the Trinity.

The cross reveals God's presence with us as one of solidarity, of making concrete the link of suffering-love between God and creature. The resurrection, however, demonstrates God's power and willingness to save. In Jesus Christ, God enacts solidarity with a broken creation. And this solidarity is the good news, because the God who is with us is the same God who raised Jesus from the dead. The God *with us* in Jesus Christ, who bears our guilt, shame, and alienation at the cross, is indeed the one, true God. God has come to us, dwelled with, died for, and saved us. The resurrection means there is no place that we can go beyond God's reach or without God's loving care. As Robert Jenson says, the cross reveals what kind of God it is who comes to us in Jesus Christ, and the resurrection proves that it is indeed God.[14]

Solidarity names the ministry of God in Christ and through the Spirit. It also, however, names the witness of the church, as Bonhoeffer

---

[12] This is a point often made by Dr. Gary Simpson in graduate seminars at Luther Seminary in Saint Paul, Minnesota.

[13] Moltmann imagines the cross as a Trinitarian event, where the Father experiences the loss of Son, and the Son bears the abandonment of the Father. See Moltmann, *The Crucified God: The Cross of Christ as the Foundation and Criticism of Christian Theology*, 346.

[14] Paraphrasing Robert Jenson – the cross demonstrates what kind of God it is that Jesus reveals, the resurrection proves *that* this is, indeed, God. See Jenson, *Systematic Theology*.

said: "bearing constitutes being a Christian."[15] Being with God in Jesus Christ is linked to our being with one another. We receive the gospel of Jesus Christ by participating in Christ's ministry among us, which means solidarity with a sinful and suffering humanity. Samuel Wells describes solidarity as "the word 'with' turned into practical action, the word 'understanding' turned into courageous acts of witness."[16] We bear witness to the gospel of Jesus Christ by living in the world with others in the way of Jesus, seeking to hear, understand, and advocate for one another. Solidarity describes the life of the church, since the world will know us by our love for one another (as Jesus says in the "upper room discourse"), but it also describes our relationship with the world.

In practicing solidarity with those to whom God sends us, we witness to the gospel of Jesus Christ. However, because the *missio Dei* names a relational ecology, we also *receive* the gospel when we learn to be with others. We learn to participate in God's mission by learning to be with those to whom God sends us. In the parable of the Good Samaritan, Jesus takes a legal question from a lawyer seeking to justify himself ("who is my neighbor?") and tells a story in which the lawyer doesn't easily fit, asking the lawyer at the end "which one . . . was a neighbor?" While popular interpretation takes Jesus' question here as a moralistic one, encouraging us to be "Good Samaritans" in our dealing with those in need, Wells reads the parable differently. He recognizes the awkward position of the lawyer by the end of the parable. With whom can the lawyer identify? Certainly, he will not identify with the Samaritan, nor the Priest or Levite. Perhaps only the man beaten and left for dead at the side of the road speaks to the lawyer's condition. After all, as Wells and others point out, this was the national mood of Israel in the First Century. Israel had been beaten by a

---

[15] Bonhoeffer, *Discipleship*, 91.

[16] Ibid., 78.

series of robbers—Babylonian, Persian, Greek, and Roman—and left for dead.[17]

While the Priest and Levite pass by the wounded and beaten man, a hated outsider, one imagined as religiously and racially impure, stops to care for the man at great personal cost.[18] Salvation comes through the goodwill of an enemy and outsider as an "unclean" stranger's hands tend to his wounds. Wells argues that we can recognize Jesus in the Samaritan. Jesus is the one rejected and hated, who rescues at great risk to himself. In such a reading, Jesus' imperative "go and do likewise" does not encourage imitation of the Samaritan, but rather the full subversion of the lawyer's self-justifying assumptions, encouraging him to recognize his own need and dependence upon others. Our interdependence with one another and ability to recognize and receive Jesus are interconnected. Are we willing to receive God's salvation in whichever way and through whomever it comes? Are we willing and able to admit our own need and dependence, and so open ourselves to the many ways in which God gifts and cares for us? "Go and do likewise," for Wells, means: "Go and continue to see the face of Jesus in the despised and rejected of the world. You are not their benefactor. You are not the answer to their prayer. They are the answer to yours . . . Do not assume that others will see Jesus' face in you: go, and expect to see Jesus' face in them."[19] If, as Wells insists, the gospel addresses us in our isolation, then the response of faith has distinct social consequences—it has everything to do with the neighbor and the stranger not as ethical demand, but as the means for our own salvation.

In *The Open Secret,* Lesslie Newbigin draws from Paul's extended reflection on election in Romans 9-11 to conclude that we do not receive

---

[17] The fact that Israel in the First Century still imagined itself in exile is a key component of N.T. Wright's interpretation of NT texts. See Wright, *The New Testament and the People of God.*

[18] Wells, *A Nazareth Manifesto: Being with God,* 88-93.

[19] Ibid., 96.

the gospel apart from learning to receive one another. Paul's surprising success among the Gentiles, Newbigin suggests, creates a situation where all who receive the gospel must do so from an outsider, an-other. In receiving Jewish messengers, Gentiles have received the gospel. And in receiving Gentile witnesses, Israel has received Christ. For Newbigin, this is not accidental to the gospel, but rather central. The good news of Jesus Christ is restored relationship with God, one another, and creation. We do not receive this good news apart from receiving one another. Furthermore, we do not experience this good news in abstraction from the particular people of God, the church, as the "sign, instrument, and foretaste of God's redeeming grace."[20] For Newbigin, relationships across difference anticipate the healing and reconciling grace of Jesus Christ. However—and this is crucial to the metaphor of solidarity—the establishment of relationships across difference does not, by itself, bring about salvation or healing of the nations. Paul's development of Romans 9-11 makes clear God's action in salvation and reconciliation. It is ultimately God's kindness that matters, and God's action that is unsearchable. By learning to receive others, we anticipate the healing work of God and cultivate an open posture toward the reconciling work of God. Solidarity, then, *participates* in God's healing work, preparing us to receive God's promised future.

The gospel proclaims God with us in the person, work, death and resurrection of Jesus Christ. The cross of Christ makes concrete the link between God and a rebellious creation, signaling the death of sin and the emergence of the new creation. In developing this theme, I have used *solidarity* to describe the active presence of God in Jesus Christ and the response of the church to the gospel. In bearing witness to this reality, the church goes to the fringes and edges, stands with and develops concrete links between themselves and the godforsaken spaces in their particular

---

[20] Newbigin, *The Gospel in a Pluralist Society*, 235.

communities. In being with the "others" to whom God sends us, we bear witness to the good news of God with us. 'Being with' testifies to the saving action of God in Jesus Christ. However, the church is also the man beaten at the side of the road, whose own healing depends upon trustworthy relationships with strangers, in whom the care and presence of Christ might be mediated. 'Being with' names the participation of the church in mission, while also disclosing the hope of the church for healing. In this way, we suffer God's mission, responding to God's call and to the many different ways in which God invites, teaches, and speaks to us in relationship with God's world. Thus, solidarity offers an entirely different framework from the modern missionary imagination, and leads the church to consider structuring its missionary activity in a way that builds interdependence and trust, connectivity and community. In short, we learn how to cultivate healthy partnerships with those people to whom God calls us and those agencies that contribute to the peace and wellbeing of our neighborhood.

Toward Trustworthy Public Companionship

Solidarity presents an attractive and elegant idea, but it is meaningless apart from real presence, real relationships. How might a congregation like Midtown remain faithfully present within its neighborhood? What concrete form might solidarity take? In the previous chapter, I highlighted the work of Keith and Sara in building significant connections between Midtown and the congregation. Drawing from a particular missionary imagination, I suggest that Midtown envisions Keith and Sara as heroic missionaries sent on behalf of the congregation to witness to the gospel in its neighborhood. The past two chapters have described dimensions of this missionary imagination as it has functioned historically and theologically. This chapter offers a different theological and sociocultural understanding of the church in mission, suggesting an approach within which identification with the other outflanks changing the other. To claim mission as suffering-love does not, however, suggest inaction or congregational passivity. Rather, it suggests a different kind of agency. The church exercises solidarity with its neighbors by cultivating space for connectivity and community, which means forming, nurturing, and discovering missional partnerships. While this can happen in a variety of ways, I offer two spaces within which congregations can cultivate public companions in ministry: (1) learning the "art of neighboring,"[21] or loving one's actual neighbor, and (2) cultivating civil society partnerships and contributing to a robust, trustworthy, and healthy civil society. Both are important and interrelated.

The "Art of Neighboring"

To describe our current context as late modern is to acknowledge widespread cultural and institutional instability. For Zygmunt Bauman, we are living through "liquid modernity," where the formerly "solid" and secure institutions, practices, and assumptions of the modern Enlightenment project have now melted, leaving us awash in practices, institutions, and assumptions which continue to destabilize our common life.[22] We are highly suspicious of the authorities and institutions necessary for modern democracy, such as news media, government programs and information, the police, organized religion, and the like.[23] While this suspicion undermines our trust in these institutions, it does not necessarily increase our freedom or agency. A veritable cottage industry has grown up trying to both diagnose and treat the garbled politics and moral assumptions of late modernity. Some see in our current malaise evidence of dissolution and fragmentation. Losing clear authority structures or

---

[21] Jay Pathak and David Runyon, *The Art of Neighboring: Building Genuine Relationships Right Outside Your Door* (Grand Rapids: Baker, 2012).

[22] Zygmunt Bauman, *Liquid Modernity* (Cambridge: Polity Press, 2000).

[23] Kellerman, *The End of Leadership*.

common cultural identities has created a void that is now filled by the inanities of mass consumer culture. We are all free to be whomever we want, and yet we all strangely look the same, living lives sponsored by the same collective of transnational corporations.[24]

Our awareness of anomie, consumerism, and dissolution has brought a renewed interest in neighborhoods for social scientists, theologians, city planners, and (hopefully) churches. Modern life subjects us to faceless bureaucracies that both solve our problems and create new ones. When the power goes out and I call an automated service that registers my address and then promises to fix the power lines, I'm grateful for such efficiency. A computer somewhere added my address, connected with a computer somewhere else, which brought a nameless, faceless worker to some downed power line somewhere on an invisible (to me, anyway) power grid to restore my power, all in just over two hours. But when my power goes out, as it did last summer, and my phone call to the computer yields no discernable difference four, five, six hours into the pitch black night, I start to get frustrated. More calls bring more promises from the computerized voice, but no power. Now, anonymity and bureaucracy become a barrier. I want to know what is going on. I want to know that someone is aware of my situation and working on it. But I can only talk with a computer. This happens when we try to access customer service, pay our taxes, or even navigate our education. The governmental and economic organizations that govern large parts of life today often operate at a scale that allows for efficiency, but not necessarily human contact. Our relationships are fragmented, our social network feeds full of people we barely know.

---

[24] See Naomi Klein, *No Logo* (New York: Picador, 2000). See also Michael Sandel, *What Money can't Buy: The Moral Limits of Markets* (New York: Farrar, Strauss, and Giroux, 2012).

According to Kirkpatrick Sale, we no longer order our lives at a "human scale."[25] What he means by this is that the structures of modern life make consistent meaningful interactions between people increasingly difficult. We may receive efficient services and products, but such systems undermine relationships, communal memory, and identity. Except, of course, when we think about the actual neighbors we greet and the sidewalks where we walk, the parks in which we play, the places we frequently shop, and the schools we attend. The narrow geographic parameters within which we live, play, garden, party, shop, and work potentially constitute a "human scale" environment where we make connections, build memories, and live our lives. These geographic parameters "potentially" describe a human scale environment because modern mobility means that we can often transcend the limitations of neighborhood and place. We can live in one community because of its low taxes and good schools, while commuting on a freeway into another community for work, while shopping in a third community and attending church in a fourth. Physical disconnection from our neighborhoods and moral fragmentation are, in fact, related.[26]

However, we all live somewhere, and so "the neighborhood" can describe an intentional return toward a "human scale" geographic and subjective reality. A geographic reality, "neighborhood" describes the small-scale environment within which we can live, work, play, and shop.[27] It is bigger than the family home or even the block, but smaller than the city or the county. It is a place that can host a broad range of interactions and provide the basic elements of human community. Subjectively,

[25] Kirkpatrick Sale, *Human Scale* (Gabriola Island: New Catalyst Books, 2007).

[26] This interconnection is now largely assumed in popular and scholarly literature. See, for example, this recent op-ed by David Brooks: David Brooks, "One Neighborhood at a Time," *New York Times* (May 17, 2016), Accessed June 2, 2016. https://www.nytimes.com/2016/05/17/opinion/one-neighborhood-at-a-time.html.

[27] Sale, *Human Scale*.

neighborhood describes an identifiable group, naming a personal identity that can be connected to place. It is one way of saying where we are from and to whom we belong. Not all neighborhoods have a sense of identity, but this is, in part, the task of building connectivity and community in our cities, towns, and rural spaces. Learning to live in and be good neighbors to one another can facilitate the building of community and the cultivation of a shared identity. Sale describes the goal of a "human scale" environment to provide "regular associations between people, easy access to public officers, mutual aid among neighbors, and open, trusting social relations."[28] For such things to take place, we need what Sales calls "smallness." We need to live in a physical space that makes such interconnections possible.

In late-modern American society, congregations can build connectivity and community, bearing witness to the gospel of Jesus Christ, by learning to live in and attend to their neighborhoods. A broad range of literature points congregations back to their neighborhoods. It seems to me that two big trends can guide our movement from recognizing the cultural need for building neighborhood connections and the specific way in which the church bears witness to the gospel by facilitating neighborliness. First, congregations should attend to geography alongside concerns for community. Second, congregational ministry should consider itself a participant in a neighborhood economy.

The Church in the Neighborhood

Southside Community Church in British Columbia started in the Edmonds neighborhood of Burnaby (an inner ring suburb of Vancouver) in the early 1990s. Given a building by the Canadian Baptists of Western Canada, the planting team made a critical decision to buy or rent houses near the church property. They moved into the neighborhood and decided

---

[28] Ibid., 189.

to cultivate a church community attentive to neighborhood dynamics. As the church has grown over the years, this critical move remains central to its identity, a church *in* the neighborhood, but also *for* it. Very few original members remain in the congregation, and yet the congregation remains a church of the neighborhood, organized by neighborhood-based missional communities. On Wednesday nights, the majority of Southside's missional communities can walk to one another's homes to share a meal and practice the five shared practices of the church together.

Linking one's neighborhood and church community provides an opportunity for Southside to not only facilitate deep bonds of communion with one another, but in a way that integrates with the neighborhood. Living within walking distance of one's church community creates the possibility not only for neighborly connection with one another, but also for shared rhythms of Christian practice throughout the week. It also helps the church community to recognize the ways in which its worship and shared practices witness to the good news of Jesus in the neighborhood. A common neighborhood challenge, such as unaffordable housing or an under resourced school, is shared across both the church and the neighborhood. Picking up these concerns, books like *The New Parish* and *Missional: Joining God in the Neighborhood* provide not only the case for the church in the neighborhood, but also offer different models for how congregations might connect life in the neighborhood with the life of the church.[29] *The New Parish,* for example, encourages a commitment to stability and the establishment of a faithful presence in a place. Critical of seeker-sensitive and program-driven approaches to church, which extract people from their neighborhoods and segregate them by stages of life, *The New Parish* names the neighborhood as a principle of social organization

---

[29] Sparks, Soerens and Friesen, *The New Parish: How Neighborhood Churches are Transforming Mission, Discipleship and Community.* See also Roxburgh, *Missional: Joining God in the Neighborhood,* 196

that can force the integration of community, mission, and spirituality. Congregations can rediscover faithful Christian community if they can learn to be good neighbors together, seeking the welfare and wellbeing of a place together.

Both Southside and *The New Parish* suggest radical reorganization of congregational structures in relationship to the neighborhood. Alan Roxburgh's *Missional: Joining God in the Neighborhood,* while no less challenging, imagines what it might be like for congregations to "join" the neighborhood where they are located. Roxburgh considers the fate of established churches like Midtown, that, despite having congregants scattered throughout the city, organize neighborhood ministries focused on the church building. While not prescriptive, Roxburgh directs congregations to pay attention to both communities—where congregants live and where the church building is located. How can church members build community within their own neighborhoods? And how might the church seek the peace and wellbeing of its own neighborhood? While Midtown has built neighborhood connections through Keith and Sara, they have not—collectively and as a church—joined in with the neighborhood. Nor do congregants think about the ways in which they might participate in the wellbeing and care of their own neighborhoods.

The Church with the Neighborhood

Over the past couple years, the city of Edmonton, Alberta has begun what they call ACE (Abundant Community Edmonton), which aims to turn "strangers into neighbours."[30] Drawing from the principles of Asset-Based Community Development, and fanned by the enthusiasm of some local church leaders experimenting with this material, the city began to equip and empower local neighborhood associations for building a sense

---

[30] See "Abundant Community Edmonton," https://www.edmonton.ca/programs_services/ for_communities/ abundant-community-edmonton.aspx (Accessed May 31, 2018).

of community pride and care. Throughout the city, "block captains" are named who help residents identify gifts they are willing to share, and who help residents connect gifts and needs. Inspired by *The Abundant Community* by Peter Block and John McKnight, the program enacts a gift based approach to neighborhood renewal.[31] Our problem, Block and McKnight argue, is not that we lack resources for flourishing neighborhoods, but that the gifts in our communities are not shared with one another. We will build community and renew our neighborhoods by taking shared responsibility for the place in which we live. This happens by sharing and receiving gifts—through building networks of interconnectivity and interdependence.[32] When congregations move into the neighborhood, they should not do so as a provider of services, but rather as a participant in, and perhaps an instigator of, a gift economy.

A church like Midtown would be wise to move from a focus on programs to relationships. When Keith described to me his thought process for bringing unchurched volunteers into his ministry, he was describing something closer to Block and McKnight's vision for neighborhood-based community building than a traditional approach to running a youth ministry program. Keith looks to connect the gifts and passions that he sees in people with needs that he can identify in the neighborhood. Keith and Sara already have dense networks of relationships utilized for running programs. Can they imagine these relationships, and the passions/gifts that these people bring, as contributing more broadly to the flourishing of the neighborhood? For example, can they connect interested college students with other agencies doing significant work? However, the invitation to the neighborhood also

---

[31] John McKnight and Peter Block, *The Abundant Community: Awakening the Power of Families and Neighborhoods* (San Francisco: Berrett-Koehler Publishers, 2012).

[32] Block and McKnight describe their vision in this way: "The community described in this book has at its center two sources of power: the expression of our gifts and their manifestation through association with our neighbors." Ibid., 109.

invites Midtown to think beyond its heroic missionaries, and to consider the ways the whole church might learn to be present in their own neighborhoods for the sake of participating in God's gifts of community and connectivity.

Cultivating Civil Society Partnerships

The previous chapter described how Keith and Sara draw from networks of volunteers well beyond the membership of the church to staff different programs. They offer tutoring programs in partnership with a local university while the ministry, which houses homeless families each September, draws volunteers and help from a wide variety of churches and non-profits. Even though Midtown imagines these partnerships in instrumental terms, the theological work of this chapter offers a different interpretation. Rather than means to the end of certain ministry goals, Midtown's various partnerships with the community offer a critical element of faithful Christian witness. Because the gospel names an economy of restored relationship between God and creation, faithful Christian witness in our time of isolation requires us to cultivate connectivity and community in the neighborhood and civil society. On the one hand, we live together in a way that develops, connects, and shares the gifts of a neighborhood. Joining the neighborhood does not mean offering programs, it means cultivating opportunity for connection and wholeness, which we can do as a part of congregational organization and community development. On the other hand, we facilitate partnerships with other civil society organizations to help cultivate space for public moral deliberation about the ends and goods of our community.

Our political life depends upon a robust civil society sector, where we learn communicative practices and cultivate "free spaces" for deliberation and collaboration.[33] Congregations, I suggest, can play a

---

[33] For an overview of civil society theory, see Simpson, *Civil Society and Congregations as Public Moral Companions*, 420-27 See also Jean L. Cohen and Andrew Arato, *Civil Society and Political Theory* (Cambridge: MIT Press, 1994).

particularly significant role in cultivating a healthy civil society by discerning and cultivating civil society partnerships. As a public companion with civil society, congregations cultivate virtues for healthy communication as well as more human and humane spaces for community flourishing. Given the deep divisions and cynicism stalking our national politics, such spaces are necessary and increasingly rare. While civil society theory is complex and contested, its basic contours follow the social theory of the German philosopher Jürgen Habermas and imagine a public space constituted by norms of deliberation and communicative ethics rather than governmental or political rationalities.[34]

Communication, by nature, connects us to others and performs action in the world. For Habermas, civil society is a space constituted by open, fair, and just conversation that facilitates solidarity and shared action. [35] Because open, fair, and just conversation seeks to include everyone who could be affected by an issue, and because it seeks to speak as well as to listen, communicative action shapes a space increasingly free from the instrumental rationality of the marketplace or the political economy. Communicative action is human-oriented action. In America, voluntary associations, non-profits, neighborhood groups, and sports leagues provide structural support for civil society. These associations and networks operate, not for the sake of accruing something else, but for the sake of human flourishing (however that might be defined). They create space for gathering and even equip us for communicative action. Conversations just might change the world.

---

[34] Simpson, *Critical Social Theory: Prophetic Reason, Civil Society, and Christian Imagination.*

[35] Ibid. See also Jürgen Habermas, *The Theory of Communicative Action*, trans. Thomas McCarthy, Vol. 1: Reason and the Rationalization of Society (Boston: Beacon Press, 1984).

I draw upon Habermas because I think he articulates the space within which the church speaks and acts in late-modern democracies as organizations within which our public and private lives overlap.[36] Moreover, a communicative vision of civil society can shape how we think about the prophetic, public witness of the church.[37] That is, our witness is not only one of verbal proclamation to the gospel, but also one of shared practice and prophetic imagination. How we speak and discern together, whom we include, and how we develop partnerships takes on significance in Habermas's vision. We develop partnerships, not only for the sake of continuing an important ministry, but also for the sake of establishing healthy, open-ended communicative practices and spaces. As Gary Simpson says, the congregation as "public companions" with civil society enables a particular kind of prophetic witness for the congregation.[38]

Cultivating companionship with civil society organizations enables the church to bear faithful witness within their community, and it contributes to the health of civil society more generally. Ten years ago, I worked with a grant to train four rural congregations in a conversation method for moral and spiritual discernment. The congregations were located in communities that had undergone rapid social and cultural change due to an influx of large numbers of immigrants. The congregations studied the conversation model, and then practiced it on various decisions the church faced. Once the congregations became comfortable with the model, the grant application encouraged them to host public forums where people could come together and talk about the changes in their community. Groups needed to attend to all voices in the room, and groups needed to commit to speaking honestly as well as listening to one another.

---

[36] Simpson, *Critical Social Theory: Prophetic Reason, Civil Society, and Christian Imagination*, 144.

[37] This, after all, is what Gary Simpson does in his book *Critical Social Theory* and in many articles. I am indebted to his reading of Habermas and the insight connecting the theory of communicative reason and action to the public vocation of congregations.

[38] Ibid., 141-144.

Congregations struggled to move from hosting internal conversations about the church to hosting public forums to discuss things that mattered to the broader community. Over the year, congregations stumbled and struggled in various ways to practice this approach in relationship to the broader community even though they immediately sensed its importance. By offering space for deliberation and public conversation, these congregations hoped to function as companions to civil society, modeling a structure for open, fair and just communicative action. Our communities desperately need more congregations to step into civil society in this way.

But there are other ways that congregations might participate in civil society. Besides helping shape moral deliberation in our communities, we should look to establish partnerships with other people and organizations that contribute to the overall wellbeing of our community. This approach requires a great deal of discernment, communication, and care. Churches often find it easier to create their own program to meet a need, so when we can afford to, we typically do. Working with partners to address homelessness, for instance, adds significant complexity to our ministry. We will constantly need to talk about values and goals, articulating where we might differ. We might feel at times that our witness is crowded out by the personalities or intentions of a partner. However, in this care and communication, we establish relationships and model the solidarity of the gospel of Jesus Christ. When we navigate between our Christian vocation and the people with whom we work to live that vocation, we bear witness to the beautiful complexity of the Word made flesh. Moreover, we act in the world in a way that anticipates the saving, reconciling, and healing work of Jesus Christ. Solidarity, expressed as neighborliness and civil society companionship, participates in God's promised future for our neighborhoods and our churches.

Navigating civil society and developing deeper connections in our neighborhood, however, requires us to learn new things. It requires the church to engage in experimental action even as we exercise the "attend, risk, act" of ongoing missional discernment. The final section of this chapter attends to the shape of such experimental action by drawing from improvisational theories of leadership. Because mission joins God in the world, we will need to learn as we go. I think improvisational models of leadership provide three critical practices for navigating the crisis of companionship, enabling us to find ways of dwelling with those to whom God sends us.[39]

Public Improvisational Leadership

Karl Weick tells a story about a group of Hungarian soldiers who lost their way hiking in the Alps. They wandered for days, running out of ideas and energy. Despondent, the group lost hope until one soldier discovered a map deep in one pocket. The group huddled around and they began to problem-solve together until they found their way out to safety. It was only after the fact that they realized that the map that directed their path was of the Pyrenees Mountains and not the Alps.[40] The map, it turns out, did not so much direct the soldiers as it gave them "a temporary sense of confidence that there was enough structure within the chaos and a loose belief that if they started down the path, they would eventually find their way out of the dilemma."[41]

The map helped them to engage their problem in a particular kind of way: "Act first 'as if' this will work; pay attention to what shows up; venture forth; make sense later." [42] If 'public' describes the space congregational leaders must hold for reflection (leadership attends not only to congregation but also neighborhood and city), then 'improvisation'

---

[39] See also Scott Hagley, "Improv in the Streets: Missional Leadership as Public Improvisational Identity Formation," *Journal of Religious Leadership* 7, no. 2 (2008), 61-85.

[40] Frank J. Barrett, *Yes to the Mess: Surprising Leadership Lessons from Jazz* (Boston: Harvard Business Review Press, 2012), 10-11.

[41] Ibid., 11.

[42] Ibid., 11.

discloses the way in which we exercise leadership in such spaces. When cultivating space and process for public, reflective conversation, congregational leadership engages similarly to what is described in Weick's anecdote, providing enough structure in the chaos in an appreciative, hopeful way so that space for risk, experimentation, and learning can emerge. It all begins in the practice of "yes."

We commonly understand improvisation to mean an extemporaneous performance composed or "made up" on the spot. While this is true to an extent—improvisational performances in theatre and jazz do provide moments of discovery—such an understanding overshadows the disciplines, habits, and practices that constitute improvisational performances. In the last decade, the disciplines, habits, and practices utilized by jazz and theatre performers have helped to frame organizational studies, leadership, and even ethics. For our purposes, we focus on three different dimensions of the improvisational "yes": *yes . . . and* (yes to who and what lie before us); *yes . . . let's* (yes to positive action, acting our way into understanding); *yes . . . we are* (reflection).

Yes . . . and . . .

A well-known rule in improvisational theatre is that of acceptance.[43] We see the rule of acceptance at work during improvisational comedy routines when one actor lobs an absurd situation toward another, who must take it in stride while stretching plausibility to keep the comedy sketch going. The same is true of jazz improvisation; a soloist cannot stop and ask the band to play differently, they must continually work with one another into our out of whatever musical situation they have created. The moment of tension, when performers and audience interact in a way that

---

[43] Sometimes using a strategy of "over-acceptance." the actor receives the situation and then draws it back into the broader narrative arc. See Samuel Wells, *Improvisation: The Drama of Christian Ethics* (Grand Rapids: Brazos Press, 2004).

launches them together into unknown territory is part of the thrill of improvisational arts and performances. Audience and performer feel the tension as the performers take a cue from one another and/or the audience, and then launch forward with their contribution: "yes...and..."

A good improvisational moment, however, is not only inventive and responsive to the situation; it is also plausible or coherent with what has gone before. A jazz soloist might begin with the melody of the song and then change certain elements of the melody or even begin with random sounding notes and build them back into something reminiscent of the melody. Similarly, improvisational comedy keeps us laughing when the absurd somehow is reconnected with the theme that began the sketch in the first place. The hope for the soloist and the actor is not sheer invention, but plausible and coherent innovation or even discovery. Weick says, "The important point is that improvisation does not materialize out of thin air. Instead, it materializes around a simple melody [or, we might say, plot] that provides the pretext for real time composing."[44] Thus, improvisation first masters the "simple melody" and composes in "real time" an innovation on that melody in response to audience, the moment, and other musicians. Within acting circles, improvisation masters the basic plot of the sketch or the rules of the improvisational game, along with the restraints of character and setting in order to innovate in real time with the audience and the other actors. In the practice of acceptance, actors and musicians acknowledge what has come before and all the limitations of the situation without being determined by the limitations of melody and plot.[45] The performance event and the moment when they are put on the spot provoke the possibility of the new.

---

[44] Karl E. Weick, "Introductory Essay: Improvisation as a Mindset for Organizational Analysis," *Organization Science* 9, no. 5 (1998), 546.

[45] Weick says it this way: "Wherever the notes [in a jazz solo] come from, their value is determined by the pattern they make *relative to* a continuing set of restraints formed by melody." Ibid., 547.

It is not difficult to see how this practice might shape congregational leadership. In the practice of attention so crucial for discernment, congregational leaders must cultivate spaces for listening to the reflections, voices, and offers of others. Some of these offers and voices will be expected and ask very little of the congregation. However, if we take our public identity seriously, if we respond to the call of God to participate in God's love in God's world, then we will find ourselves listening to and responding to the voices of others that challenge, provoke, and surprise us.

We may feel tempted to silence these voices, but doing so closes down discernment and limits our ability to respond to the Spirit of God. Nevertheless, listening to the voices in our neighborhood and community can also be incredibly confusing and painful, as we encounter myriad ideas, perspectives, and hopes. This is where the practice of improvisation intervenes. We must say "yes" to these voices, and listen to them.[46] But we must listen in a way that is authentic to our own identity as the church and our calling as a congregation. How might we listen and respond in a way that is plausible with the gospel story that is coherent with our calling as the Church of Jesus Christ? Listening to these voices demands that we know our own plot and melody well. Who are we as a particular congregation with particular gifts and histories? Who are we, as the Church of Jesus Christ, and what are we called to do? As we listen, we receive the words and actions of others, and then we risk connecting this to the gospel story: yes . . . and . . .

"Yes . . . let's try . . ."

Frank J. Barrett can pinpoint the exact moment in which he became a jazz soloist. As a young pianist, he was called upon to back up an

---

[46] Pat Keifert has a memorable phrase about the effects of such listening, that when we do so, we listen one another into free speech. See Keifert, *We are here Now: A New Missional Era.*

up-and-coming clarinet player named Ken Peplowski in a Houston club. In the middle of one song, the rhythm section and the piano were supposed to drop away and allow Peplowski to solo. However, the rhythm section and Barrett missed each other, leaving Barrett playing piano by himself with the 5,000-member audience and band all looking at him. He said "yes . . . and . . ." playing some random notes, then adding some chords, repeating and building a theme, Barrett found himself playing something he had never played before. At one point, he heard Peplowski say "yeah" and he heard a member of the audience shout. The band came back in and the audience applauded. Barrett reflects, "I said yes to the mess I was in and followed what I was hearing myself play."[47]

Barrett's experience underscores the retrospective nature of improvisation. Barrett entered a risky moment uncertain where it would lead. He played a couple notes, and then, hearing what he played, he added some chords, and hearing the chords, he continued to build a coherent musical response to the silence of the band. By playing *something* and then *paying attention* to what he just played, Barrett improvised a solo. Ted Gioia says that improvisation does not work from plans, but from retrospect, for one in the midst of a solo cannot "look ahead to what he is going to play, but he can look behind at what he has just played; thus each new musical phrase can be shaped with relation to what has gone before. He creates his form retrospectively."[48] We can understand improvisation as both a noun and a verb. As a noun, it describes the transformation of something. As a verb, it describes precisely what Barrett did. It is the risk of taking action when the future, outcome, or even next step remains unclear. Barrett said yes, let's try this . . .

Barrett's story underscores one way in which we develop creativity and innovation: we risk taking action before we even have a plan, and we

---

[47] Barrett, *Yes to the Mess: Surprising Leadership Lessons from Jazz*, 28.

[48] Weick, Introductory Essay: Improvisation as a Mindset for Organizational Analysis, 547.

learn from this action even as we continue to improvise. Like the Hungarian soldiers, some situations require us to take positive action and build capacity and knowledge as we go. Learning remains a risky business. Thus, congregational leadership that cultivates space for discernment and builds capacity for discernment does not only listen, but helps the congregation to take risks in response to what they have learned. Yes . . . let's try . . . This practice of improvisational leadership helps enable the congregation to be adaptive, to develop the capacity to learn from and with those in its community.

In the past ten years, the work of Ronald Heifetz and Marty Linsky has popularized the adjective "adaptive" for describing successful organizations in the modern world.[49] An adaptive organization is one that builds capacity to address the ever-changing risks and demands of a fluid and unstable world. We live in an era characterized by "discontinuous change," which means that the usual methods of planning and strategy are too slow and internally focused for organizations to address dynamic challenges of the marketplace or the environment. An adaptive organization, instead, internalizes processes of risk and reflection, taking action and learning from failure, among other things. Congregational leadership nurtures adaptive behaviors in the congregation by taking action in response to cues it encounters from the neighborhood. Some things, we can only learn by saying "yes to the mess." Leadership in the new missional era will learn ways of doing this, and by saying yes, begin to cultivate capacities for practicing discernment in the congregation.

"Yes . . . we are . . ."

Leadership exercises improvisational competence by saying yes to interruption and surprise by learning to listen to the outsider and stranger

---

[49] Ronald A. Heifetz and Martin Linsky, *Leadership on the Line: Staying Alive through the Dangers of Leading* (Boston: Harvard Business School Press, 2002).

in our midst. Like an improvisational actor receiving a surprising cue while on stage, leadership in its public dimensions that is concerned with building capacity for theological discernment remains open in posture and practice to those outside the usual power structure of the congregation. Such openness can lead to confusion and uncertainty. Leadership attentive to theological discernment learns from improvisational practices by seeking opportunity to learn and experiment in the midst of such uncertainty, to say "yes . . . let's try . . ." as a response to what was heard or observed. Such a practice recognizes that learning happens while doing and not only while thinking or talking. Like the Hungarian soldiers lost in the mountains, or Frank Barrett's risky foray into a piano solo, experiments are not ends in themselves, but rather moments of learning that beg to be named and described. An improvisational sketch or solo eventually finds its way back to the melody of the song or the arc of the narrative. Whatever we discover in the improvisational moment becomes integrated back into the song or the story by the performers, otherwise it remains interesting noise but relatively meaningless.

The work of improvisational leadership, then, leads toward practices of reflection and sense making, where participants in the experiment or the disturbance or interruption are brought into a shared space to reflect on what was learned. In such settings, leadership works to help the congregation, alongside shareholders in the community, to regularly articulate "we are here now," as a means of making sense of what the congregation and neighborhood has heard and experienced.[50] This practice of reflection often needs the practice of simple, repeatable questions, such as, "What did we learn?" "What did we hear God say?"

---

[50] See Patrick Keifert, *We are Here Now*. The title of Keifert's book is as much about understanding the current "new missional era" as it is about practices of "discovery" regarding the identity of the congregation and the work of God in its midst. Sensemaking constitutes important features of the text, and results in making a claim regarding one's current situation. Organizations, as well as people, function by continually making sense of oneself and one's situation. This last practice of improvisational leadership draws upon that fundamental insight. See also Karl E. Weick, *Sensemaking in Organizations* (Thousand Oaks: Sage Publications, 1995).

"What surprised us?" Regular engagement with such questions builds reflexive capacity in the congregation, shaping the posture of the congregation for missional discernment.

Conclusion

When speaking with a Midtown Sunday School class, I asked some questions about the ways they imagine the church bearing public witness to the gospel. In the middle of our conversation, one woman blurted out her view on abortion: she thought evangelicals have largely been wrong on the issue, and argued for "a more compassionate stance." The entire group grew tense. Midtown was an activist congregation, but largely followed evangelical norms on issues such as this. The woman's statement obviously crossed a line and articulated a clear moral difference. The silence was broken by another woman, who began by saying she is troubled by abortion, but then told a story about a friend of hers with an unwanted pregnancy. She articulated her inability to really understand the woman, and, searching for common space, also suggested that the church needs to meet people wherever they are and not pass judgment. The exchange set off an open conversation, with several others weighing in with different means of evaluating the moral choices involved in terminating a pregnancy, often punctuated with personal stories.

It was a remarkable moment, which made me ask how Midtown learned to do this. The answer? These conversations happen whenever Midtown engages with other neighborhood partners to meet common goals. Pastor Robert cultivates space for this type of interaction by his non-anxious and permission-giving approach to leadership and critical members of the church practice open-ended, morally discerning conversations at all levels of the congregation. They are practiced in communicative reason and action, and so able to navigate complex moral issues in ways that build trust and find space for shared action across difference. This is what public companionship teaches the congregation.

CHAPTER 7

THE CRISIS OF CONTEXT

"Do not move about from house to house."
Luke 10:7

Introduction

When approaching Midtown Baptist Church from the North on foot, one must chart a course through bodies slouched, peering into smart phones, and swaying to the silent rhythms of noise canceling headphones. Diesel hangs in the air. City buses exchange passengers, who maneuver through crowds and wait with the kind of disinterested attentiveness that characterizes public transit regulars in cities across North America. Once past the crowds, one will see a small Lutheran church perched one block from the bus stop before coming across Midtown. A beige, three-story rectangle structure built right up to the sidewalk, Midtown projects pragmatic symmetry; evenly spaced two-tone stained glass windows adorn the sparse south side of the building with a flat, featureless roof devoid of a cross or steeple.

Crossing the street and heading south from the Lutheran church, one can walk up alongside Midtown and take in the whole front of the building. Two identical entrances greet one with symmetrical features and a sign that says "NOT AN ENTRANCE" blocking the steps up to the doors. To enter the church, one needs to walk further south, where the bricks change into a vertically aligned pattern, with rows alternating like opened vertical blinds. Sidewalk-to-ceiling glass signals the functioning entryway, next to a sign that says "Midtown Baptist Church: God's Love, Alive in the West End." In some ways, the building footprint tells the story of Midtown.

The original building was completed in 1913. Orderly and symmetrical, the building exudes the clear sense of ethnic identity that once characterized the congregation. An immigrant church in a thriving Swedish neighborhood at the center of the city, Midtown's early years featured services in Swedish and English, amidst a growing Scandinavian community. In the middle part of the twentieth century, the congregation enjoyed the intellectual and cultural benefits of students and professors in regular attendance from a denominational college and seminary located just up the road. As more women joined the workforce through WWII and beyond, Midtown discerned a need for childcare in the neighborhood, culminating in an education wing, completed in 1948, and a preschool for neighborhood children.

Midtown's place in the neighborhood began to change in the 1970s when surging suburban development, expanding freeways, racial tensions, and growing perceptions of urban crime contributed to what is commonly called "white flight" from the city. The college and seminary bought a large tract of wooded land several miles outside the city limits and sold its urban campus. Church members also moved away from the city center in search of the space and perceived safety of the suburbs. The professors, students, and young families who once constituted the Midtown community became less prevalent. Looking out at expanding freeways and flourishing suburbs of the early 1970s, Midtown toyed with visions of a brand new building, green grass, a parking lot, and room to grow. Inspired by church growth principles that emphasize the importance of homogeneity for growing congregations, Midtown wondered whether its future, and its white middle class sense of identity, was now located in the suburbs.

The most recent modification to the facilities, completed after the church discerned its call to the city in 1975, involved building a new sanctuary and converting the 1913 building into a community center and gymnasium for neighborhood youth. They closed the arched entryway to the 1913 building, creating a new glass entryway and foyer with a gas fireplace, marking a new era for the congregation. Thus, the current footprint of Midtown witnesses to three separate eras of church faithfulness and discernment. The 1913 facility provided a sanctuary and fellowship hall, followed by the education wing completed in two different projects (1948 and 1962), followed by a new sanctuary and a conversion of the old sanctuary into a gymnasium in 1975. Built to the edges of the property, the new and old sections of the facility lie uneasily next to each other, with competing architectural styles and a maze of hallways. The buildings could easily represent the uneasiness in Midtown's own story. For in the same way that perduring presence is an ongoing invitation, where congregations must actively discern the call and leading of God, so also perduring presence provokes an ongoing identity crisis, where congregations must learn to cultivate Christian community in the places they are located. In Luke 10, Jesus instructs the seventy-two to remain *wherever* they have been received. They are to remain where they encounter a person of peace and are not to move from house to house. So also the prophet Jeremiah instructs exiles in Babylon to plant gardens and seek the welfare of the places they are located (Jer. 29:5-7). The apostle Paul refers to churches based on the city where they are located, recognizing different *charisms* and crises for churches in different places.

Place matters for the mission of God. Place matters for the formation of community and spirituality. The mission of God *places* us among people, institutions, nations, cultures, and languages that offer new possibilities for Christian community and faithfulness: *where* we are inevitably shapes *who* we are. When it comes to congregations, remaining present in a dynamic urban context introduces dynamism into its own life. Perduring presence requires an acceptance of ambiguity within the life of the congregation, as new forms of community and church life rest (at times) uneasily next to older ones. New and old constitute a crisis of context, presenting both risk and opportunity to the congregation. Similar to Midtown closing the entrance to the 1913 building, congregations risk losing critical elements of their self-understanding through the crisis of context. To remain in a place and cultivate connection to it, congregations will put their own preferred vision(s) in jeopardy. Elements of Midtown's Swedish-Baptist identity are no longer plausible. That door is no longer open. Yet, the decision to remain in the neighborhood gifts Midtown with an opportunity for renewal and discovery. The crisis of context invites the congregation to discover new dimensions of the gospel and a renewed vision for faithful Christian witness.

I have suggested that the mission of God precipitates a crisis in the life of the church. When Jesus sends the seventy two-by-two in Luke 10, they go out into God's world as sheep into the midst of wolves, bearing witness to the coming kingdom not through their activism or sheer creativity, but rather their solidarity with the stranger. In chapter 3, we explored theological dimensions of this crisis, observing the dynamic in the Scriptures between love and mission to argue that we suffer participation in the mission of God. By using the term "suffer," I am not primarily talking about martyrdom or violence, but rather the way in which love, passion, and affection are intertwined: to love is to suffer, to love is to be moved by an Other, both God and neighbor. In addition, this suffering marks the crisis of mission, for when God calls and sends us to participate in God's mission, we suffer the dynamic movements of God in the world. In the last two chapters, I explored the sense of dislocation caused by remaining in a fast changing neighborhood, suggesting the need for Midtown to cultivate new forms of community with the neighborhood by tending to neighborhood gifts and civil society partners. Learning to dwell with the people to whom God sends them will require a shift in both imagination and practice. In both cases—the crises of call and cultivation— the congregation in mission finds itself shaped in surprising ways by both God and God's work in the world. For Midtown, such crises come as a gift, providing opportunity for Midtown to learn certain core organizational competencies for engaging with its dynamic urban context.

These last two chapters sketch the third crisis Midtown encounters in mission as the crisis of context. If the crisis of cultivation confronts a sense of dislocation by directing the church to think and live *with* the neighborhood, then the crisis of context invites the church to discover new forms of faithful witness *within* the neighborhood.

Sketching the Crisis: How Does One Join a Family?

Silence descended like an early morning fog as eyes nervously scanned the room, searching for inspiration. I had just asked the Midtown leadership team to tell me a story about a stranger who joined their community and served in congregational leadership. I anticipated a well-rehearsed narrative that might display congregational aspiration more than daily reality. I had already heard several such stories regarding young people coming to faith, families staying together, addicts experiencing healing. When such dramatic events occur, congregations tend to tell and retell such stories to communicate their hopes and values. People do not experience such healing every day, but telling stories like Gary's in chapter 1 offer a picture of possibility, as if to say "we are the kind of community where people are loved and transformed." I expected a similar story to emerge from the leadership team regarding an individual who entered the church and successfully joined the "family." Instead, my question invited silence and searching before Ruben, an affable, young professional, ventured an interpretation: "well, this seems to be a problem for us." Ruben would know. His wife grew up in the church and his in-laws exercise significant influence in the community. Ruben loves Midtown and serves the ministry of the church in many ways, but he also knows that he married into the church family. When younger members of the church serve in leadership, they tend to have a pedigree similar to Ruben. "Church family" extends from metaphor to bloodlines. "How does one join a family?" Ruben asked aloud.

Midtown's robust engagement with the neighborhood intensifies this question. On the one hand, Midtown is a close intimate family with clear boundaries reinforced over many years. On the other hand, Midtown is a congregation that is incredibly inclusive of the outsider and the stranger. On Sunday mornings, Midtown hosts a wide variety of people with warmth and grace. The homeless will occasionally attend not only services but also Sunday school classes. The worship team makes room for those with disabilities, and services are sometimes punctuated by spontaneous shouts from those who have come to the church from an assisted living facility. The life of the church throughout the week engages the neighborhood even more directly, with a variety of children's ministries and other partnerships bringing kids, families, and folks seeking housing and/or food through the church every day.

All of this is done under the banner of family; Midtown is a family that prepares a large banquet table, welcoming the neighborhood to come take a seat. However, the boundaries between family and stranger are always clear. For example, Midtown has some university students who are at the church building nearly every day to run after school programs and to connect with kids. However, they would not be referred to with family language. Similarly, those in the church will talk about the "church kids" and the "community kids" that participate in the youth ministry. The "church kids" are not those who participate in the youth ministry, but rather those related to members of the intimate core, whether they attend the church or not. Such use of language might seem inconsequential, but it foregrounds key strands of Midtown's identity, which are subsequently challenged by Midtown's own faithful presence in the West End neighborhood. For Midtown's ministry subverts its own conflation of "family" and "intimacy."

Family Intimacy

Many congregations describe themselves as a family. It is often the closest metaphor that we have to describe the type of belonging, longevity, and community that we hope to experience in a church. Family describes certain features of congregational life while also naming some of our deepest aspirations, such as intimacy. A quick glance at pop culture should convince us that our age desires intimate connection. Consider the format for syrupy romantic comedies, like the 2003 Christmas movie *Love, Actually.* The film seemingly condenses all the usual storylines of the romantic comedy into a single film, with several stories told at the same time. In the end, various characters must make decisions between public and private life, between career and family. In one plotline, the British Prime Minister chooses to pursue a relationship with one of the staff at the Prime Minister's residence at risk to his political agenda (and, one must note, with a troublesome disregard for the power differential).[1]

To the viewer, the choice is obvious: happiness and fulfillment depend upon choosing the beloved over career and public service. Even movies that work against this format uphold the abiding value of intimacy. For example, the 2009 movie *(500) Days of Summer,* tells a story of heartbreak, connecting unrequited love with personal growth and self-discovery. Told through a series of flashbacks, the film plunges into the confusing aftermath of a breakup with a woman named Summer. Despite the longing of the protagonist, the relationship is over. He is left to make meaning with fragments and memories. Yet, the film cannot resist bringing the viewer back to the all-encompassing good of intimacy. In the final scene, the protagonist meets a woman who agrees to meet him for coffee. Her name, not surprisingly, is Autumn. Intimacy, or the desire for

---

[1] In light of recent allegations of sexual misconduct and assault leveled against powerful men in virtually every industry in 2016-17, this plotline looks more ill-conceived every day.

intimacy, trumps all other possible goods. Usually, such a revelation takes the leading actor an extended video montage, where she/he comes precipitously close to the edge of loneliness and suddenly sees what the audience knew all along, that intimacy offers itself as the pearl of great price. The story resolves itself through some series of highly improbable events that make possible a final, impassioned speech, where the lead actor revalues all values before the call to intimate connection. We know how it ends. A pithy, memorable response and the closing kiss.

Such films portray a particularly romantic understanding of intimacy, ending before the problems, possibilities, riches, and conflicts of intimacy really begin. Furthermore, they assume intimacy as an exclusive good, an end or *telos* for relationships that excludes other ends or goods for relationships, such as those with strangers or even colleagues. Such movies rarely end with a speech regarding the value of friendship, or the importance of collegial relationships with neighbors. They end with a strong valuation of romantic intimacy that subsumes all other outcomes for fulfilling human relationships. Something like this romanticizing of intimacy happens when strong value is placed upon the family metaphor for congregations. Midtown does not speak of "family" with notions of romantic intimacy, but its image of family closeness does relativize all other possible goods for relationship. One either belongs to the family and enjoys warmth and closeness or does not. Family intimacy constructs a good that revalues all other values. The power of this metaphor drives Ruben's inquiry: "How does one join a family?"

Leaders and congregants alike describe Midtown as a family. Family, if it means anything at all, requires clear boundaries. When a person says, "We are like family," the statement assumes clarity regarding who "we" are. If I stand in the middle of a busy shopping mall and gesture to those hurrying in and out of the mall and say "we are like a family," my statement will be confusing at best and meaningless at worst. When a hockey player says the same thing while sitting in the locker room, the referent is much clearer. The team functions as family. Now imagine the hockey player is sitting in a locker room after a late night drop-in hockey session at a public ice rink. The statement becomes more difficult to understand. Not everyone in the room comes to play every week; he may never step on the ice with a handful of the players ever again. It is a transient, public gathering of athletes. What does this statement mean?

Who is the "we" referred to that functions like family? Most likely, if the statement has any meaning, it refers to a small group of players who have committed to drop-in hockey, who know one another and have played together for some time. If "family" has meaning in this setting, it is because those on the inside have established a clear and tightly managed boundary. The players serving as "extras" know that they are not a part of the "family." Those who attend regularly but do not have the longevity or personal relationships or social capital to be included with the insiders are also not part of the "family." Not everyone in the locker room can become part of this "family;" it will take time, commitment, and some intentional acts of welcoming by those already on the inside. To be "family" in such a setting means to cross a boundary, and to be acknowledged by those on the other side of the social boundary. For anyone who participates in public recreation events: drop-in basketball, hockey, soccer, even tennis or swimming, we all understand this dynamic. The same thing happens with congregations.

Congregations, like other voluntary associations, must exercise some formal intentionality in managing their boundaries. They have membership classes and lists, they ask for tithes and offerings, they invite members to serve on boards and committees, to lead or serve. But, like showing up to play drop-in hockey, a name on the membership list or participation in committee work does not necessarily make one a member of the family. Imagining the congregation as family extends beyond formal means of participation or membership and suggests another, invisible yet tightly managed boundary between insider and outsider.

The clarity of this boundary between insider and outsider can also be seen in Midtown's youth and children's ministry. At one time, 'church families' constituted the majority of Midtown's children/youth ministries. Then, youth group was an unambiguous part of the church's cradle-to-grave family care. The youth ministry was a service to the family, an extension of the boundaries drawn more broadly. Now, however, large numbers of students from the neighborhood whose families are only marginally involved constitutes these ministries. Furthermore, some 'church families' send their children to other, more suburban congregations for mid-week programming. These factors combine to force some ambiguity regarding these ministries. Are they 'church' ministries constituted by congregational 'insiders' or 'family'? Or are they considered church 'outreach' and thus mission-to the neighborhood or care-for a people and thus an extension of the church family?

Intimacy is a basic human longing that requires certain boundaries to be drawn and maintained. For Midtown, the problem is not the good of intimacy or the metaphor of family, but the way in which intimacy subsumes other goods or ends for relationships. In its changing context, its sense of family has become strained by the many invitations to strangers offered by different congregational ministries. How does one join the Midtown family? When Ruben asked his question, the leadership team imagined a problem of assimilation. How do we help *them* join *us*? However, like the aesthetic jigsaw of Midtown's building, which surrounds a symmetrical 1913 brick building with additions reflecting the architectural designs of the 1940s and 1970s, assimilation will not happen without massive reconstruction. The differences between Midtown's core identity and current neighborhood dynamics remain too great. A shrinking, ethnically homogenous family has stood the test of time and tumult in the West End neighborhood. It now faces, not a crisis of connection or sustainability, but of creating a contextual Christian community in the West End neighborhood.

Outside the church, a sign reads "God's Love, Alive in the West End." Does this mean that the core family exists as a light on the hillside for the neighborhood to see the love of God? Or does this mean that the love of God is being cultivated anew in the dance between constituencies and partners in relationship to Midtown Church? This ambiguity not only discloses the crisis, but also clarifies what is at stake. While better assimilation of newcomers might sustain the status quo, it does not address the growing gap that exists between Midtown membership and the West End neighborhood in terms of race, ethnicity, socioeconomic status, and culture. If Midtown addresses this crisis, seeking to cultivate new community in the spaces between church and neighborhood, it will discover for itself the profound missiological truth expressed in its sign. God's love is alive and giving life to the church and through the church in the West End neighborhood. The difference between the two interpretations of the sign lies in the gap between assimilation and contextualization. To confront the crisis of context, Midtown must aim for the latter.

Contextualization and Assimilation

John William Colenso began his call as the Anglican Bishop of Natal (now in South Africa) in 1853.[2] An advance of the "civilizing" mission

---

[2] For what follows, I follow Willie James Jennings's excellent and insightful portrait of Colenso in *The Christian Imagination*. See Jennings, *The Christian Imagination: Theology and the Origins of Race*, 119-68. Jennings's chapter on Colenso is followed by another, where he explores the life and work of Olaudah Equiano, a freed slave whose autobiography, *Interesting Narrative,* demonstrates for Jennings the dimensions of "black life forcibly formed inside the market . . ." Equiano published and distributed his book without white redaction, which allowed him to expose "the echoes of a commodified existence" and to lodge "within it the protest for intimacy, for acceptance, and relationship for his people and for himself" (189). Both chapters together demonstrate the interrelationship between commerce, colonialism, slavery, and mission work throughout the eighteenth and nineteenth centuries. Neither the work of translation nor the translating work of the slave

of the English Empire, Colenso arrived in Natal eager to "to convert and to educate" the Zulu in the Christian faith.3 A skilled linguist and conscientious worker, Colenso built relational bridges with several indigenous men and immersed himself in local language and culture. Colenso's productivity is hard to imagine. Three months after landing in Natal, Colenso produced a dictionary, grammar, and revised translation of Matthew's gospel in Zulu. Within seven years, he translated the entire New Testament and parts of the Hebrew Bible into isiZulu.4 Not content with translation, Colenso also invested himself in educational empowerment for the Zulu, providing indigenous students tools for participation in the new economic order wrought by England. An agent of "benevolent colonialism," conversion and education produced "proper colonial subjects" among the Zulu.5

Colenso's vigorous translation, cultural sensitivity, and friendship with his African congregation might appear as effective contextualization. However, it is not that simple. Colenso served in Natal as an emissary of the English church and society. Alongside his translations, Colenso also published books in England, with the intention of bringing insights from "the African mind" into English theological debates. While his body was in Africa, Willie James Jennings insists, his mind remained in England. Thus, his contextual work among the Zulu alongside his attempts to educate the English with regard to Africa, served to create space within the English world for his African congregants. With perhaps the best intentions, Colenso prepared the ground for Africans to assimilate to a world remade by colonialists.

---

narrative is straightforward. Both are caught in broader racial ideologies, market forces, and political considerations.

3 Ibid., 122.

4 Ibid., 132-33.

5 Ibid., 132.

Figures like Colenso demonstrate the deep ambiguities of Christian mission. On the one hand, Colenso models the type of sensitive cultural study and translation work necessary for contextual, indigenous mission. On the other hand, mission, translation, and discipleship all functionally assimilated the Zulu into Anglican ways as subjects of the Empire. Translation and education prepared the way for English mastery over the region. Colenso's missionary work presents a thick, ambiguous stew of contradictions: contextual ministry can serve assimilative ends. It is a stew served many decades later as congregations wrestle with the shape of contextual ministry in changing contexts. The right instincts toward neighborhood engagement and education can be placed in service of larger assimilative ends. Congregations engage their context so that those in their context might join the congregation, so that *they* might become like *us*. Something like this names Midtown's tension between its robust social services and its awareness of a shrinking, intimate "church family." Midtown's service in the neighborhood, like Colenso's translation and education, is not the problem. What is the problem, however, is their confusion between assimilation and contextualization. As I discuss below, assimilation domesticates the unpredictable dynamism of contextualization and assumes theological passivity on the part of one's context.

A Primer on Contextualization

In Missiology, "contextualization" refers to the process by which the Gospel is made authentic and understandable within a cultural context. [6] Contextualization takes cultural agency seriously as theological work, acknowledging the ways that vernacular cultures will innovate and

---

[6] Darrell Whiteman, "Contextualization, Models of," in *An Encyclopedia of Mission and Missionaries*, ed. Jonathan Bonk (New York: Routledge, 2007), 90-95.

improvise with the gospel on their own terms and in their own way.[7] As such, contextualization clarifies the cultural, congregational, and theological importance of context for faithful Christian witness.

Contemporary notions of contextualization stem from modern anthropological theories of culture and cross-cultural engagement. In anthropology, the *ubiquity* of culture contributes a non-hierarchical and nonjudgmental starting point for studying culture.[8] Cultures cannot be differentiated into "higher" or "lower," "primitive" or "developed" because no single vantage point exists outside of culture from which one might evaluate cultural differences. For example, an American anthropologist studies another culture as an American, while in turn people from the other culture view the American from their own perspective. Human cultures exist as the means by which we live in and understand our world. A nonjudgmental, relativist understanding of cultures places the missionary and the host on level ground and requires a reevaluation of the dynamic between gospel and cultures. Simply put, contextualization imagines shared agency between missionary and host in the transmission of faith. No longer does the missionary accommodate features of the host culture, but rather the host, in partnership with the missionary, discovers faithful, articulate, witness in her own cultural setting.

Contextualization resists abstract or non-cultural notions of the gospel.[9] Reflecting on issues related to contextualization, Andrew Walls imagines the whole human community as sitting in a giant theatre watching the "Christ play." In such a theatre, each seat provides a different

---

[7] While "contextualization" became a formal topic for missiological conversation in the 1970s, the basic idea has been carried with other terms. For example, the "accomodationist" approaches of people like Matteo Ricci and Francis Xavier, who adopted, respectively, Chinese and Japanese dress, intellectual traditions, and ways of life explores the same terrain as contextualization by giving some agency and priority to one's cultural context.

[8] See Kathryn Tanner, *Theories of Culture: A New Agenda for Theology* (Minneapolis: Fortress Press, 1997).

[9] Walls, *The Missionary Movement in Christian History: Studies in the Transmission of Faith*, 43-54.

view of the play. Because we are cultured creatures, Walls insists that we cannot view the Christ event from any other position. Conversion, in Walls's model, is not the assimilation into the culture of the missionary, but rather the beginning of the conversion of the host culture. It is the recognition of the Christ event from within one's own setting. One does not enter the gospel's culture, but rather the gospel begins to grow and flourish in the new culture. The missionary cannot see the Christ event from the new cultural perspective, she must learn from those indigenous to the cultural setting what Christian faithfulness looks like.

The thoroughgoing importance of culture for receiving and understanding the gospel bears significant implications for how congregations engage mission. In the 1990s, the Gospel and Our Culture Network (GOCN) and its seminal text *Missional Church* engaged questions of contextualization in relationship to North American congregations. However, many early proponents of "missional" have grown disconcerted with its popular appropriation, which envisions context as a target for mission rather than a generative partner.[10] Alan Roxburgh, for example, critiques what he calls the "ecclesiocentrism" of the missional church conversation.[11] When congregations struggle for people or experience dwindling funds, they focus outward in hope that they can draw more people into the church and (perhaps) expand their territory. Ecclesiocentrism makes the church rather than the world the center of mission and it makes the church the primary agent of mission rather than God. If congregations draw from the cultural relativity assumed in contextualization,[12] they will move away from ecclesiocentrism and expect

---

[10] See Van Gelder and Zscheile, *The Missional Church in Perspective: Mapping Trends and Shaping the Conversation.*

[11] Roxburgh, *Missional: Joining God in the Neighborhood,* 196.

[12] "Cultural relativism" is not the same as "moral relativism." Here I refer to a non-judgmental understanding of cultures and cultural differences. Culture just simply *is.* The gospel of Jesus Christ addresses us in and within our cultural setting.

new cultures and peoples to make constructive contributions to the life and ministry of the congregation. In short, mission demands contextualization rather than assimilation. In addition, while there are good cultural criteria for insisting upon contextualization over assimilation, *missio Dei* offers us theological criteria as well.

In fact, mission theology attentive to the relationship between God and world requires the cultural relativity and congregational flexibility outlined above. In chapter 3, I argued that the *missio Dei* describes God as the agent and end of mission. In Trinitarian theology, *missio* names the interrelatedness of Father, Son, and Spirit. The Father sends the Son, and Father and Son send the Spirit, who gifts and sends the church into the world. Mission names the availability of God in the world, while also revealing the nature and character of God. As Catherine LaCugna says, it reveals "God *for us*" and "*God* for us."[13] Given this theological frame for mission, openness to cultural difference at the congregational level is sustained by both divine mystery and worldly encounter. First, theological work bears a light load because it is done against an unsearchable and inexhaustible horizon. We must not take ourselves too seriously, for God's judgments are "unsearchable" and God's paths "beyond tracing out" (Romans 11). We come to know God in fits and starts; we confess our trust in God without ever seeing the whole picture. Throughout the biblical tradition, God's name is unutterable because God cannot be controlled or fully known. When Israel or the church claims more for God than possible or wise, they fall into idolatry. When we insist upon mission as *God's,* then we must also accept an unsearchable horizon for our missionary activity. Just like no one theology exhaustively lays claim to God's nature, so also no single understanding of mission settles the question.

Second, because mission names God's sending in relationship to the world, our growing understanding of mission takes place in dynamic

---

[13] LaCugna, *God for Us: The Trinity and Christian Life.*

relationship with the world. Roxburgh traces this thread throughout Luke-Acts, demonstrating the way in which conversation with strangers—Hellenists, Samaritans, Ethiopians, and Gentiles—helps the early church understand the gospel of God.[14] These are not only evangelistic encounters, but also divine encounters. Lamin Sanneh identifies something similar in the Acts narrative as the confession of the early church moves from a focus on Jesus as Messiah to Jesus as Lord.[15] The use of "Lord," as Sanneh points out, is a concept explicitly borrowed from the Greco-Roman context, which the church would have learned as the gospel took root in Hellenistic settings. In conversation with context, the church not only learns to engage contextualized ministry, but also encounters the good news of God in new and unexpected ways.

Dwelling with and within our context changes us, whether we are prepared for that change or not. We can see this in the broad arc of Colenso's life. Early in his career, Colenso's mind was in England even if his body was in Africa. However, the integrity of Colenso's work would not allow this dichotomy to remain. His mind eventually caught up to his body, and he found himself in between the English and the African. He found himself joined to the African in ways that his English superiors could not understand. Colenso began to turn toward context by giving voice to perspectives he encountered among the Zulu. In his commentary on the Torah, Colenso addresses questions and offers interpretive frameworks that arose from his Zulu interlocutors.

The inclusion of African voices and perspectives raised eyebrows in England, offending some reviewers as tolerating heresy. Several years later, Colenso presented theological insights he gained in conversation with one of his students, a Zulu man named Ngidi, while lecturing in

---

[14] See Roxburgh, *Missional: Joining God in the Neighborhood.*

[15] Sanneh, *Translating the Message: The Missionary Impact on Culture*, 324.

England. Several critics challenged Colenso's presumptuous pluralism, and he soon found himself embroiled in a heresy trial. In the view of some, he gave too much ground to African voices. The trial put him at odds with English colonials and shaped him into an advocate for the Zulu. Colenso ended his days in tension with the tradition that nurtured him, working tirelessly against the British campaign to subdue Zululand.

Herein rest the deep ambiguities of God's mission. Colenso might be remembered as an overly contextualized heretic, a repentant colonialist, or perhaps a missionary. In all cases, Colenso points toward the tensions of genuine contextualization, where the persons in a context do not simply receive a message, but take an active role in shaping, interpreting, and discerning the gospel together. Colenso bears this tension in his own body, for a crisis of context confronts him as his translation work moves from assimilative to contextual concerns. Rather than translate, Colenso *joins with* the Zulu, which creates tension within his own theological paradigms and ecclesial community. The implication of missionary work is not only the translation of texts, but "loving, caring, intimate joining" which is "a sharing in the pain, plight, and life of another." The missionary vocation expressed in the work of translation, according to Willie Jennings, "cost Bishop Colenso everything."[16]

Colenso intended to help the African assimilate into English patterns and communities. Nevertheless, his faithful presence among the Zulu cultivated in him a new Christian identity, formed in empathy and co-suffering with his African congregation. God's mission precipitates such crises, what I call here the crisis of context. Whatever our intentions, perduring presence in the places and among the people God calls us inevitably shapes us. New communities and identities are cultivated in the act of translation that takes place between groups and people. As the sordid history of colonialism and the ambiguous nature of Colenso's life

---

[16] Jennings, *The Christian Imagination: Theology and the Origins of Race*, 156–57.

demonstrate, such a crisis is neither simple nor unproblematic. Yet, I contend, it is unavoidable.

Bishop Colenso's story remains instructive for congregations like Midtown. In a short period, Midtown observed rapid change in the surrounding neighborhood and, more broadly, in the city and region. Some of these changes are due to broad cultural and social phenomena like "post-Christendom" and globalization; others are due to the localized shape of such forces, incentivizing where immigrants settle and the growth of suburbs and the decisions made by the metropolitan transit council. In less than fifty years, Midtown's Sunday morning worship has gone from a reflection of the neighborhood to an anomaly in the neighborhood. The bus stops and businesses, the houses and community centers reveal a population younger and significantly less homogeneous than Midtown on Sundays or Midtown's leadership. Midtown's decision to remain in the neighborhood and its achievement of a perduring presence in the West End neighborhood means that Midtown bridges a variety of cultural, socioeconomic, linguistic, and racial differences when hosting ministries and programs for the community.

In Midtown's understanding, such bridges are a means for bearing witness to the gospel in the neighborhood. Congregants can tell stories of families reconciled, of young people coming to faith, of God's love, alive in the West End and reflected in the ministries of Midtown. Like Colenso's early work, these stories suggest assimilation. Midtown's many neighborhood ministries make it possible for people to enter the Midtown community, to assimilate to its rich spiritual tradition, to "join" the church and all that this entails. Yet, bridges allow for two-way traffic. And, like Colenso late in his life, Midtown's perduring presence confronts Midtown's self-understanding, disclosing not only a gap between church and neighborhood, but also the real challenge Midtown faces to join the neighborhood. Like Colenso, Midtown's intention to serve with other West

End inhabitants cultivates the possibility of significant change in the congregation, which is ambiguous and risky. Like Colenso, Midtown's building and bodies may be in the pluralist realities of the twenty-first century, even if its minds are still in the homogenous neighborhood of the mid-twentieth century. Ineffectual assimilation at the level of leadership presents a symptom of what is a struggle to shape identity at the boundary between congregational identities and contextual ministries. In this tension lay the crisis of context.

The remainder of the chapter, I link cultivation and context to move the congregation away from its assimilationist tendencies. Contextualization engages both people and place. Thus, the congregation cultivates partnerships with people and connection to place.

Cultivating Connection to Place

At various times, my wife and I imagined ourselves gardeners. We started with houseplants, which would thrive for a while until we forgot to water them or the plant outgrew the pot. During graduate school in Minnesota, we attempted guerrilla gardening, planting tomato plants, peppers, and flowers in places amenable to gardening but not visible to people on the street. Because our townhouse association required uniformity between units, we grew tomatoes in window wells, interspersed pepper plants behind shrubbery, and planted flowers in an empty lot across the street. When we moved to Vancouver, we experimented with gardening on our balcony, growing flowers and vegetables in pots and discovering that many favorites struggled to grow in the cooler Vancouver weather and partial sun of our deck. However, we discovered new favorites more amenable to the climate and context.

Our first spring in Pittsburgh, we decided to build a 4' x 8' raised garden bed in our front yard. I picked up cedar boards from Home Depot, dug up a rectangle of dirt near the sidewalk, and filled the box with soil from a local gardening store. We talked with people about the growing season, the soil, and gardening strategies for Western Pennsylvania, and then planted the garden and began to water and wait. As spring eased into summer, green shoots appeared throughout the bed. Neighbors walking by on their way to the store, coffee shop, or bakery would stop and take note of our progress. Some older women in the neighborhood began to linger at our property and offer Maribeth and me advice about plants not growing, on spacing of existing plants, and on general care for the garden. Collard greens, Russian kale, and cucumbers thrived and threatened to overtake the garden. Peppers and squash, carrots and radishes were limited. Of course, various neighborhood gardeners and urban farmers gave us opinions and advice; we learned much and approached the next year with great anticipation.

In each place we have lived, cultivating plants and planting gardens looked different. In each case, a particular vision of abundance, greenery, and flowers engaged the possibilities and limitations of housing, land, weather, soil, and neighbors. Gardens do not display ubiquitous universal principles, but rather the particularities of place. In this way, gardening attends to a variety of local limitations, some that are obvious and others that must be learned from local experts or through trial and error. For instance, our condo in Vancouver provided an obvious set of structural obstacles for gardening. We could not change the orientation of our unit to get more sunlight, nor could we plant vegetables in the common area. However, other limitations of gardening on a patio we needed to learn from others. We initially did not know how to keep the soil nutrient rich. We also had to learn the delicate balance between over- and under-watering potted plants. Other obstacles were social. In Minnesota, we had to abide by social expectations of uniformity between townhouse units, so we needed to cultivate our garden in particular places that would not draw the ire of our neighbors. In Pittsburgh, we placed our garden in the front yard on a busy street because we do not have a back yard. But this placement made our experiment public and vulnerable to the inspection and judgment of people passing by or waiting for the bus. Still more obstacles are creational; we are limited by the soil quality, weather patterns, rodents, bugs, disease, even faulty seeds. We cultivate a garden by working with and within all of these limitations of place. We cannot combine all the ideal conditions of Minnesota, British Columbia, and Pennsylvania in gardening. We garden in just one of those places at a time. Cultivation depends on place; and places are *made* through the relationships and connections that thrive or struggle in that locale.

Cultivate

Gardening discloses the relationship between the verb "cultivate" and the noun "place." When we cultivate ground for gardening, we work within and respond to the particular features of a particular place. In cultivating soil, the gardener both *shapes* and *responds* to a place. The gardener, as cultivator, prepares ground and creates conditions for growth and change; yet, the gardener is limited in what she can do. Cultivation is not the same thing as causation. The gardener cannot cause growth; often the success or failure of a crop is due to a variety of causes. But the gardener can cultivate possibility for success. We understand in gardening that "cultivation" describes a limited and contingent form of human agency, which responds to the nuances and unexpected challenges brought by cultural, economic, creational, and social dynamics.

Culture and community formation work similarly. Kathryn Tanner notes the connection between our modern word "culture" and the agrarian connotations of "cultivate."[17] Before our modern anthropological understanding of culture, the term "culture" named the best of a particular civilization (however that might be determined). To be "cultured," in such a view, one must cultivate appreciation for and skill in the arts, literature, manners, and accomplishments of high society. We still sometimes talk

---

[17] Tanner, *Theories of Culture: A New Agenda for Theology.*

about cultured people in such ways: cultured people go to the ballet, not pro wrestling. In this older understanding of culture, we recognize awareness of how differences in people's values, hopes, and aesthetics can be traced to community and formation. The modern anthropological understanding of culture, however, does not rank cultural values hierarchically, but rather studies the ubiquitous fact of culture. To be human is to be cultured; the communities we belong to do not only shape us, they make us who and what we are. We can interact meaningfully with others because we are cultured in a particular way; something we take for granted until we have a misunderstanding or difficulty communicating across cultural difference.

Yet, we are also participants in culture making.[18] When we communicate or use a cultural symbol or participate in a cultural event, we contribute to the cultural flows that have and will shape us. For example, when my family moved from Canada to the United States, my kids had no idea about the "Pledge of Allegiance" to the American flag. Schoolchildren in Canada sing the national anthem, but they do not have any practice comparable to pledging to the flag. When they arrived at school and the students stood up, covered their hearts, and said the "Pledge," my girls did not participate. Their cultural formation did not prepare them for this moment. However, they stood silently and covered their heart. What was cultural ignorance to them was interpreted as intentional protest by their classmates, which led to a series of conversations at school and then at home about what the "Pledge" means, and whether Christians should make such a pledge in the first place. The point is, their stoic (and culturally ignorant) presence made a cultural contribution, modeling an alternative practice which called the "Pledge" into question in subtle ways.

---

[18] Andy Crouch, *Culture Making: Recovering our Creative Calling* (Downers Grove: IVP Books, 2008).

We are cultural creatures, in the sense that we are made by the various social, linguistic, and formational flows of culture. This basic anthropological insight informs my use of "cultivate" to describe a chastened understanding of human agency. We are cultivated cultivators in our social and moral life, both shaped by context and culture even as we give shape to it. The term "cultivation" thus describes a particular kind of human agency, where our actions both shape and are shaped by broader cultural contexts and flows. Such cultivation, however, always depends upon place. The task of *cultivation* outlined in the previous two chapters necessitates attention to *place,* to context. If contextualization will avoid becoming a means for assimilation, Midtown must become responsive to both people and place.

Place

I use the term "place" to describe, as richly as possible, the locale for cultivation. In the case of gardening, place describes land, weather, history, social/cultural expectations, laws, etc. Successful cultivation of a garden will need to attend to all of these factors, and more. Cultivation is a particular kind of placed agency. In using "place" so expansively, I follow theorists who recognize a distinction between generalized environments and the rich contexts to which we attach meaning, make memories, and form communities.[19] For example, when I ask someone, "Where are you from?" I am asking about not only a geographic location, but also one's identity. I am asking where this person has made significant memories, the geography, seasons, weather, and cultural factors that have shaped this person's outlook, interests, and capacities. It makes a difference if the person answers "Hamilton, Ontario" or "New Orleans, Louisiana." "Where are you from?" asks about a place. However, if I ask "how did you get

---

[19] See Mary McClintock Fulkerson, *Places of Redemption: Theology for a Worldly Church* (New York: Oxford University Press, 2007). And Len Hjalmarson, *No Home Like Place: A Christian Theology of Place* (Portland: Urban Loft Publishers, 2014).

here?" I ask an entirely different question about one's movement through space. I am not asking a question of identity, but rather mobility.

John Inge distinguishes between these two different ways of talking about environment by making a distinction between "space" and "place."[20] For Inge, "space" names the general environment through which we move: the neighborhoods and farmland that hurtle past us on the freeway or the experience at an airport or shopping mall. The freeway moves us *through* places that exist for others, but the very design of the freeway detaches us from the unique contours of place. We do not interact with people, hills are flattened and low places are raised, local histories are largely erased except, perhaps, when a "historical marker" is placed beside the road. When we pull off the freeway, interchanges are noticeable only for their homogeneity and predictability. The same gas stations and fast food chains dot the landscape. Any memories we make or identities we form in relationship to freeway travel are bound to be transient and shallow. The freeway is not designed for living, but for movement. The same dynamics hold true in air travel. Airports are designed to move us through spaces with efficiency, but not for building connection or community. Airport food, security, and aesthetics are all vaguely familiar no matter where one travels; local customs and even languages are erased or made subservient to the custom, language, and aims of air travel. These are spaces.

"Place" names the contexts where we make meaning and that, in turn, make us. We move through space, but we *make* and are made by place. We do not easily connect to place in the modern world, however. Technology, transportation, and global economics invite unprecedented global mobility. We move through even the neighborhoods and cities we call home, forming identities and living lives largely disconnected from the

---

[20] John Inge, *A Christian Theology of Place* (Burlington: Ashgate, 2003).

contours of place. In the modern world, we might as well be citizens of anywhere, diminishing the local differences between Hamilton, Ontario and New Orleans, Louisiana. However, place making, the establishment of roots and joining the rhythms and histories and general contours of a particular locale, remains significant for moral and community formation. As embodied creatures, our identity and agency must always be connected to the limits and possibilities of our locale. Communities and people fashioning themselves in universal, placeless terms can be morally incoherent and reckless.

The popular 2009 movie *Up in the Air* explores the relationship between place and identity through the story of Ryan Bingham, a corporate downsizer who travels for a living. He prides himself on a life without limitations, baggage, and aspirations. The airline miles he has amassed mean that all relationships in his life are pleasantly commodified due to his "elite" status in all things travel. Facing downsizing at his own company, Bingham is forced to travel with Natalie Keener, a young woman who represents all of the relational and emotional messiness that Bingham largely avoids.

In *Up in the Air,* a small life is given greater weight or significance. The people who appear on screen for thirty seconds to be fired by Bingham and Keener demonstrate depth of care, grief, responsibility, and love for family in comparison to the flat, dispassionate sketch of Bingham. It is not until Bingham himself lives small and attends to relationships that he also appears a more richly developed character. It is when Bingham is 'grounded' from his travels and attempts to join himself to the lives of others that he also experiences disappointment, grief, and pain. On the ground, Bingham risks relationship with others and encounters emotional baggage, suffering inconvenience, disappointment, and hurt. When Bingham is 'up in the air,' he pleasantly moves through space, but remains only a two-dimensional character.

Up in the Air offers a subtle plea for place. Character is not developed by hurtling through space, but rather through the kinds of connections facilitated by time, stability, and patience. While traveling, Bingham has no accountability or connection. He has no history that is not commodified, no relationship to local time zones, and no enduring memories as he drops into batches of nameless, contextless faces to fire them before going back to the airport. Bingham's life rings hollow even while it offers a mild form of pleasure. Living with no restrictions means he can be anything. However, without context, history, time, and connection, Bingham's *anything* is revealed to be *nothing*. It also, however, issues a warning. When Bingham goes to visit family or attempts to meet a romantic partner outside of his travel schedule, he must suffer the whims and expectations of others in relationships free from commodification. "On the ground," we are vulnerable; we can be rejected, fired, or left behind. This represents our creaturely conundrum. What makes life rich also makes us vulnerable to one another. When I use the term "place," I am referencing this broader context of our creatureliness, the lives we live cultivated within and dependent upon the land, histories, institutions, communities, and economics of our time and place. Place names where we are *from* and where we are. Like the gardener, the dynamics of place provide both challenge and opportunity for cultivation—of plants as well as community.

Congregations are also *from* somewhere. They are placed, in the sense that their history, culture, practices, and sense of the possible are rooted in a particular community and neighborhood, reflective of numerous local factors, much like a garden.[21] The congregation's own story

---

[21] Mary McClintock-Fulkerson draws from place theory to suggest congregations themselves as places for gathering, as places that are constituted through the practices, habits, and narratives of a people who gather there. I want to draw from this approach, but extend it into the neighborhood, to think about how the neighborhood is also a place within which the congregation does its work and meaning-making. See Fulkerson, *Places of Redemption: Theology for a Worldly Church.*

inevitably interacts with the story of its neighborhood and its neighbors; the shape of its community inevitably reflects the neighborhood it calls home. Pittsburgh congregations will narrate their own life by reference to the boom and bust of the steel industry, and the emerging revitalization and gentrification of the city. As Nancy Ammerman demonstrates in *Congregation & Community,* congregations that are not *from* somewhere are less likely to thrive in their context.[22]

We can say, then, that congregations are *placed* at a number of levels. First, as a public gathering, they are located somewhere. While pop theology chastises anyone who refers to "the church on 10th Street" as a building, preferring instead to describe the church as a people, our colloquial conflation of "church" and "building" reveals something important. Public gatherings happen *somewhere*. Second, congregations are placed in a more significant way, sharing in the same features we might associate with the question "where are you from?" Like the question of hometown, congregational location informs the narrative and self-understanding of the congregation. Location contributes something to congregational identity and story. A third level deepens this insight with regard to location, for place not only provides a setting, history, and shared social memory for a congregation, it also provides the conditions of possibility, the limitations and challenges, for the congregation. Congregations *are placed,* and unless they pick up and move, they must learn to cultivate missional community within that context.

Thus, *place* poses a challenge to congregations, because congregational identity and its locale are so interconnected. In Midtown's early years, its congregational life and neighborhood were inextricably linked. They worshipped in Swedish in a largely Swedish neighborhood. They facilitated Christian formation for young people who attended the denominational college and seminary just down the street. The language,

---

[22] Ammerman, *Congregation & Community.*

economics, ethnicity, and even work of the congregation overlapped with its immediate neighborhood in sufficient measure. Without much work, Midtown displayed the kind of contextual awareness that comes from overlapping worlds and experiences. However, neighborhoods do not stay the same. Place makes us, but we also make place. Thus, a community formed by the rhythms, language, and dynamics of one particular place finds itself uprooted without ever having left the neighborhood. Midtown's various building projects represent new attempts to cultivate soil, put down roots, and flourish in new settings. At one stage, Midtown added an education wing to address community need. Later on, Midtown converted the old sanctuary into a gymnasium to facilitate space for neighborhood youth to gather. These were not initiatives of Midtown, but rather attempts to respond to changes in their neighborhood. Place or neighborhood contributes a dynamic energy to congregational life. If a congregation will remain faithfully present in any one place, it must inevitably respond to contextual dynamics, a crisis of context. Here the crises of cultivation and context constitute one another: Midtown must learn to cultivate new community in a new context.

Conclusion

In a meeting with Midtown leaders, Ruben asked, "how does one join a family?" Midtown's effective engagement with its context has disclosed a gap between the identity of the congregation as an intimate family and the numbers of strangers that participate in the life of the church throughout the week. The context precipitates a crisis for the congregation that initially appears as a challenge for assimilation. How can we help all these people join us? How can we share with the neighborhood our wealth of love, intimacy, and pastoral care? However, such questions do not meet the basic challenge of gospel contextualization, which aims to facilitate space for local and indigenous expressions of the gospel to emerge within new contexts. While contextualization doesn't *exclude* the possibility of assimilation, it certainly cannot begin with assimilative goals. The crisis of context raises for Midtown the challenge of cultivating a placed identity. This means the possibility of adaptive change for the congregation. Like a gardener moving to a new city, Midtown must learn what authentic, faithful, Christian community looks like in this place at this time.

We should not be surprised that this is the case. Mission participates in the suffering-love of God. In mission, we suffer God's call and the place to which God sends us. In the next chapter, I will explore Midtown's practice of hospitality as a critical way in which congregations can learn to cultivate placed Christian identity.

CHAPTER 8

DISCOVERING GOD'S LOVE IN THE NEIGHBORHOOD

How could we sing the songs of the Lord
in a foreign land?
(Psalm 137:4)

The weather recently turned cold. The first snow of the season dusted the sidewalk and promised more cold days to come while a steady stream of bodies wrapped in coats and scarves and mittens pushed through Midtown's entryway, their presence announced with a blast of cold air and the scent of fresh snow. It was the Wednesday evening before Thanksgiving. Friends and strangers, church folk and neighbors gathered for Midtown's annual Thanksgiving feast. Circular tables filled the space outside the sanctuary. A gas fire flickered in the fireplace. Over one hundred people ate their fill, some taking home plates of leftovers. For several years, Midtown's Thanksgiving meal had developed from a shared meal for the elderly and homeless in the neighborhood into a full-blown neighborhood event. A team of competent women choreographs the event each year, cooking multiple turkeys, soliciting side dishes from members of the congregation, and organizing a team of volunteers.

Among the different ways that Midtown serves the neighborhood, this event stands apart in its graceful hospitality. Apart from the team serving in the kitchen, the line between 'insider' and 'outsider' blurs during the event. Church members share tables and conversation with neighborhood families and people who walk in off the street. While the meal clearly serves a need in the neighborhood, its energy emanates from this practice of hospitality—the church risks hosting and sharing with strangers around the table. It is an event formed by the Christian practice of hospitality, with its open door and round tables and uncertainty regarding insiders and outsiders. In church lore, the event stands as a highlight year after year.

The last chapter explored the crisis of context for Midtown, which appears in the tension between Midtown's sense of identity and its public ministry. When congregations like Midtown are called to participate in God's mission and follow the invitation of God to venture into their neighborhoods in faith and hope, they inevitably encounter certain differences that provoke and challenge the congregation in surprising ways. Because congregations assume that mission extends care for the neighborhood, they are unprepared for the ways that relationships in the neighborhood might act back upon them. The public life and ministry of the congregation precipitates a crisis, for relationships formed in the neighborhood may challenge cherished notions of the congregation.

In the case of Midtown, growing ministries and public partnerships challenge Midtown's sense of "family." A powerful metaphor of belonging and intimacy, "family" also obfuscates pathways or processes for belonging. As Ruben asked, how does one join a family? An insider-outsider dynamic persists despite Midtown's robust, benevolent, and hospitable service in the neighborhood. In the previous chapter, I suggested that issues of belonging and intimacy signal a deeper identity crisis precipitated by mission, a crisis of context. Just as the congregation suffers the call of God to participate in mission and the cultivation of new relationships, it will also need to discern faithful witness in its place. The congregation will do this *with* those to whom God sends it and *in* the place where God leads it.

Exploring the difference between contextualization and assimilation in mission, I conclude that the crisis of context presents *formational* challenge for the congregation, as they must discover a new identity attentive to the changing dynamics of the place they are located. While Midtown's failure to assimilate newcomers into their Swedish, pietist family heightens this challenge, it is an inevitable part of mission, sharing in the concerns of contextualization in mission history. This chapter explores the practice of hospitality as a means for discovering and cultivating a renewed contextual identity for the congregation. In this respect, Midtown's thanksgiving dinner shows great promise, for in practicing hospitality, Midtown learns the profound truth of God's love, alive around the tables of the West End.

The chapter is organized into two different parts. First, since the connection between contextualization and Christian formation may not be immediately apparent, I outline the formational possibilities for contextualization. The church-in-mission discovers new shades and hues for the gospel, which shapes not only the congregation's self-understanding, but also its public practice of the Christian faith. Second, I explore Christian hospitality as a practice for cultivating Christian identity attentive to time and place. As a practice, hospitality forms particular capacities for listening, attending, and responding. As participation in God's mission, hospitality publicly performs the gospel story.

Contextualization and Identity

A couple of years ago I was with my family in Whistler, British Columbia for a day of skiing. Late one afternoon, we were walking through the crowded village, carrying skis over our shoulders and weaving our way through the snow-greased streets. As we were crossing a square, we heard throbbing dance music from invisible speakers and noticed a couple people near us moving to the music in a coordinated fashion. We were not sure what was going on, but we stopped to watch and also backed up from the dancers to gain perspective. Suddenly, by some unheard cue in the music, the people next to us began to dance also. Clearly, they were practiced in this performance, and we found ourselves still in the middle of the dance. We were carrying skis, we did not know the moves, and so we backed up again. As the song continued, more and more people joined the dance. Soon, bystanders who clearly did *not* know the moves also ran in to join in the festivities, slowly and awkwardly picking up the patterns in the coordinated movement. At another imperceptible cue, the entire street froze, the music stopped, and a man dressed in a lion costume appeared to propose to an unsuspecting woman. The crowd cheered, smiled, clapped, and then dispersed talking about their participation in this shared "flash mob" experience.

At Thanksgiving, Midtown performs its own flash mob. By hosting a public meal, it turns a family spiritual practice inside out. Midtown's table opens up, not primarily as an act of service, but of hospitality and sharing. At Thanksgiving, neighbors, strangers, and church family all gather around the table to eat and give thanks; a core practice of the church family—hospitality and fellowship—is turned outward and made public. The event is, at the same time, a practice hosted by the church that is performed *with* neighborhood partners, *in* the neighborhood. The final performance of the meal requires the "insiders" who planned the meal to rely upon the participation of those on the "outside." It is a public and improvisational performance of a particular Christian practice. It also shows the unsettling elements of contextualization when it comes to Christian identity.

Understanding Identity

In popular speech, "identity" names a response to the question: "Who am I?" Depending on the context, questions of identity can be answered with reference to one's history, upbringing, hobbies, likes/dislikes, or social location. Such responses, however, remain insufficient. Identity describes these features, but so much more. One's sense of self is a moral horizon, orienting the person within the world in a particular way. A similar dynamic prevails when thinking about congregational identity. At a basic level, it refers to congregational self-understanding, by which a congregant might refer to elements of history, commitments, social location, or numbers in worship. However, such uses of the term "identity" miss the more profound ways in which identity functions.

Charles Taylor insists that the question "who am I" can only be answered in relationship to commitments and values, for they constitute a "horizon" within which the "I" makes sense.[1] As Taylor says, "To know who I am is a species of knowing where I stand. My identity is defined by the commitments or identifications which provide the frame or horizon within which I can try to determine what is good, or valuable, or what ought to be done."[2] In Taylor's view, identity is inseparable from the communities to which we belong or claim allegiance. To identify as Christian means I continue to navigate some relationship to a broader Christian tradition. I determine where I am and what I ought to pursue based on the moral horizon or set of "goods" that I have inherited from Christianity. As such, identity is formed in relationship to particular moral goods that we value above all others. However, what happens when some moral goods that we strongly value are questioned or revealed as implausible? What happens when, say, the strong value we place on evangelism is suddenly experienced as conflicting with the value we place on tolerance? Such conflicts go to the heart of identity for individuals and communities, affecting not only their sense of self, but also the coherence of their life in the world.

---

[1] Charles Taylor, *Sources of the Self: The Making of the Modern Identity* (Cambridge: Harvard University Press, 1989).

[2] Ibid., 27.

Take, for example, the contemporary debate about the "real" America.[3] When Coca-Cola aired its "America the Beautiful" ad during the 2014 Super Bowl, the interrelationship between identity, moral horizon, and intelligible action came into clear focus. Sweeping, panoramic shots of breathtaking scenery fade into one another, offset by intimate portraits of multiethnic, multigenerational people singing "America the Beautiful" in different languages keeping perfect time and harmony. Of course, Coca-Cola bottles are also artfully placed throughout the commercial. The advertisement simultaneously drew cheers and criticism on the internet. Congressman Allen West wrote in a blog "If we cannot be proud enough as a country to sing 'America the Beautiful' in English in a commercial during the Super Bowl, by a company as American as they come—doggone we are on the road to perdition."[4] West disagreed with the portrayal of America in the advertisement, and understood that a different American identity compels different moral action. The "road to perdition" that West fears is a multilingual cultural identity, one with perhaps less pressure on newcomers to learn English and more pressure on native English speakers to accommodate other languages and cultures. In such a case, identifying as "American" entails a multilcultural awareness and sensitivity. Of course, West contests this picture of America, implying not only a different picture but also a different ethic in relationship to immigrants and native English speakers. It is not just that the advertisement and West have different ideas of an "American," but that they imagine fundamentally different goals or goods for American identity. In each case, different conceptions of "beauty" are implied in the term "America." In one vision, multilinguistic diversity names the good and beautiful for America, while another hopes

---

[3] This debate seems to surface in every election cycle, where candidates claim to speak for the mythical "real, hardworking Americans," implicitly excluding people of color and those who vote for the "other" party.

[4] Ashley Kilough, "Coca-Cola Superbowl Ad Ignites Online Debate," *CNN* (February 3, 2014), Accessed December 15, 2016.
http://politicalticker.blogs.cnn.com/2014/02/03/coca-cola-super-bowl-ad-ignites-online-debate/

for multicultural assimilation into a shared language. Coca-Cola celebrates America as diverse. Congressman West celebrates America as united by shared language and cultural goals.

According to Taylor, the differences between West and Coca-Cola are not simply aesthetic preference, but moral and imaginative. While both claim allegiance to America, they imagine different things by this term and, therefore, suggest rival or conflicting moral actions. How one lives as an American depends upon what one intends by the term "American." The goods implied in the phrase "America the Beautiful," that is, what one considers the aim or the *telos* for America, provide a constructive and evaluative vision for action in the world. Identity assumes our participation in a broader set of commitments; how we imagine the aim or "good" of these commitments constitutes the moral space within which we act.

In the case of Midtown, some preferred self-perceptions of the congregation have come under pressure because it has chosen to remain faithfully present in the West End neighborhood. Several new communities now gather at the boundaries of the Midtown family because of the youth ministry, tutoring program, childcare center, and the homeless ministry. These communities owe their existence to Midtown, but they do not yet identify as part of the family. As with "America the Beautiful," diverse communities and experiences raise questions of belonging and participation. How does one join the Midtown family? Who are we, as the Midtown family? Midtown's future is at stake in these questions arising through experience. Events like the Thanksgiving meal and ministries that feed and shelter homeless families are not means for assimilating outsiders into the family, but rather legitimate expressions of the church in mission as public, improvisational communities.

In the previous chapter, I argued that contextualization assumes indigenous cultures and peoples will improvise and innovate with the gospel in their own way and on their own terms. As such, I distinguished contextualization as a mode of missionary participation with different ends than assimilation, concluding that contextualization cannot help but shape the church as well as the context. In what follows, I clarify this statement by drawing contextualization and identity together, to demonstrate how it is that the church-in-mission submits to an ongoing dialectic with regard to its identity. Coming to terms with one's context, or place, inevitably shapes the identity of the congregation.

Context and Identity

The transmission of the Christian faith across cultural, linguistic, or geographic boundaries is full of possibility and pitfalls. Yet, as difficult and problematic as contextualization might be, it is a necessary and constitutive element of Christian identity. Through processes of contextualization, Christian identity is constructed through encounters with difference. For example, when a person converts to the Christian faith, she does so from within her cultural context. That is, she does not abandon her cultural location and to join some new "universal" perspective, but rather her conversion begins a long, uneven, ambiguous process of contextualization. Conversion "does not isolate the convert from his or her community; it begins the conversion of that community. Conversion to Christ . . . produces distinctive discipleships, as diverse and variegated as human life itself."[5] The contextualization of the Christian faith, by which I mean the process of discovering a faithful Christian identity in our time and place, is the ongoing task of the congregation. Situated within the horizon of *missio Dei,* Christian identity is an ongoing discovery, constructed in relationship to God's work in the world.

The crisis of mission presents both a *challenge* and a *gift* for the church, as dynamic cultural contexts both confront and contribute to the

---

[5] Walls, *The Missionary Movement in Christian History: Studies in the Transmission of Faith,* 51.

richness and flourishing of the faith. The improbable innovations, the fresh questions, even the wrong turns, are contributions to the renewal of the Christian faith connected to a particular people and place. Another way to say this is that the identity of a congregation cannot be discerned apart from the contributions of neighbor, for if the congregation will bear witness to the gospel among *this* people in *this* place, it must allow the peculiarities of people and place a constructive voice. To shift back to the flash-mob, it must find ways of learning from and acknowledging that the *whole dance,* and not just those who have already practiced and memorized the parts, is the public performance of the gospel.

The particularity of people and place is critical for understanding what I am proposing with contextualization and identity. Missionary and congregational obsession with method and strategy in the contemporary era obscures the way that contextualization-as-discipleship must always be a local process of discovery. For at least fifty years, approaches to congregational leadership and renewal have tended to work from the abstract to the particular, from the level of the 'universal law' back to means and methods for congregational renewal.[6] The same habits tend to accompany discipleship literature and promises to make congregations "relevant" in their neighborhood. What all these approaches have in common is their *place-less-ness.* Congregations factor into the work as a placeholder or as an example for the universal principle already deduced from social science, leadership, or a biblical interpretation. No actual congregations emerge in the work, with the idiosyncrasies of place and the histories of people at stake.

---

[6] I'm thinking here of approaches to congregational health and mission that assume universal principles for congregational success, such as "Natural Church Development" and some generalized leadership literature. See Milfred Minatrea, *Shaped by God's Heart: The Passion and Practices of Missional Churches* (San Francisco: Jossey-Bass, 2004); Christian A. Schwarz, *Natural Church Development: A Guide to Eight Essential Qualities of Healthy Churches* (Carol Stream: ChurchSmart Resources, 1996).

However, if Walls is right, and if the crisis of context is a challenge for congregations, then there can be no abstract universal method to which a church can adhere. The very crisis is one of actual bodies and actual place as constitutive of Christian identity. This, in the end, is why Midtown must find new articulation and expression: the inner realities of transformation and the visions of family intimacy must again be placed in the neighborhood and among its people. The crisis of context poses a deep challenge to Midtown's identity, calling into question the goods of intimacy and security. However, it also offers the possibility of discerning new textures of the gospel, new means of organizing the church around the mission of God in the West End neighborhood. The challenge, as I hinted in the last chapter, is one of discovery through an intentional connection and openness to the places where God has called them. They must discover a faithful Christian identity with and among the people to whom God has called them. To do this, Midtown needs to connect mission and formation in the practice of hospitality.

Hospitality and Missional Formation

After being driven by hurricane force winds and buffeted by waves for fourteen days, morale on Paul's prison voyage to Rome was low. The sailors attempted every trick of the trade, dragging the sea anchor at times and throwing nonessentials overboard. They had not seen sun, moon, or stars for days, and they gave up all hope of being saved. Two different times over the previous days, Paul encouraged those on board the ship to stick together, insisting that God would save all on board together. Now, under the molasses blanket of a moonless night and driven by wind across the Adriatic, the sailors suspect land approaching, throw down anchors and pray for daylight. With the anxious nighttime hours ticking away, Paul gathers the 276 people on board to remind them of God's promise given earlier: that all on board will be saved, and he urges them to eat. Paul says, "You have been in suspense and . . . without food, having eaten nothing.

Therefore I urge you to take some food, for it will help you survive; for none of you will lose a hair from your heads" (Acts 27:33-34). After this, he takes some bread and gives thanks to God in front of the whole ship before breaking and eating it. Paul's act encourages his shipmates, who then eat until they are satisfied. The ship eventually runs aground in the light of day and the whole ship, fortified by their feast, makes it to shore safely.

Paul's intervention on the high seas marks the sixteenth descriptive meal scene in the Luke-Acts narrative, and echoes many previous ones.[7] By drawing the whole ship together, the meal expressed fellowship and unity. Throughout the ordeal, Paul insisted that the whole ship would be saved together (31-32). Here, the table-fellowship initiated by Paul reflects the table fellowship of the early church in Acts 2 and Jesus' regular practice of creating fellowship with unlikely characters, from tax collectors to Pharisees. When Paul encourages his shipmates to eat so they might be strengthened and saved, he echoes Jesus' announcement of salvation to Zacchaeus in Luke 19 and Peter's meal with Cornelius, for salvation comes to both homes, and now to the ship.[8] The cluster of verbs Luke uses to describe Paul's actions—take, give thanks, break, and eat— evokes the Eucharistic meal, which adds theological depth to a story about survival in a storm.

In Luke, the Eucharistic table constitutes fellowship with Jesus and one another, while also physically sustaining the disciples for the long night ahead and promising the salvation of God ("do this in remembrance"). As with the other gospels, the Lukan last supper brings the eschatological echoes of table fellowship into the foreground, where Jesus says that he will not eat this meal again until it is fulfilled in the Kingdom of God. Throughout Luke-Acts, the table evokes elements of the

---

[7] See John Paul Heil, *The Meal Scenes in Luke-Acts: An Audience-Oriented Approach*, Vol. 52 (Atlanta: Society of Biblical Literature, 1999).

[8] See Ibid., 295-296.

Eucharist, pointing toward fellowship with Christ and the promised salvation of God. Much like Peter with Cornelius or Jesus in the house of Zacchaeus, Paul and his companions host a meal in the middle of a stormy sea, among prison guards and distraught sailors to announce, demonstrate, and actualize the promised salvation of God.

Of course, Paul does not explicitly celebrate the Eucharist with his shipmates, and the immediate meaning of "salvation" here is that no one on the boat will die at sea. However, Paul's intervention draws deeply upon the ministry of Christ and the practice of the church. The echoes of other meals are cues given in Luke's storytelling, and I think they provide critical insight for Midtown in navigating the crisis of context. While a prisoner, Paul publicly witnesses to the grace and promise of God in a way that builds fellowship and invites participation. By providing echoes to other meal scenes, Luke reveals how Paul learned to do this: he created table fellowship in the way Jesus and the church did before him. Paul's action on the boat is linked to his participation with Christ and at Christ's table. In broad categories, we can call this an exercise in hospitality. In what follows, I explore the formational and missiological dimensions of hospitality, insisting that in this practice, the church both learns to cultivate contextual community and bears witness to the gospel of God.

Discerning Shared (Worldly) Practices

Our practices—the shared, meaningful, and repetitive actions that constitute our lives—both *form* us and *perform* particular beliefs and values. Before considering hospitality as a formative and performative practice for renewing Christian identity in the crisis of context, we need to explore the nature and functioning of practices as both performative and formative.

What is a Practice?

In a well-known *Seinfeld* episode, George and Jerry pitch an idea for a television show to NBC executives. George enthusiastically describes a show with no stories, no development, and no point: a show about nothing. Confused, an executive tells George that he doesn't understand— how can a show be about nothing? George answers: "it's like life: you eat, you sleep, you read, you go to work . . ." And in a comedic instant, *Seinfeld* captures something of our modern mood. Our lives *are* fragmented. The discrete activities of our lives do not always add up to "mean" something. Drawn out between multiple communities and stories, our lives feel disconnected from any over-arching sense of belonging or purpose. George's show is like life: meaningless.

The absence of story is critical for George's sense of meaninglessness. Without stories, Alistair MacIntyre reminds us, we are "anxious stutterers," unable to see the action of our lives in relationship to other concerns and human aims. [9] We rely upon stories to make sense of our lives, and to provide connection between our experiences and those of our community. We are, in the end, story-telling and story-formed creatures who live from and within narrative structures given and performed by the practices of our community. Practices, and communities of practice, integrate our lives and make us whole by performing or enacting the story of a community while also equipping us to achieve and participate in that story. An apprenticeship to a woodworker or a surgeon functions this way. So does the church. In the introduction to *Practicing Theology,* Dorothy Bass says, "Christian practices are patterns of cooperative human activity in and through which life together takes shape over time in response to and in the light of God as known in Jesus

---

[9] This is a highly condensed version of Alistair MacIntyre's framing of practice in *After Virtue.* While MacIntyre's definition of practice is too technical and limited for the work here, it remains a helpful starting point in thinking about the dynamic relationship between holistic integration, belonging to a community, and moral formation. The examples I provide of apprenticeship as a community of practice also borrow from MacIntyre. See MacIntyre, *After Virtue: A Study in Moral Theory.*

Christ."[10] This definition provides several important hooks upon which we can understand the formative and performative dimensions of Christian practices.

First, Bass states that practices are "patterns of cooperative human activity." Practices are *shared* or cooperative patterned activities. That is, they are not individual personal performances or expressions of individual subjectivity. They are means of participation, they are activities shaped through cooperation and learned through sharing life with one another. A woodworker learns her trade when others share wisdom and patterns with her; so also the practices of medicine or Christianity. Even a practice that might be highly internalized and that rewards individual experimentation, such as contemplative prayer, is *shared* in the sense that the contemplative enters into and makes sense of his experience through his particular community. Even hermits in the desert found ways to share in practices, or we would have never heard of them!

Second, the shared activity is patterned, which means that it is not random and participants do not make it up as they go. Part of what is shared in a practice is a sense of tradition, excellence, capacities, and boundaries that make the practice the practice. As Charles Taylor says, a practice is "a stable configuration of shared activity, whose shape is defined by a certain pattern of do's and don'ts"[11] In the long tradition of Christian spirituality, we have a treasure-trove of guidance on the basic practices of the Christian faith: prayer, engaging the Scriptures, hospitality, simplicity, fasting, and many others. This tradition helps to establish the patterns of the practices even as practitioners continue to sharpen or innovate within these practices.

Third, Bass insists that the life of a community takes place over time "in and through" these shared cooperative activities. The practices of

---

[10] Miroslav Volf and Dorothy C. Bass, eds., *Practicing Theology: Beliefs and Practices in Christian Life* (Grand Rapids: Eerdmans, 2002), 3.

[11] Taylor, *Sources of the Self: The Making of the Modern Identity*, 204.

a community constitute that community. They are the shared activities through which the life of the community takes shape. They are what the community does together. The life of a community occurs through a practice, like dwelling in the Scriptures or hospitality, over time. However, the life of the community also takes place *in* its practices, which means that the patterns governing a practice exercise some formational pull on the community. A practice like dwelling in the Word, for example, will shape the possibilities and imagination for a community in a way that a different practice, like watching TED talks, will not. The two practices will generate different kinds of communities.

Finally, Bass directs the entire conversation toward a theological center. Christian practices are not only descriptive of a life of a community of Christians, they are also *normative*, or perhaps prescriptive, in the fact that *Christian* practices are those shared activities that *respond to* and which take place *in the light of* the God we know in Jesus Christ. Christian practices are those shaped by and in response to God. Even more, they make sense in the light of Jesus. They emerge from within and point back to a particular theological vision of the crucified and risen Christ. They enact and embody a set of theological convictions and perform a particular narrative construal of the world. This is where the Christian tradition enters yet again, for any list of the basic Christian spiritual disciplines is rooted in particular convictions regarding the nature, presence, and work of God.

Practices Perform the Gospel

When Paul gathered the 276-crew members together to give thanks and break bread, he performed in their midst what he had previously claimed: that God would save the whole ship together. A skeptical and worn-out crew first watched Paul (and perhaps his traveling companions) eat, and then they found the courage and encouragement to do the same. If God indeed was going to save the whole ship together, then the crew needed to stay together and eat for strength. Paul's public action and invitation gave concrete, embodied, and public expression to his belief. In the West, we are accustomed to thinking that belief directs action in such ways. We have what James K.A. Smith calls an "intellectualist" preference, which holds belief and ideas as prior to action and bodies.[12] In such a view, Paul first believed God's promise, and then acted on it.

Yet, something more complicated takes place here. For the way in which Paul demonstrates God's promise to save is in the form of the Lord's Supper. This comes about, not because Paul thinks he is at a church service, but because this is a practice Paul has performed repeatedly in congregations across the ancient world. The practice of giving thanks and breaking bread is *habitual* for Paul because he and his companions have been shaped by the practice of the Eucharist into a Eucharistic community. Paul lives and acts within a Eucharistic-kind of story. Whatever one *thinks* when participating in the rhythms and liturgies of Christ's table, one's body, senses, and stomach are also involved. The literature on practices insists that this embodied participation matters. Sometimes it shapes us even despite our beliefs. Moreover, Paul's meal *really does save* the crew.[13] They fought wind, waves, and their own anxiety for fourteen days without food. The ship will soon crash on a sandbar and they will all need to kick and paddle their way to shore. By offering the meal in the way he does, Paul bears the mark of one who has sat around Christ's table. By receiving the meal, the crew receives nourishment and grace. Like the flash mob at the beginning of the chapter, the public practices of the church perform the gospel even while they form the congregation.

---

[12] James K. A. Smith, *Desiring the Kingdom: Worship, Worldview, and Cultural Formation* (Grand Rapids: Baker Academic, 2009), 28.

[13] Heil, *The Meal Scenes in Luke-Acts: An Audience-Oriented Approach*, 295-296. Heil clarifies Luke's broad use of "saved" in this text and throughout Luke-Acts. This is not a text about the conversion of those on the boat, but rather their rescue from a dangerous situation.

Christian practices perform the gospel, then, in two different ways. First, they bear witness to the gospel by making visible its claims and promises through the Christian community in the world. By habit and by performance, they demonstrate the gospel story in their very structure, rhythm, and action. Second, and perhaps more controversially, they are the means of grace by which the news of the gospel is lived, received, and experienced. The first claim is not terribly controversial. It leaves largely unchallenged the priority we give to ideas, by claiming that the community lives its beliefs publicly. The second statement, however, needs a little more unpacking.

In *Hospitality and the Other,* Amos Yong outlines what he calls a "pneumatological and performative theology" whereby "many tongues equals many practices."[14] Because words do not only *describe* the world, but also *shape* and *create* worlds, Yong argues for a much closer link between theology, theological speech, and performative practice. In philosophy, speech-act theory explores the different things that sentences do. They can perform what is called a "locutionary act," which describes something: "The woman walked into the street." They can also do something in the world, shaping or changing the circumstances: "Do not go into the street!" This is called the illocutionary act. Finally, words can describe the effect that they have had: "You stopped her from entering the street." This is called the perlocutionary effect.[15]

When we consider how the Bible functions, and how sentences intending Christian theology function, speech-act theory helpfully places practice and theology together. George Lindbeck, for example, argues that Christian theology both forms and is formed by the practices of the

---

[14] Amos Yong, *Hospitality and the Other: Pentecost, Christian Practices, and the Neighbor* (Maryknoll,: Orbis Books, 2008), 39.

[15] Yong develops J.L. Austin's Speech-Act theory here. Ibid., 48-49.

church.[16] For Lindbeck, the Bible and theology perform an illocutionary function by providing rules for practice, in much the same way that grammar provides rules for language. Yet, the ongoing work of Bible interpretation and theological reflection also records the perlocutionary effect of Christian practice. In the same way that we cannot learn language without using it, and by using it participate in shaping it, Lindbeck suggests Christian theology requires Christian practice, and vice versa. We make theological claims from within the logic of Christian practice; Christian practice is the end toward which we make theological claims.

This link between language and practice means that the Pentecost points toward not only a diversity of languages in witnessing the gospel, but also a diversity of practices. When the Holy Spirit is poured out on all flesh, the disciples participate in a miracle of speaking and of hearing, as those feasting in Jerusalem hear the gospel in their vernacular languages.[17] Pentecost, then, is not the reversal of Babel back to a singular cultural-linguistic expression, but rather its healing. It is, as Michael Welker says, where "a ruptured world begins to grow together."[18] Thus, the "many tongues" of Pentecost implies many different cultural expressions of the gospel: "many tongues equals many practices." Practices perform Christian claims, and different cultural-linguistic communities will perform these claims differently through the same Spirit.

The church, then, understands and performs the gospel differently depending on context. To change Andrew Walls's theatre analogy, it is not only that each seat in the theatre occupies a different socio-cultural perspective on the Jesus act, but also that the Jesus act is performed in theatres all across the world and throughout history. In addition, this act is

---

[16] George A. Lindbeck, *The Nature of Doctrine: Religion and Theology in a Postliberal Age* (Philadelphia: Westminster Press, 1984).

[17] Michael Welker, *God the Spirit*, trans. John F. Hoffmeyer, (Minneapolis: Fortress Press, 1994), 230.

[18] Ibid., 230.

performed in the public life of local church communities, who explore the meaning of this act even as they perform it. In the shared practices of the local church, the congregation's own understanding of and encounter with the gospel is publicly performed. These practices—such as worship, prayer, Sabbath, and hospitality—form the congregation in the Spirit-led way of Jesus. However, the shared life of the church in the world also provides the basis from which its own understanding of the gospel is formed, and through which the church receives the gospel. The practices of the congregation make its public witness possible, as a "hermeneutic of the gospel."[19]

As a community of practice, Midtown enjoyed decades of growth in the West End neighborhood based around a particular gospel-shaped identity. The homogeneity of the neighborhood and the context of Christendom enabled the congregation to shape its life around a desire for intimacy. A particular synthesis emerged between congregation and context. The connection between performance and theology, and the awareness of cultural plurality in performances, thus clarifies the nature of Midtown's challenge in cultivating faithful presence in a changing neighborhood. They must cultivate particular Christian practices that will enable them to not only perform the gospel within a changing context, but to allow them to be shaped into the kind of community that can bear witness in the West End. In the next section, I consider the practice of hospitality as one way in which the congregation publicly performs the gospel while also renewing Christian identity.

Practicing Hospitality

Christine Pohl argues that a closer reading of the Christian hospitality tradition will enable us to see that "hospitality is central to the

---

[19] Newbigin, *The Gospel in a Pluralist Society*, 224ff.

meaning of the gospel," for it is a "lens through which we can read and understand much of the gospel, and a practice by which we can welcome Jesus himself."[20] In *Making Room: Recovering Hospitality as a Christian Tradition,* Pohl distinguishes between modern assumptions and the traditional practice. By "hospitality," most people think "Martha Stewart" before "Francis of Assisi." In the modern imagination, good hosts are those who have a clean house, good manners, and better food. However, hosting dinner parties or having friends over for coffee tends to confuse entertainment and hospitality. Often, when we entertain friends and strangers, we do so to impress them or to raise our social status. The hospitality tradition, however, is not about entertainment or climbing the social ladder. It is, rather, the costly Christian practice of welcoming the stranger, or—to use Pohl's metaphor—making room for the other. The hospitality tradition was formed in ancient times when travel was risky and hotels scandalous. It was formed as a means to create space for, welcome, and care for the vulnerable. Paul encourages congregations throughout his letters to exercise hospitality toward those sent to them: "welcome one another, therefore, just as Christ has welcomed you" (Rom. 15:7). Over the centuries, monastic communities have engaged in radical practices of hospitality, committing themselves to welcome anyone who shows up at their door, as if receiving Jesus himself.

Hospitality has deep theological resonance in the biblical story. It is not only a good practice, but, indeed, central to understanding the gospel for several reasons. First, Yahweh-God appears, in several points throughout the Scriptures, as a stranger. Genesis 18 provides the paradigmatic example, where God appears to Abraham while he sits at the entrance of his tent, in the heat of the day by the oaks of Mamre. These details set up a story where three strangers appear near Abraham, who comes out to them and asks them to stay with him while Sarah prepares a

---

[20] Christine D. Pohl, *Making Room: Recovering Hospitality as a Christian Tradition* (Grand Rapids: Eerdmans, 1999), 8.

meal. In a time and climate where hospitality can mean the difference between survival and death, Abraham's offer sustains an important element of the social fabric. During the course of the meal, the strangers affirm God's promise to Abraham and Sarah, while also revealing to Abraham God's intentions to judge Sodom and Gomorrah. Theologians debate the exact identity of these strangers. Are they messengers, angels, a theophany of the Trinity? Regardless, the implications for hospitality are clear. In welcoming the stranger, Abraham heard from and encountered God.

In the Gospels, Jesus also pairs hospitality with encountering God. In Matthew 25, those who inherit the Kingdom of God are those who have welcomed the hungry, thirsty, the stranger, and prisoner. For in welcoming the dispossessed and strange, the disciples welcome Jesus himself. When the disciples on the road to Emmaus welcome the stranger, they realize at the breaking of bread that they have welcomed the resurrected Christ. Hebrews 13 picks up this same tradition, warning the church: "do not neglect to show hospitality to strangers, for by doing that some have entertained angels without knowing it" (Heb. 13:2). While God reveals Godself in the traditions, texts, and teachers of God's people, the Scriptures are also clear that God comes to God's people in the guise of the stranger, the alien, the downtrodden, and dispossessed.

Second, God *welcomes us* in Jesus Christ. The hospitality tradition is not only about God's people welcoming others, it is also, perhaps more important, about God welcoming *us*. The hospitality tradition discloses an "economy of grace," essential to understanding and participating in the gospel of Jesus Christ.[21] We see glimmers of this economy even in the examples just given. Although Abraham hosts the strangers, he becomes the guest of God when they speak God's promises. In the space created by

---

[21] Kathryn Tanner, *Economy of Grace* (Minneapolis: Fortress Press, 2005).

Abraham, the strangers become the host, blessing Abraham and Sarah. Around the dinner table in Emmaus, the resurrected Christ takes the bread and gives thanks. Here, again, is a break in protocol, where the guest takes initiative and becomes the host. Throughout Jesus' ministry, he "characterizes the hospitality of God in part as the exemplary recipient of hospitality."[22] In receiving hospitality, often around the table, Jesus "announces and enacts" the Reign of God.[23] Mutual hospitality, marked by fellowship around the table, participates in the Trinitarian hospitality of God, where the Father receives the sinner in solidarity with the Son in the Spirit; as Jesus says to Zacchaeus, "salvation has come to this house" (Luke 19:9).

Third, Jesus' disciples who have welcomed Jesus and been welcomed by the Father are sent into the world to be guests as well as hosts in the way and name of Jesus. In Matthew 10:40, Jesus instructs the disciples to depend upon the hospitality of others, for those that welcome the disciples also welcome Jesus and the Father. Of course, in Luke 10 the seventy are deliberately sent out with nothing so that they must depend upon the hospitality of those to whom they are sent. The seventy only offer blessing—healing the sick and announcing the reign of God—from within the room created by their hosts.

Hospitality is "central to the meaning of the gospel" because of the relational, participatory, nature of its practice.[24] It performs the gospel message, even as it forms communities capable of bearing witness to the gospel. It performs the gospel because it both depends upon and reveals the suffering-love of the Triune God. Catherine LaCugna claims that the doctrine of the Trinity reveals God's life as "the mystery of love among

---

[22] Yong, *Hospitality and the Other: Pentecost, Christian Practices, and the Neighbor*, 101

[23] Ibid., 101.

[24] Pohl, *Making Room: Recovering Hospitality as a Christian Tradition*, 8.

persons."[25] In Christ and through the Spirit, the Triune God reveals to us the means to live in the joy of the divine love. Christ reveals to us a new *oikos,* a new household with a new social order, where "the Samaritan woman, the tax collector, and the leper are equally at home."[26] Jesus performs this social order at numerous tables and throughout his parables. Jesus consistently overturns expectations about whom God welcomes and includes with the righteous.

When confronted by his family because they worried for his sanity, Jesus turns toward the crowd and asks, "Who is my mother, and who are my brothers?" Turning toward the disciples, he answers his question: "For whoever does the will of my Father in heaven is my brother and sister and mother" (Matt. 12:48, 50). For LaCugna, the new social order marked out by Jesus' ministry displays the *economy* of God's salvation, an economy marked by grace. Ephesians describes this social order as a household wherein the Spirit of God through the cross of Christ unites Jew and Gentile. However, LaCugna insists, the new social order created by Jesus reveals the character and life of the Triune God. The God we know in Jesus Christ is *this kind of God:* the God who receives the ones received by Jesus, the God who remains with the community of Christ in the Holy Spirit.

The God we know in Jesus is, in fact, God. The Triune God, in Jesus Christ, does not only *receive* sinners, but also *shares* Godself with them. God's hospitality offered in Jesus Christ *seeks out* the outcast and outsider while welcoming and receiving them. The same mutuality we observe in table fellowship, where host and guest receive and welcome one another, finds its theological center in the *missio Dei.* We noted in chapter 3 that "missio" names the sending activity of God: the Father sends the Son, Father and Son send the Spirit, who sends the church. God seeks to

---

[25] LaCugna, *God for Us: The Trinity and Christian Life,* 378.

[26] Ibid., 378.

redeem and reconcile a lost and broken creation. The parable of the lost coin and the lost sheep display this sending nature of God. However, under the rubric of Triune hospitality, sending and welcoming, sharing and receiving are understood together, such that we recognize suffering-love as the means of God's mission. When Jesus breaks bread and says, "This is my body," we recognize the relational dynamic between sharing and receiving that constitutes the divine hospitality. Jesus hosts the disciples around the table in that moment, offering his broken body.

In Luke-Acts, the Eucharistic table provides a key to understand all the other tables. The broken bread and poured out wine join the disciples to Christ and to one another. Receiving from Jesus, and sharing among themselves, they re-member Christ and anticipate the divine banquet feast. Meals throughout Luke-Acts are less explicit, but they reflect these themes, where fellowship is sustained and Christ is revealed or recognized. The fellowship the Son shares with Father and Spirit is made available to those who receive from Jesus, and who make room for such Eucharistic encounters. The gospel is, therefore, the good news of human fellowship with God and one another; it is participation and co-suffering-love. For this reason, hospitality performs the gospel and reveals the character of God. Pohl remarks: "A shared meal is the activity most closely tied to the reality of God's kingdom, just as it is the most basic expression of hospitality."[27] As an enduring Christian practice, however, hospitality continues to perform the good news of God as well as form communities capable of bearing public witness to the gospel. We can see how hospitality not only enacts something we believe to be true about God's hospitable welcome for the other, but how it might *form* new gospel-shaped identities within the church. In the remainder of the chapter, I want to explore how it is that the practice of hospitality can cultivate a contextual identity for congregations. Thinking in particular about

---

[27] Pohl, *Making Room: Recovering Hospitality as a Christian Tradition*, 30.

Midtown, I suggest the recovery of hospitality as means for addressing the crisis of context.

Rhythms of Welcome: 'Making Room' in the Congregation and Community

When Midtown opens its doors for Thanksgiving, it *makes room* for the community in ways that Pohl attributes to the hospitality tradition. Midtown intentionally sets up round tables and provides food in a way that builds fellowship and community. Guests are invited to sit and to stay. Persons are encouraged to wait on one another. Food is intentionally abundant so that persons are invited to seconds, thirds, or even to take plates to go. The congregation literally makes room for the other by clearing the main foyer and dedicating it to tables, food, and fellowship. It is a beautiful evening of shared community, food, joy, and laughter.

Another ministry regularly feeds the homeless throughout the year. This group operates with another non-profit, and so must abide by the policies of the organization. While this group provides a good service to the neighborhood, they must work harder to create fellowship. The distinctions between benefactor and client are more demonstrable. Yet, this also provides a practice whereby the congregation makes room for those that are need in the neighborhood in a devoted and ongoing way. During the month of September, Midtown also opens up its building as an emergency overflow homeless shelter for families, because county facilities cannot keep up with demand. During this month, hundreds of volunteers provide space in the church as well as breakfast and a snack for anywhere from five to twenty-five people finding shelter in the church. Again, because of county policies, the church is obviously providing a service to the community. Yet, it is a tangible way that the church makes room for the stranger, the homeless, the outsider, the one who is vulnerable.

These ministries, while providing powerful connections for Midtown in the community, also exacerbate the crisis of context. As highlighted in chapter 5, these relationships provide services without connection. In fact, Midtown has few stories of building deep connections, of cultivating fellowship with their neighbors that they serve. While they enjoy deep familial connections with one another, they do not yet know how to help the newcomer, the outsider, or the stranger to assimilate into their family. Pohl argues that the hospitality tradition connects household and private space with more public social services. One of the challenges Midtown faces is that while it makes room for the other in providing space and services for those in need, it is done in its official capacity as a congregation. Midtown has actual programs and services for meeting needs in the neighborhood. Thus, while volunteers from the church help Midtown welcome strangers, outsiders, and the vulnerable into the building, the welcome remains institutional rather than interpersonal. It is a table without fellowship.

Approaching hospitality as a *practice* for the congregation, however, invites improvisation and conversation about the means by which Midtown can make room for others. Practices, as I mentioned earlier, are shared meaningful activities governed by "dos and don'ts." As such, practices require ongoing conversation and often apprenticeship in their performance. They require, in short, *practice*. For example, we learn to pray by praying, but also by praying with others, who might be spiritual directors, friends, pastors, or mentors; and we often learn to pray by apprenticing ourselves to our spiritual mothers and fathers in the faith, long-since dead. Prayer, as a shared meaningful activity with its own sense of what is better and best, demands that we continuously learn from others within the practice. Midtown, in addressing its crisis of context, should approach the hospitality tradition as a shared practice of making room.

This means that the ministries of service and outreach, which Midtown so faithfully staffs, must be seen as only one component of the congregation's hospitality. Besides creating room in the church building for providing goods and services, Midtown members must recognize God's invitation to make room in their homes for church members, neighbors, and even strangers. I do not suggest blurring lines between official services the church offers through intermediaries, but rather a shift in orientation for the congregation, recognizing the opening of one's home as part of Christian hospitality and discipleship. For example, the church I currently attend names one shared practice as "eating together." We practice eating together every week when we take communion. However, the hope and intention of this practice is for us to eat in one another's homes throughout the week. When someone joins the church, they are encouraged to write a rule of life in relationship to our shared practices, to discern and define how it is that she or he will practice eating together. The practice of table fellowship, spread out through the week, builds capacities in congregations that connect church and household more directly.

However, eating together weekly or even multiple times a week only takes a step toward the kind of integration that the practice of hospitality creates. Opening our homes to friends can easily blur the line between entertainment and hospitality. We learn to open our homes and our lives by eating at the Lord's Table and eating together throughout the week, but we must practice hospitality within our own neighborhoods and among our neighbors. Thus, the second way to engage the practice of hospitality is to provide space, encouragement, and accountability for congregation members to welcome and eat with neighbors on a regular basis. In eating with others, welcome is not only offered, but new communities are formed. Congregations will need to figure out the right rhythms, training, and encouragement for such engagements.

Discerning Welcome: Cultivating a Connection to Place

Hospitality requires us to be both guest and host. Jesus hosted outsiders by receiving their invitation to be a guest. The seventy sent out in Luke 10 do so empty-handed for the same reason. As congregants discern rhythms of welcome that might be shared and learned together, they must also learn to discern and respond to the invitations of others and outsiders. Congregants should not only see themselves as showing hospitality to their neighbors, but also as receiving the hospitality of their neighbors as well. In Vancouver, I led a missional community that had covenanted together to share a meal with another person or family at least once a week. Sometimes, we would all eat together. Other times, we would encourage each member to eat with a neighbor. When we reconvened, we would talk about the difficulties and joy of this practice, together learning the "do's and don'ts" of the hospitality tradition. Through this practice, we learned how to integrate newcomers into our community, and we grew over time.

Our church, however, also wanted us to articulate a mission. What shared work was God calling us to? This encouragement from church leadership initiated months of conversation and discernment, where we learned about the plight of refugee families in our neighborhood. After doing more investigation, we learned about a ministry in our community that provided services for refugees, and was looking for 'ordinary Canadians' to join the refugee community on Tuesday nights for a weekly dinner. One of the biggest needs the ministry identified for refugee families was in building connections and friendships in a new place. We responded to the invitation, and began to show up at the Tuesday meal. Often, we did not cook, but came to receive the hospitality of a refugee family who prepared the meal, and enjoyed table fellowship with anywhere from fifteen to thirty people from around the world. In discerning welcome, our group learned how we might become more hospitable to refugees in our neighborhood . . . because now we knew many of them! We learn the practice of hospitality by making room to welcome others, but also (and perhaps more importantly) by making room in our own lives to receive the welcome of others.

God's Love, Alive in the West End: Conclusion

In the last chapter, I used the metaphor of gardening to frame the challenge Midtown faces with regard to the crisis of context. I suggest that the place Midtown is located poses challenges to the congregational identity. Its members must learn to cultivate new life, new community, attentive to the demands and dynamics of their context. Even though Midtown has not moved, its environment has changed. It is as if they are gardening in a new context. While they cannot grow things on their own volition, they must cultivate the land in a way that is attentive to the new context. Moreover, like a gardener, their own hopes and dreams will be conditioned by their context. What missiologists call "contextualization" precipitates an identity crisis for Midtown.

Midtown's sign out front says "God's Love, Alive in the West End." I suggested at the beginning of chapter 5 that this sign could be interpreted one of two ways. It could mean that Midtown is somehow the embodiment of God's love, alive in the neighborhood. Under this meaning, the problem of Midtown's relationship with the neighborhood can be seen as one of assimilation. Midtown is and has a certain kind of 'good' in the neighborhood that must be shared with the outsider. However, this interpretation of the sign misses God's invitation to connect more deeply with its context, to root itself in this dynamic neighborhood and learn to make room for the newcomer and the stranger. The sign, of course, could also mean that the Triune God's love is indeed alive and at work in the neighborhood through and quite apart from Midtown. In such a meaning, Midtown members can go from the congregation, extend out beyond congregational programs, in hope and confidence that they will encounter "people of peace" who will make room for Midtown folks. The practice of hospitality enables the church to imagine this second meaning and it builds Midtown's capacity to enact it.

EPILOGUE

In common parlance, we don't think of staying in one place as missionary movement. We hear texts like "As the Father has sent me, so I send you" and wean our congregations on stories of the heroic missionaries who crossed oceans, leaving children and family for the sake of evangelistic passion. We tend to imagine missions in relationship to terms like "mobilization," "strategy," or "impact." Throughout much of the modern missions movement, our language and practice assumed a certain division of labor between congregations and missionaries. Congregations nurtured the faithful, whose monetary gifts mobilized the missionary to evangelize peoples far away. After the Second World War, however, we have begun to imagine mission as *missio Dei,* the life of the Triune God for the sake of the world, which shapes and gives life to the church of Jesus Christ in the Holy Spirit to the glory of the Father. This shift has been termed the "Copernican Revolution in missions" because it has reversed the emphasis from mission as a human activity performed by special individuals toward mission as naming the way in which God's people participate in God's Triune life.[1]

Along with *missio Dei,* we in the West have become increasingly aware of our complicity in colonialism and the fast decline of Christian

---

[1] Van Gelder, "How Missiology can Help Inform the Conversation about the Missional Church in Context," 20.

practice at home. We recognize that benevolent intentions only veiled the paternalistic assumptions and controlling postures of the Western Church. In addition, while the modern missionary movement can look to a global Christian presence as an amazing accomplishment, we must listen to stories from our Christian brothers and sisters that report our colonial complicity. Furthermore, a deep irony persists in the fact that missionary enthusiasm abroad coincided with Christian disaffection at home. Our theology and experience over the past sixty years certainly complicates our understanding of mission. That is, *missio Dei*, along with the experience of the Western Church after colonialism, has begun to clarify the fact that "mission" refers to a complex relational dynamic and not only the sending of one party to another. I offer "perduring presence" as one such way of shifting our missional imagination from a goal-oriented activity to the realm of relationship. We discover this precise dynamic in Luke 10, where Jesus sends his disciples out ahead of him to the places where he intends to go.

Jesus sends the disciples "like lambs into the midst of wolves," encouraging them to go directly to the towns empty-handed so that they might depend upon the hospitality of those in the town (Luke 10:1-12). Finding a person upon whom the peace of God rests, they are to stay in that house and to avoid moving about from house to house. Instead, they are to dwell with that person of peace, "eating what is set before" them, "healing the sick who are there," and announcing that the reign of God has come near. If the disciples are not shown hospitality, their verbal message remains the same: "yet know this, the reign of God has come near." It is an odd text. An odd set of instructions that has not been used to frame missionary activity until very recently. Because of the shifts listed above, the text now offers several significant insights into thinking about mission as the participation in a kind of presence, where we might imagine mission as both going and dwelling. A couple final observations can be made.

First, the Church encounters God in a new way as it is sent to the Other in mission. The disciples go in vulnerability and openness. They dwell among the townspeople to whom they are sent, and they come back to Jesus with stories of discovery, not only accomplishment. While dwelling in openness and dependence, they discover the power and presence of God: "even the demons submit" they exclaim (Luke 10:17). Recent studies of mission have reflected this theme from Luke 10. Lamin Sanneh's *Translating the Message* explores at the experience of the early church and mission history to argue that whenever the gospel moves across a cultural and linguistic boundary, the new cultural-linguistic community does not merely receive the gospel passively, but rather, actively provides insight into the Jesus story. He uses the expansion of Jesus' title from "Messiah" to "Lord" in the mission to the Gentiles as paradigmatic for his argument.

Second, the townspeople are, in a way, co-participants in God's mission. The disciples are instructed to protest and leave if the town does not show hospitality. The disciples do not function as self-sufficient emissaries dispensing God's gifts to a receptive audience. They are folks in need of shelter and food. Jesus instructs them first to stay in the same house and to eat with and among those to whom he sends them before he mentions healing the sick and proclaiming the good news. Mission historian Andrew Walls notes the ways in which the evangelized have shown agency in their own adaptation of Christian belief and practice over the centuries. He argues that the gospel of the incarnate Christ makes its home in the world; in mission, it is translated into the vernacular of new cultures and societies. When the gospel of Jesus Christ is received, it turns all things in a culture toward itself and so develops new indigenous forms.

Third, the disciples sent by Jesus provide a physical, embodied link between the townspeople and the good news of the gospel. In fact, their presence does make a difference in the town. Not only are they sitting around tables, but also they are healing the sick that they find and proclaiming the nearness of God's reign. They embody and anticipate the coming of Jesus himself, and so connect the town to the broader Jesus-movement in their very bodies, in their presence, and in their speech and act. Andrew Walls also helps us see this in light of global mission. For the gospel both makes its home in indigenous expressions and witnesses a movement greater than any one people or culture. This is due to how the gospel is received: always from an Other, and to the nature of the gospel itself. The trans-national and trans-historical movement of the gospel and its eschatological character mean that it never can become totally at home in any one culture, but must always call us out of whatever culture we find ourselves. The gospel makes us at home and calls us out to become pilgrims.

These themes come together around the table. Whatever it is that Jesus sends the disciples to do, embodied presence—sharing space, food, proximity—constitutes the bulk of Jesus' instructions. Proclamation and healing assume shared space around a table; they depend upon the hospitality of the stranger. The disciples' ministry shares in the service of the townspeople to the disciples. Tables factor into the Luke-Acts narrative at several critical points. On the night Jesus is betrayed, he reinterprets the basic elements of Passover as a participation in his own body and blood: "this is my body;" "this is my blood;" "take and eat;" "take and drink." While the Church has long debated how literally to interpret these sayings, the Eucharist has always included human bodies gathered around a physical table eating real bread and drinking some kind of grape beverage.

Near the end of Luke, two unnamed disciples receive a stranger on the road to Emmaus. They discuss together the recent tragic events in Jerusalem and rumors of Jesus' resurrection. While the disciples chastise the stranger for not hearing of the recent events in Jerusalem, the stranger, in turn, instructs them in biblical themes regarding the suffering of the Messiah the disciples had previously overlooked. The impassioned conversation stretches into the evening, and the disciples invite the stranger in to their home to stay. They prepare food and sit down to eat with him. At the table, the stranger becomes the host, takes up the bread, gives thanks, and breaks it. Suddenly the disciples see who the stranger has been all along: Jesus. Along the road, the one teaching them from the Scriptures, the stranger they welcomed into their home, who set before them broken bread . . . this, they recognize, is Jesus. "Were not our hearts burning within us?" they ask each other. In that moment, an ordinary table becomes Christ's table in a way that causes the disciples to think differently about their experience and their future. And from the table they rush back to Jerusalem to tell their story—no doubt around another table!

We often see the Emmaus table as a Eucharistic moment. It comes in the narrative immediately after the last supper. While the bread is broken, the disciples certainly re-member the risen Christ, recognizing his presence with them on their journey, causing them to reimagine the whole exchange with the stranger, and to rush out to share the good news with others. In our rush to discuss the meaning of this text, however, we can miss the simple fact of embodiment. Whatever their experience, however they finally recognized the stranger as Jesus, wherever Jesus went after the moment of recognition, it all depends upon embodied presence.

This is no flighty spiritual escape from corporeal existence. The encounter with Jesus occurs with tired legs and breathless conversation while climbing hills and trying to put words to ideas while navigating the road. The encounter with Jesus takes place when all parties are tired from their journey, requiring food, rest, and water. The recognition happens when they sit face to face, give thanks, and break bread. When we break bread in our own congregations, we participate in this act of recognition gathered together, with all the concomitant aspects of embodiment: growling stomachs, tired postures, making eye contact, speaking and hearing, breaking bread, tasting wine. Within this physicality, we remember and participate in the table of Christ. When we receive the broken bread from the hand of another, we enact, recognize, remember Christ's table. In the act of receiving and giving thanks, we are invited to reimagine Christ's presence in our lives in the world and among strangers. In the act of receiving the benediction, we go out to share the good news.

Later in the book of Acts, Peter shares a table with the Gentile Cornelius. It takes the intervention of an angel and tri-fold vision and the clear empowerment of the Spirit to keep Peter in the home of this Gentile. However, Peter recognizes God's power and presence in that place. As he tells the Jerusalem church later on, he could not stand in the way of God's clear action. It is not Peter's action in going or preaching to Cornelius that raises concern, but Peter's presence at Cornelius's table. In eating at the table of a Gentile, Peter's body risks defilement. He bears in his flesh solidarity with Cornelius, and so scandalizes some in the Jerusalem community. Cornelius, in keeping with the Luke 10 tradition, receives the Word of God by welcoming and showing hospitality to the one sent by God.

More deserves to be said about each of these tables, but they together demonstrate something long overlooked when considering the mission of the church: the vulnerability of human bodies. The table is a place of shared vulnerability. However exalted our prose, however fulfilled our spirit, if we do not eat, we die. Moreover, when we eat, we share in a visceral solidarity with one another. Anyone who has suffered food poisoning from a buffet intuitively understands this risk. Furthermore, the rituals of table fellowship in any culture disclose a dance between initiative and response between host, cook, guest, and stranger. Each person around the table is an agent and responder, *actio* and *passio*. It is a dance of reciprocity, which assumes real, embodied presence. Table fellowship cannot be downloaded or captured as an essence. It can only be embodied and shared.

In the popular narratives of mission, which involve going somewhere or extending the love or reach of Christ into some other part of the world, such emphases on bodies, tables, shared hospitality, and vulnerability become less prominent. The practice of short-term mission trips provides one example of how mission is understood apart from such concerns. By nature, the trip does not invite participants to stay in one place or to go in need and vulnerability. Solidarity around a table remains abstract or fleeting. Urban mission work can suffer from similar limitations, in that the relational sharing of vulnerabilities marked by the table never occurs because the church is too busy preparing meals to serve the underprivileged and homeless. However, there are situations where the missionary remains among and with the people to whom God called her, and where the congregation discerns God's call to stay, to remain, to dwell in its urban neighborhood. These commitments of stability, perduring in one place, provide the possibility for mission attentive to the relational dynamics we see in Luke-Acts. It provides a post-colonial way to imagine the invitation of God to participate in God's mission in this Post-Christendom era. Eat what is set before you: mission as perduring presence.

APPENDIX:

LIVING AS A GUEST

The crisis of mission prods and provokes congregations to learn new things in relationship to both God and world/context. While this study focuses on Midtown's particular experience of this crisis, their story can function allegorically for any congregation, as context will inevitably raise questions and post challenges for the congregation. In my work with congregations and congregational leaders, I have developed, borrowed, and adapted a number of different experiments and practices for helping congregations to develop capacities for both learning from context and cultivating new Christian identity from within a context. I offer some ideas below, organized around the rhythm of a meal: receive, pray, and eat.

Receive

1. Learn to *see* your neighborhood.

Learning to *see* and *hear* what is before us remains a critical capacity for both discernment and improvisational leadership. For our congregations to enter the journey outlined by Midtown, we need to attend to our capacities for perception, particularly in relationship to voices, people, and social realities that our current social location or assumptions immediately exclude. We need means for paying attention to the "Chuyias" in our midst.[1]

---

[1] I am referencing the protagonist in the movie *Water* who disrupts the life and rhythm of an ashram. See chapter four for more details.

I begin chapter 2 referencing Alexandra Horowitz's book *On Looking,* where she walks her block in New York City with eleven different "experts," to record what they notice, see, hear, etc. It offers fascinating insight into the beautiful complexity of any place, street, or neighborhood, as well as the social dimensions of perception. One way to *see* and *hear* our neighborhood(s) in new ways is to make a commitment to walking them in a similar way.

Invite the congregational leadership team to walk the church neighborhood five different times over the course of five weeks with a different neighborhood "expert." This expert can be a family pet, a local business owner, a long-standing friend, a person who occupies a different social location, etc. Congregational leaders should record descriptive answers to a consistent set of questions after each walk, to be shared with the community. Some sample questions might be:

- What do you notice? See? Hear? Feel?
- What did you talk about?
- What new questions emerge for you about our neighborhood or the role of the church in the neighborhood?

2. Learn to *hear* your congregation

When confronted with the crisis of mission, congregations often look for technical solutions to adaptive problems. Faced with difficult questions related to the future of the church, they desire new leadership, or outside expertise to fix or save them: If only we had younger leaders! If only we had more committed members! If only we had a wealthy donor!

I am committed to the idea that congregations are communities gathered by Christ and gifted through the Holy Spirit. This is one reason why the text of this book adheres closely to Midtown's story: we can encounter theological wisdom through attentive engagement with what is particular and local.

When it comes to cultivating congregational habits for addressing the crises of mission, we need to learn how to pay attention to the stories, gifts, and commitments of our particular congregation. Congregations do not need a program developed in another church to navigate the crisis of call, they need to be aware of their own history, gifts, and passions so that they can recognize where these passions intersect with the particular context in which God has placed them. Congregations must recognize and receive the gifts, hopes, and passions of both the congregation and the context.

Many different models exist for learning to pay attention. Mark Lau Branson's book *Memories, Hopes, and Conversations* outlines a process called "Appreciative Inquiry," which is incredibly helpful in learning to pay attention to the congregation.[2] I highly suggest this book as a resource. However, we can also develop this attentiveness through a regular practice of storytelling.

Choose one appropriate venue in the life of the church, and then prepare people to tell stories about mission, about passion, about witness, about the neighborhood, their work, etc. Develop a pointed question, and then use it as a prompt over a period of time. Pay attention to what is said, and begin feeding back to the congregation what you hear about the history, hopes, passions, and anxieties of the community.

For example, at Southside Community Church, we began asking in our missional communities: "where have you encountered God or seen the work of God in the past week?" We asked this question every week. At first, participants were unable to respond to the question because it was not the way we typically talked to one another. However, over time, we learned to

---

[2] See Mark Lau Branson, *Memories, Hopes, and Conversations: Appreciative Inquiry and Congregational Change* (Herndon: Alban Institute, 2004).

both tell and attend to the work of God in the lives of one another. As a part of the Church Planting program here at Pittsburgh Theological Seminary, we ask one another whenever we gather: "When have you felt closest to your vocation in the past couple weeks? When have you felt far away?" This question helps us not only pay attention to our own passions, joys, challenges, and opportunities, but it also teaches us to testify to these things in our own lives and see them in the lives of others.

These questions can be adapted to help people identify the work of God in one another: "When have you heard the voice of God in worship or through another person?" These questions can be adapted to tell about the life of the congregation: "What gives you joy in this congregation?" Or, they can be adapted to reflect on our life in the neighborhood, as I will demonstrate with the "Dwelling in the World" practice below in the "Pray" section. The point is that a regular reflective question should be part of or gatherings to enable us to reflect on the theological contours of our own lives, and to attend to God's work in the lives of one another.

Pray

1. Dwelling in the Word

In order to discern calling, and to reform congregational identity in light of one's neighborhood partners and context, congregations need to develop a capacity to risk theological speech. We need to learn how to both attend to our experience and make theological sense of these experiences.

Dwelling in the Word is a powerful and portable practice developed by Church Innovations Institute. It can be done at the beginning of a leadership meeting, with neighbors, in a small group, or even with a whole congregation.[3] When groups dwell together regularly and remain in the same text, they begin to cultivate capacities for both speaking and listening theologically. Pat Taylor Ellison and Pat Keifert have published a handbook outlining this practice, called *Dwelling in the Word: A Pocket Handbook*.[4]

The basic structure of the practice, however, is to read a text out loud in a group, instructing the group to remain wherever in the text their attention rests. After a moment of silence, participants will find a "reasonably friendly-looking stranger" in the room and share where their attention rested. After some time of conversation, the whole group convenes and participants share, not where *they* rested, but where their partner rested.

2. Dwelling in the World

Dwelling in the World is a companion practice to Dwelling in the Word. It, too, is both portable and powerful. It, too, can be done in large and small groups. It also works best if practiced consistently over a period of time.

Dwelling in the World asks a simple question: "Where have you encountered a person of peace? And, can you go back to this person or place?" Drawing from Luke 10, the question asks congregants to reimagine their previous week in light of the hospitality that others have shown them. When practiced over time, we begin to recognize persons of peace as we encounter them rather than only in retrospect. As with Dwelling in the

---

[3] Church Innovations equips congregations in Dwelling in the Word, Dwelling in the World, and several other "disruptive" missional practices. See "Six Missional Practices," http://www.churchinnovations.org/what-we-do/events/recent-events/ (accessed, December 15, 2017).

[4] Pat Taylor Ellison and Patrick R. Keifert, *Dwelling in the Word: A Pocket Handbook* (Saint Paul: Church Innovations Institute, 2011).

Word, Dwelling in the World shapes a social imagination, preparing the ground for the partnerships encouraged throughout this book.

3. The Daily Examen

When I was a pastor at Southside Community Church, we recognized a prevailing practical atheism throughout our congregation. We certainly believed that God was present and working in the world, but we struggled to recognize this activity and talk about it. Recognizing this, we began to offer guidelines for morning and evening prayer for our congregants. We encouraged the congregation to begin the day with a prayer of openness, and close the day with the practice of Examen.

While we would write different prayers for different seasons (often praying the Psalms as well), the morning prayer always included something like: God, help me to hear you, see you, recognize you this day." The evening prayer, then, would invite the congregation into the practice of Examen, asking them: "What was life-giving today? Where was God close to you? What was life-taking today? Where did you feel far from your calling, or God's absence?" These questions would then lead us into prayer for the night. Such a rhythm of prayer helped us to develop habits of attention and speech that integrated our experiences with our theological commitments. They prepared the way for us to not only discern our calling, but to respond to God's promptings and leadings in our everyday life.

Eat

1. Practicing Hospitality

I argue in chapter 8 for hospitality as both a formative and performative practice. In practicing hospitality, we learn to receive the gospel and grow in capacities necessary for navigating the crises of mission. But we also bear witness to the gospel in the practice as well. But, as with all practices, we need to learn how to do this, we need to be formed in the rhythms and disciplines of the practice. It does not just happen; we need to experiment with it, reflect on these experiments, and apprentice ourselves to others.

I have belonged to two different congregations that explicitly state their intention to share meals with one another and with neighbors. In both congregations, this intention was not only stated, but also encouraged through specific experiments, instructions, and challenges. At Southside Community Church, we would encourage congregants to say "yes" to every invitation (within reason) offered by a neighbor during a period of time. During this time, we would provide room for congregants to talk about this experiment with their missional community, and help them to recognize the importance of *being welcomed* and *being hosted* for the practice. In other seasons, we would share meals regularly as a missional community, or free congregants up to consider eating one meal a week with a neighbor. Intentionality, reflection, and organization are critical for developing the practice of hospitality. Of course, the practice is about more than meals, but mealtime is a great place for congregations to begin cultivating an imagination for hospitality.

2. Learning with Neighborhood Partners

Both the 'art of neighboring' and 'public companionship' from chapters 5 and 6 assume a shift in congregational life from a provider of goods and services to a participant and co-learner in the work of God. We will not cultivate or discern good partnerships if we are not able to learn from and with others in our community. Thus, whenever our congregation identifies a need in the neighborhood, or sees an opportunity for mission and witness, we should recognize the opportunity to learn from others in our community/neighborhood who have expertise and experience in the area. Doing this shifts our posture from "for" to "with" (following Samuel Wells).

A congregation in New England hoped to start a youth ministry several years ago. They gathered several adults passionate about youth, planned a program, advertised it, and then opened their doors. Nobody came. After several frustrating months, one of the leaders began to form a relationship with a young man who ran a youth drop-in center down the street. Several conversations into the relationship, the youth leadership team enrolled in the volunteer training and began to volunteer at the drop-in center. They became learners, drawing from wisdom in the neighborhood while also sharing their gifts with the local youth drop-in. We must look for similar opportunities to become learners in our neighborhoods.

BIBLIOGRAPHY

"The New ŠKODA Fabia Attention Test." YouTube. Accessed August 20, 2015. https://www.youtube.com/watch?v=qpPYdMs97eE.

"Spiritual Discernment for Thriving in Change." Church Innovations Institute. Accessed September 8, 2015. http://www.churchinnovations.org/events/recent-events/spiritual-discernment/.

"Why Missions? Report of Commision I on the Biblical and Theological Basis of Missions."Princeton Theological Seminary, Box 41.2, Princeton, NJ.

Ammerman, Nancy Tatom. *Congregation & Community*. New Brunswick: Rutgers University Press, 1997.

Anderson, Rufus. "The Time for the World's Conversion Come." In *To Advance the Gospel: Selections from the Writings of Rufus Anderson*, edited by Beaver, R. Pierce, 59-76. Grand Rapids: Eerdmans, 1967.

Barrett, Frank J. *Yes to the Mess: Surprising Leadership Lessons from Jazz*. Boston: Harvard Business Review Press, 2012.

Bauman, Zygmunt. *Liquid Modernity*. Cambridge: Polity Press, 2000.

Blauw, Johannes. *The Missionary Nature of the Church: A Survey of the Biblical Theology of Mission*. Foundations of the Christian Mission. New York: McGraw-Hill, 1962.

Boersma, Hans. *Violence, Hospitality, and the Cross: Reappropriating the Atonement Tradition*. Grand Rapids: Baker Academic, 2004.

Bonhoeffer, Dietrich. *Discipleship*. Dietrich Bonhoeffer Works. Vol. 4. Minneapolis: Fortress Press, 2001.

Bosch, David Jacobus. "The Structure of Mission: An Exposition of Matthew 28:16-20." In *The Study of Evangelism: Exploring a Missional Practice of the Church*, edited by Chilcote, Paul W. and Laceye C. Warner, 73-92. Grand Rapids: Eerdmans, 2008.

———. *Transforming Mission: Paradigm Shifts in Theology of Mission*. American Society of Missiology Series. 20th anniversary ed. Vol. 16. Maryknoll: Orbis, 2011.

———. *Transforming Mission: Paradigm Shifts in Theology of Mission*. American Society of Missiology Series. Vol. 16. Maryknoll: Orbis Books, 1991.

Branson, Mark Lau. *Memories, Hopes, and Conversations: Appreciative Inquiry and Congregational Change*. Herndon: Alban Institute, 2004.

Brooks, David. "One Neighborhood at a Time." *New York Times* (May 17, 2016): Accessed June 2, 2016. https://www.nytimes.com/2016/05/17/opinion/one-neighborhood-at-a-time.html.

Brueggemann, Walter. *Theology of the Old Testament: Testimony, Dispute, Advocacy*. Minneapolis: Fortress Press, 1997.

Carey, William. "An Enquiry into the Obligations of Christians." Hodder and Stoughton. Accessed May 18, 2017. http://www.wmcarey.edu/carey/enquiry/anenquiry.pdf.

Clifford, James. "On Ethnographic Allegory." In *Writing Culture: The Poetics and Politics of Ethnography*, edited by Clifford, James and George E. Marcus, 98-121. Berkley: University of California Press, 1986.

Clifford, James and George E. Marcus, eds. *Writing Culture: The Politics and Poetics of Ethnography*. Berkley: University of California Press, 1986.

Cohen, Jean L. and Andrew Arato. *Civil Society and Political Theory*. Cambridge: MIT Press, 1994.

Crouch, Andy. *Culture Making: Recovering our Creative Calling*. Downers Grove: IVP Books, 2008.

Ellison, Pat Taylor and Patrick R. Keifert, *Dwelling in the Word: A Pocket Handbook*. Saint Paul: Church Innovations Institute, 2011.

Finke, Roger and Rodney Stark. *The Churching of America, 1776-1990: Winners and Losers in our Religious Economy*. New Brunswick, NJ: Rutgers University Press, 1992.

Fitch, David E. *Faithful Presence: Seven Disciplines that Shape the Church for Mission*. Downers Grove: IVP Books, 2016.

Flett, John G. *The Witness of God: The Trinity, Missio Dei, Karl Barth, and the Nature of Christian Community*. Grand Rapids: Eerdmans, 2010.

Frost, Michael and Alan Hirsch. *ReJesus: A Wild Messiah for a Missional Church*. Peabody, MA: Hendrickson, 2009.

Fulkerson, Mary McClintock. *Places of Redemption: Theology for a Worldly Church*. New York: Oxford University Press, 2007.

Gay, Craig M. *The Way of the (Modern) World, Or, Why it's Tempting to Live as if God Doesn't Exist*. Grand Rapids: Eerdmans, 1998.

Goheen, Michael W. *A Light to the Nations: The Missional Church and the Biblical Story*. Grand Rapids: Baker Academic, 2011.

Goodall, Norman, ed. *Missions Under the Cross: Addresses Delivered at the Enlarged Meeting of the Committee of the International Missionary Council at Willingen, in Germany, 1952, with Statements Issued by the Meeting*. New York: Friendship Press, 1953.

Green, Thomas H. *Weeds among the Wheat: Discernment, Where Prayer & Action Meet*. Notre Dame: Ave Maria Press, 1984.

Grenz, Stanley J. *The Social God and the Relational Self: A Trinitarian Theology of the Imago Dei*. Louisville: Westminster John Knox Press, 2001.

Guder, Darrell L. *The Continuing Conversion of the Church*. Gospel and our Culture Series. Grand Rapids: Eerdmans, 2000.

———. *Missional Church: A Vision for the Sending of the Church in North America*. Grand Rapids: Eerdmans, 1998.

Habermas, Jürgen. *The Theory of Communicative Action*. Translated by McCarthy, Thomas. Vol. 1: Reason and the Rationalization of Society. Boston: Beacon Press, 1984.

Hagley, Scott. "Cultivating Response-Able Leadership Postures: Ricoeur's Hermeneutic Phenomenology and the Biblical Text." *Journal of Religious Leadership* 15, no. 2 (Fall 2016): 81-108.

———. "Exiles on Main Street: Reframing Short-Term Mission." In *Cultivating Sent Communities: Missional Spiritual Formation*, edited by Zscheile, Dwight J., 56-80. Grand Rapids: Eerdmans, 2012.

———. "Improv in the Streets: Missional Leadership as Public Improvisational Identity Formation." *Journal of Religious Leadership* 7, no. 2 (2008): 61-85.

Hanciles, Jehu. *Beyond Christendom: Globalization, African Migration, and the Transformation of the West*. Maryknoll, N.Y.: Orbis Books, 2008.

Hartenstein, Karl. "Wozu Notigt Die Finanzlage Der Mission." *Evangelisches Missions-Magazin* 79, (1934): 217-229.

Heifetz, Ronald A. and Martin Linsky. *Leadership on the Line: Staying Alive through the Dangers of Leading*. Boston: Harvard Business School Press, 2002.

Heil, John Paul. *The Meal Scenes in Luke-Acts: An Audience-Oriented Approach*. Society of Biblical Literature Monograph Series. Vol. 52. Atlanta: Society of Biblical Literature, 1999.

Henig, Robin Maranz. "Taking Play Seriously." *New York Times Magazine* (February 17, 2008). https://www.nytimes.com/2008/02/17/magazine/17play.html (accessed May 31, 2018).

Hjalmarson, Len. *No Home Like Place: A Christian Theology of Place*. Portland: Urban Loft Publishers, 2014.

Hoekendijk, Johannes Christiaan. *The Church Inside Out*. Adventures in Faith. Philadelphia: Westminster Press, 1966.

Horowitz, Alexandra. *On Looking: A Walker's Guide to the Art of Observation*. New York: Scribner, 2014.

Hunsberger, George R. and Craig Van Gelder. *The Church between Gospel and Culture: The Emerging Mission in North America*. Grand Rapids: Eerdmans, 1996.

Hunter, James Davison. *To Change the World: The Irony, Tragedy, and Possibility of Christianity in the Late Modern World*. New York: Oxford University Press, 2010.

Inge, John. *A Christian Theology of Place*. Burlington: Ashgate, 2003.

Jennings, Willie James. *The Christian Imagination: Theology and the Origins of Race*. New Haven: Yale University Press, 2010.

Jenson, Robert W. *Systematic Theology*. Vol. 1. New York: Oxford University Press, 1997.

Johnson, Luke Timothy. *Scripture & Discernment: Decision-Making in the Church*. Nashville: Abingdon Press, 1996.

Juel, Donald. *A Master of Surprise: Mark Interpreted*. Minneapolis: Fortress Press, 1994.

Kähler, Martin. *Schriften Zur Christologie Und Mission*. Munich: Chr. Kaiser Verlag, 1971.

Keifert, Patrick R. *We are here Now: A New Missional Era*. St. Paul: Church Innovations Institute, 2011.

―――. *Welcoming the Stranger: A Public Theology of Worship and Evangelism*. Minneapolis: Fortress Press, 1992.

Kellerman, Barbara. *The End of Leadership*. New York: Harper Collins, 2012.

Kierkegaard, Søren. *Fear and Trembling; Repetition*. Kierkegaard's Writings. Translated by Hong, Howard V. and Edna H. Hong. Vol. 6. Princeton: Princeton University Press, 1983.

Kilough, Ashley. "Coca-Cola Superbowl Ad Ignites Online Debate." *CNN* (February 3, 2014): Accessed December 15, 2016. http://politicalticker.blogs.cnn.com/2014/02/03/coca-cola-super-bowl-ad-ignites-online-debate/.

Klein, Naomi. *No Logo*. New York: Picador, 2000.

LaCugna, Catherine Mowry. *God for Us: The Trinity and Christian Life*. 1st ed. San Francisco: HarperSanFrancisco, 1991.

Latourette, Kenneth Scott. *Advance through Storm*. A History o the Expansion of Christianity. Vol. 7. New York: Harper & Brothers, 1945.

———. *The Great Century: Europe and the United States*. A History of the Expansion of Christianity. Vol. 4. New York: Harper & Brothers, 1941.

———. *The Great Century: The Americas , Australasia, and Africa*. A History of the Expansion of Christianity. Vol. 5. New York: Harper & Brothers, 1943.

Lindbeck, George A. *The Nature of Doctrine: Religion and Theology in a Postliberal Age*. Philadelphia: Westminster Press, 1984.

MacIntyre, Alasdair C. *After Virtue: A Study in Moral Theory*. 3rd ed. Notre Dame: University of Notre Dame Press, 2007.

McKnight, John and Peter Block. *The Abundant Community: Awakening the Power of Families and Neighborhoods*. San Francisco: Berrett-Koehler Publishers, 2012.

Minatrea, Milfred. *Shaped by God's Heart: The Passion and Practices of Missional Churches*. San Francisco: Jossey-Bass, 2004.

Moltmann, Jürgen. *The Crucified God: The Cross of Christ as the Foundation and Criticism of Christian Theology*. Minneapolis: Fortress Press, 1993.

Morris, Danny E. and Charles M. Olsen. *Discerning God's Will Together: A Spiritual Practice for the Church*. Rev. ed. Herndon, VA: Alban Institute, 2012.

Moschella, Mary Clark. *Ethnography as a Pastoral Practice: An Introduction*. Cleveland: Pilgrim Press, 2008.

Newbigin, Lesslie. *The Gospel in a Pluralist Society*. Grand Rapids: W.B. Eerdmans, 1989.

———. *The Open Secret: An Introduction to the Theology of Mission*. Rev ed. Grand Rapids: Eerdmans, 1995.

Northouse, Peter Guy. *Leadership: Theory and Practice*. Seventh Edition ed. Thousand Oaks: SAGE Publications, 2015.

Olson, Roger. "A Free Church Ecclesiology and Evangelical Spirituality: A Unique Compatibility." In *Evangelical Ecclesiology: Reality Or Illusion?*, edited by Stackhouse, John G., 161-178. Grand Rapids: Baker Academic, 2003.

Pannenberg, Wolfhart. *Jesus, God and Man*. 2nd ed. Philadelphia: Westminster Press, 1977.

———. *Systematic Theology*. Vol. 1. Grand Rapids: Eerdmans, 1991.

Pathak, Jay and David Runyon. *The Art of Neighboring: Building Genuine Relationships Right Outside Your Door*. Grand Rapids: Baker, 2012.

Pohl, Christine D. *Making Room: Recovering Hospitality as a Christian Tradition*. Grand Rapids: Eerdmans, 1999.

Rahner, Karl. *The Trinity*. Translated by Donceel, Joseph. New York: Crossroad, 1997.

Ricoeur, Paul. "Imagination in Discourse and Action." In *From Text to Action: Essays in Hermeneutics II*. Translated by Blamey, Kathleen and John B. Thompson, 168-87. Evanston: Northwestern University Press, 2007.

———. *From Text to Action: Essays in Hermeneutics II*. Translated by Blamey, Kathleen and John B. Thompson. Evanston: Northwestern University Press, 1991.

Roxburgh, Alan J. *Missional: Joining God in the Neighborhood*. Allelon Missional Series. Grand Rapids: Baker Books, 2011.

———. *The Missionary Congregation, Leadership & Liminality*. Christian Mission and Modern Culture. Harrisburg, PA: Trinity Press International, 1997.

Sale, Kirkpatrick. *Human Scale*. Gabriola Island: New Catalyst Books, 2007.

Sandel, Michael. *What Money can't Buy: The Moral Limits of Markets*. New York: Farrar, Strauss, and Giroux, 2012.

Sanneh, Lamin O. *Translating the Message: The Missionary Impact on Culture*. American Society of Missiology Series. 2nd ed. Vol. 42. Maryknoll, N.Y.: Orbis Books, 2009.

Saunders, George. "The Tenth of December." In *The Tenth of December*, 215-49. New York: Random House, 2013.

Schnabel, Eckhard J. *Early Christian Mission*. Vol. 1. Downers Grove: InterVarsity Press, 2004.

Schwarz, Christian A. *Natural Church Development: A Guide to Eight Essential Qualities of Healthy Churches*. Carol Stream: ChurchSmart Resources, 1996.

Simpson, Gary M. "Civil Society and Congregations as Public Moral Companions." *Word & World* 15, no. 4 (Fall 1995): 420-27.

———. *Critical Social Theory: Prophetic Reason, Civil Society, and Christian Imagination*. Guides to Theological Inquiry. Minneapolis: Fortress Press, 2002.

Smith, James K. A. *Desiring the Kingdom: Worship, Worldview, and Cultural Formation*. Grand Rapids: Baker Academic, 2009.

Sparks, Paul, Tim Soerens, and Dwight J. Friesen. *The New Parish: How Neighborhood Churches are Transforming Mission, Discipleship and Community*. Downers Grove: InterVarsity Press, 2014.

Spener, Philipp Jakob. *Pia Desideria*. Translated by Tappert, Theodore G. Philadelphia: Fortress Press, 1964.

Stackhouse, John G., ed. *Evangelical Ecclesiology: Reality Or Illusion?*. Grand Rapids: Baker Academic, 2003.

Stott, John, ed. *Making Christ Known: Historic Mission Documents from the Lausanne Movement, 1974-1989*. Grand Rapids: Eerdmans, 1996.

Strom, Jonathan. "Problems and Promises of Pietism Research." *Church History* 71, no. 3 (2002): 536-54.

Swart, Jannie, Scott Hagley, Mark Love, and John Ogren. "Toward a Missional Theology of Participation: Ecumenical Reflections on Contributions to Trinity, Mission, and Church." *Missiology: An International Review* 37, no. 1 (2009): 75-87.

Tanner, Kathryn. *Theories of Culture: A New Agenda for Theology*. Guides to Theological Inquiry. Minneapolis: Fortress Press, 1997.

———. *Christ the Key*. Current Issues in Theology. New York: Cambridge University Press, 2010.

———. *Economy of Grace*. Minneapolis: Fortress Press, 2005.

Taylor, Charles C. *Modern Social Imaginaries*. Durham: Duke University Press, 2004.

———. *A Secular Age*. Cambridge: Belknap Press, 2007.

———. *Sources of the Self: The Making of the Modern Identity*. Cambridge: Harvard University Press, 1989.

Toulmin, Stephen Edelston. *Cosmopolis: The Hidden Agenda of Modernity*. New York: Free Press, 1990.

Van Gelder, Craig. "An Ecclesial Geno-Project: Unpacking the DNA of Denominations and Denominationalism." In *The Missional Church and Denominations: Helping Congregations Develop a Missional Identity*, edited by Van Gelder, Craig, 12-45. Grand Rapids: Eerdmans, 2008.

———. "How Missiology can Help Inform the Conversation about the Missional Church in Context." In *The Missional Church in Context :Helping Congregations Develop Contextual Ministry*, edited by Van Gelder, Craig, 12-43. Grand Rapids: Eerdmans, 2007.

Van Gelder, Craig and Dwight J. Zscheile. *The Missional Church in Perspective: Mapping Trends and Shaping the Conversation*. Grand Rapids: Baker Academic, 2011.

Volf, Miroslav and Dorothy C. Bass, eds. *Practicing Theology: Beliefs and Practices in Christian Life*. Grand Rapids: Eerdmans, 2002.

Walls, Andrew F. *The Missionary Movement in Christian History: Studies in the Transmission of Faith*. Maryknoll, NY: Orbis Books, 1996.

Walter, Gregory. *Being Promised: Theology, Gift, and Practice*. Grand Rapids: Eerdmans, 2013.

Warner, R. Stephen. "The Place of the Congregation in the Contemporary American Religious Configuration." In *American Congregations: New Perspectives in the Study of Congregations*, edited by Wind, James P. and James W. Lewis. Vol. 2, 54-99, 1994.

Weick, Karl E. "Introductory Essay: Improvisation as a Mindset for Organizational Analysis." *Organization Science* 9, no. 5 (1998): 543-555.

———. *Sensemaking in Organizations*. Thousand Oaks: Sage Publications, 1995.

Welker, Michael. *God the Spirit*. Translated by Hoffmeyer, John F. Minneapolis: Fortress Press, 1994.

Wells, Samuel. *Improvisation: The Drama of Christian Ethics*. Grand Rapids: Brazos Press, 2004.

———. *A Nazareth Manifesto: Being with God*. Malden: Wiley Blackwell, 2015.

Whiteman, Darrell. "Contextualization, Models of." In *An Encyclopedia of Mission and Missionaries*, edited by Bonk, Jonathan, 90-95. New York: Routledge, 2007.

Willard, Dallas. *The Spirit of the Disciplines: Understanding how God Changes Lives*. San Francisco: Harper & Row, 1988.

World Council of Churches. "WCC Archives, Willingen IMC." Accessed August 17, 2015. http://archives.wcc-coe.org/query/resultatliste.aspx.

Wright, Christopher J. H. *The Mission of God: Unlocking the Bible's Grand Narrative*. Downers Grove: IVP Academic, 2006.

Wright, N. T. "How can the Bible be Authoritative?" *Vox Evangelica* 21, (1991): 7-32.

———. *The New Testament and the People of God*. Christian Origins and the Question of God. Vol. 1. Minneapolis: Fortress Press, 1992.

Wuthnow, Robert. *The Restructuring of American Religion:*. Princeton: Princeton University Press, 1988.

Yong, Amos. *Hospitality and the Other: Pentecost, Christian Practices, and the Neighbor*. Maryknoll,: Orbis Books, 2008.

Printed in Great Britain
by Amazon